A MAN OF SHEFFIELD

THE ADSETTS
STORY

Chi non fa, non falla.

He who does nothing, makes no mistakes.

'The man who makes no mistakes, does not usually make anything'

Rev H C McGee, Archbishop of York 1868

Sir Norman Adsetts OBE

First published in Great Britain in 2017 by RMC Media
6 Broadfield Court, Sheffield, S8 0XF
Tel: 0114 250 6300
www.rmcmedia.co.uk

A CIP catalogue record for this book is available from the British Library.

ISBN: 978-1-907998-31-7

Design & Typesetting by Steve Levers

Printed and bound in Malta by Gutenberg Press Ltd
www.gutenberg.com.mt

WITH LOVE
TO THE ADSETTS FAMILY
OCTOBER 2016

CONTENTS

The Adsetts Story – Ernest & Norman Get to Work

The Adsetts Story – The Birth of a New Career

INTRODUCTION

My father would often share fond memories of the schoolboy paradise where he spent his youth. The village of Laneham on the River Trent, where his father had settled in retirement, left a profound and lasting impression on the young Ernest Norman Adsetts.

But there were other family legends that he recalled only vaguely. One was the tale that his grandfather had met his end while gardening with a scythe. The other was that in the east end of Sheffield there was an Adsetts St – but how and why it got its name remained shrouded in mystery.

These were not very auspicious beginnings for any attempt to write a family history, but I decided to do exactly that.

The year was 1985. It was the start of a journey into the past that turned out to be full of surprises. It also unearthed a host of characters, many of them long forgotten, from a working class Conservative politician fiercely active in Sheffield's East End to a dynasty of innkeepers in Bolsover; from a professional athlete in America to a glass designer in Sweden – and a notorious murderer in Hong Kong.

Over the years, this task expanded in two directions: back into the seventeenth and eighteenth centuries, as more was learned about the family tree, and forward into the twentieth century, as both my father and I pursued the business careers which had brought us into partnership in Sheffield in 1966. Then from 1985, when I became Chairman of SIG plc, there was a third strand of involvement in local urban regeneration as I entered into partnership with the local authority and others.

The story begins in 1633, in the village of Clowne in Derbyshire, a few miles from Eckington, where I now live, and it reaches a sort of conclusion in the year 1999 when I was knighted for 'services to the community in Sheffield'.

The College of Arms had designed an Adsetts coat of arms based on a visual pun on the name Adsetts, portrayed as a 'set of adzes' against a background of red and blue stripes with white stripes in between, depicting hot and cold temperatures separated by insulation to illustrate my chosen career!

The York Herald of the College of Arms suggested I should add a motto and I found mine in a dictionary of foreign quotations. It is an Italian proverb, 'Chi non fa non falla', which means 'he who does nothing makes no mistakes'. It's not an uncommon sentiment – my father used to say something similar, 'the person who washes the pots breaks the most', but I found its clearest expression in a saying of 1868 by WC Magee, an Irish priest who became the Archbishop of York, who said that 'the man who makes no mistakes does not usually make anything'.

The significance of this motto for me arose from my National Service in the Royal Air Force in 1951 when, as the equipment officer of a flying training school in Driffield, I lost a Gloster Meteor. The Air Ministry auditors discovered that a damaged aeroplane for which I was responsible had completely disappeared from our records. Where was it? (It had actually been repaired and was flying happily in Germany, but it took some time to find it!)

Forty years later, by which time I was the chairman of a public company SIG plc, I was interviewed in the *Independent on Sunday* about 'My Biggest Mistake', a weekly series that ran for five years. I described how I had lost a multi-million pound jet trainer and what I had learned from the experience.

In 1998, academic research based on these interviews was published in a book, *Ending the Blame Culture*, which stressed the positive value of mistakes in any learning process, quoting my final comment: 'The experience taught me a valuable and lasting lesson about paying attention to detail', and concluding that 'not making mistakes is bad for you'.

My career had barely begun when I 'lost' the Meteor, and only now do I really understand what I learned from it. My approach to delegation and leadership, negotiation and partnership, and my attitude toward trust and blame over a long business career – all have benefitted from this 'mistake'.

Apart from the genealogical research which is the basis of our family tree reaching back to 1600, I have always been interested in the origins of this uncommon name.

The Adshead One-Name Study noted in 2014 that there was an overlap of the spellings of Adshed and Adsetts in the single surname of one family in Sussex, and has also noted a possible Celtic association with Adzehead, one of the nicknames of St Patrick, which stemmed from the hairstyle of the early Celtic monks. Maybe the College of Arms has got this derivation of the surname right?

On the other hand, the linkage with a Saxon place-name may be more likely; I certainly thought so when I found the etymology of our unusual name in a book which explained that the name of Adsett, a hamlet in Gloucestershire, came from the Old English *(ge)set* – a dwelling place for animals, a stable or fold – and that the prefix *ad* is derived from a personal name such as Aeddi or Adda. Similar examples in our region include Woodsetts in Nottinghamshire or Thornsett in Derbyshire.

No Adsetts or similar surname has been found in the records of Gloucestershire or neighbouring counties, but in the parish registers of Derbyshire, Nottinghamshire and Lincolnshire there are many references to Adset, Adsett, Adsettes or Adsetts surnames from the 16th century onwards. The origin of the name may be in this region – perhaps a lost village or an alternative form of Woodsetts?

So we have a choice. Our surname has either a mediaeval connection with the adze based on the way in which early monks cut their hair, or it is a surname with a Saxon prefix that is spread widely across an area of heavy Saxon settlement. I think I prefer the second, but the evidence is sparse.

The first mention of the name appears in the church records of Worksop Priory, where in 1580 my daughter's namesake, Hellen Adsettes, married Richard Yates, and the second reference is to the 1625 christening of Ellen the daughter of Richard Adsett in Clowne in Derbyshire.

I have traced my own line of descent back to her brother, Robert Adsetts, who was born in Clowne in 1633, moving 30 years later to become the wheelwright of the neighbouring village of Elmton.

Between 1663 and the end of the eighteenth century there were five generations of the Adsetts family living in Elmton before William Adsetts married and moved to Scarcliffe-by-Palterton in 1800. His son George, born in 1806 and married in 1827, was to be my great-great-grandfather.

George's son, my great-grandfather John Adsetts, moved to Greenhill, near Sheffield, and married a local girl in 1857. A few years later he established the family home in the industrial East End, where he was a groom and gardener to one of the local industrialists.

His son William Tom Adsetts, my grandfather, worked in the rolling mill of Spear & Jackson and rose quickly to become its manager, while as a separate side-line he ran a number of retail shops with other members of his family. He died in 1913 aged 47, having retired to the Lincolnshire village of Laneham to relax and focus on his favourite sport of fishing.

This book covers the Adsetts family history in Sheffield City Region from Robert Adsetts, the wheelwright of Clowne, to my present home in Eckington – a journey of just over four miles in 400 years!

The first part follows the direct line over 12 generations from Robert Adsetts to William Tom Adsetts my grandfather. It also contains a number of interesting life stories of Adsetts men who left the main line of the family history in this period to achieve fortune fame or even notoriety!

The second part begins with the birth in 1905 of my father Ernest Norman, who forged a career that brought him through the Depression years as a hard-sell salesman and shopkeeper to become an RAF officer from 1941 to 1945 and a one-man businessman selling ice cream in the 1950's.

He and I joined forces in 1966 to turn his new company Sheffield Insulations into a multi-million pound public company SIG plc before his death in 1991 and my retirement in 1996. My father was a risk-taker, an opportunist leader, a decision-maker – a man of immense energy and charm, with a good memory. He did not delegate well but we worked together in an effective partnership, sharing a mutual regard and respect that overcame the occasional tensions.

The third part begins a few years before I retired from SIG, when I became Chairman and took an active interest in my Sheffield surroundings after years spent thinking mainly of my family and my business. I began to make the case for the public and private sectors in Sheffield to work together in partnership to achieve the regeneration of a city in decline.

I chaired the Image working party of the Chamber of Commerce, launching a Partnership in Action campaign that brought local government and business together as partners in the regeneration of Sheffield, and I got involved in the wider application of this approach to regional development, higher education and the arts. I was also engaged in promoting investment in Sheffield, and specifically in the practical support of people with autism, with which two of my grandchildren had been diagnosed.

All of this resulted in the unexpected award of a knighthood in the Birthday Honours List of 1999 for 'services to the community in Sheffield'.

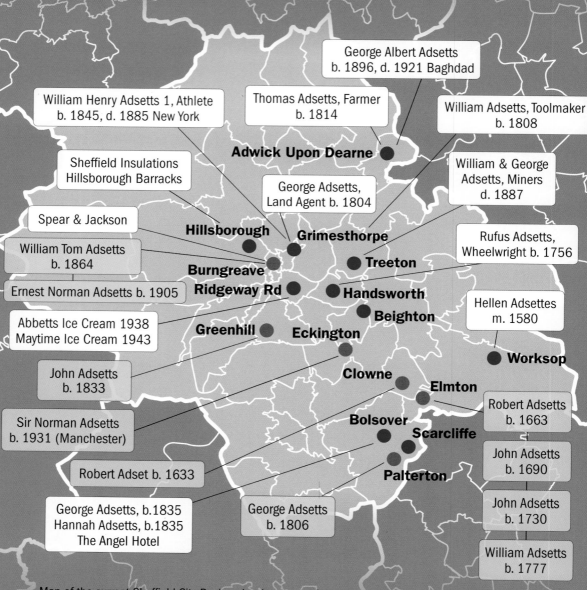

4 MILES IN 400 YEARS

From Robert Adset, the Wheelwright of Clowne to Sir Norman Adsetts OBE, the Knight of Eckington

George Albert Adsetts
b. 1896, d. 1921 Baghdad

William Henry Adsetts 1, Athlete
b. 1845, d. 1885 New York

Thomas Adsetts, Farmer
b. 1814

William Adsetts, Toolmaker
b. 1808

Adwick Upon Dearne

Sheffield Insulations
Hillsborough Barracks

George Adsetts,
Land Agent b. 1804

William & George
Adsetts, Miners
d. 1887

Spear & Jackson

Hillsborough

Grimesthorpe

Rufus Adsetts,
Wheelwright b. 1756

William Tom Adsetts
b. 1864

Burngreave

Treeton

Ernest Norman Adsetts b. 1905

Ridgeway Rd

Handsworth

Hellen Adsettes
m. 1580

Abbetts Ice Cream 1938
Maytime Ice Cream 1943

Greenhill

Beighton

Eckington

Worksop

John Adsetts
b. 1833

Clowne

Robert Adsetts
b. 1663

Sir Norman Adsetts
b. 1931 (Manchester)

Elmton

Bolsover

Scarcliffe

John Adsetts
b. 1690

Robert Adset b. 1633

Palterton

John Adsetts
b. 1730

George Adsetts, b.1835
Hannah Adsetts, b.1835
The Angel Hotel

George Adsetts
b. 1806

William Adsetts
b. 1777

Map of the current Sheffield City Region showing some of the places described throughout the book.
● Indicates the direct line from Robert Adset.

William Tom Adsetts

Ernest Norman Adsetts

THE MAYTIME ICE CREAM CO.,

FOR CHILDREN UP TO 90

THE "RAINBOW" RANGE

OF

JOLLY-LOLLY

THE MAYTIME ICE CREAM CO.,

SIX
DOZEN

Ridgeway Road,
SHEFFIELD, 12.

SIX
DOZEN

Sir Norman Adsetts

THE ADSETTS STORY

The Direct Line

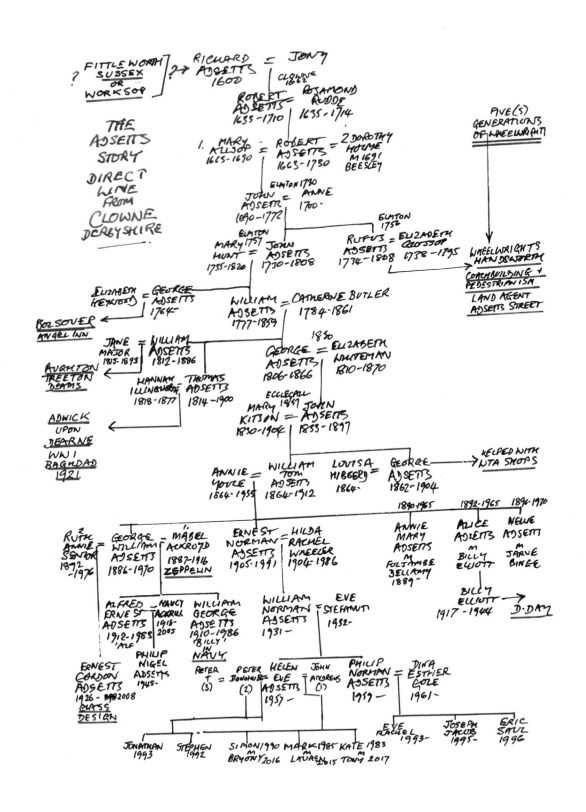

THE CLOWNE CONNECTION

ROBERT ADSETS
BORN 1633

Present-day Clowne is a village and civil parish in the Bolsover district of Derbyshire, England, with a population of over 7,500. It was mentioned in the Domesday Book as Clune, derived from the Celtic *Clun*, for a river; and in the seventeenth century it was a rural farming community with a population of just under 400, slowly recovering from the plague that struck the village in both 1586 and 1606.

There was massive growth in the nineteenth century, when Clowne became a colliery village following the sinking of a 300m-deep mine in 1877. Employing 400 men and producing 600 tons of coal per day, Southgate colliery changed the face of Clowne, with row after row of terraces built to house the mining families. Southgate survived for over 50 years, closing in 1929 after the pit flooded.

The first references to the surname Adsetts in local church records are in 1577 and 1580 in Worksop. The next occurrence is in Clowne, seven miles away, where Ellen Adsett was christened in 1625 in the church of St John the Baptist, the oldest building in the village.

Richard Adsett and Jony were the parents of Ellen Adsett, the sister of Thomas Adsett, born in 1628, and of Robert Adsets in 1633. We know very little of Richard Adsett, who is currently the first in our family line. He may well be linked to the Adsetts family in Worksop, but new information discovered in June 2017 suggests that he was born in

1600 in Fittleworth in Sussex and this will need to be checked.

Clowne and Bolsover were closely linked, and the hearings of the Bolsover Court Leet contain a fairly continuous record of petty misdemeanours involving the people of both villages. On 12 April 1658, 32 Clowne men, including Rob Adsotes, were fined 2d each for failure to attend a meeting of the court. This was clearly the Robert Adsets who married Rosamond Rudde in Clowne four years later, on 22 April 1662, moving shortly thereafter to become the wheelwright of the neighbouring village of Elmton where his first son, also named Robert, was baptised on 22 November 1663.

THE ELMTON CONNECTION

ROBERT THE WHEELWRIGHT
BORN 1663

Elmton is a small village with a long history. It appears in the Domesday Survey of 1086 as Helmetune, an Anglo-Saxon name referring to the elm trees that were once a feature of the local landscape. They fell victim to Dutch elm disease and were all cut down in the 1970s, but in 2012 a sapling from an elm that withstood the disease was planted on the village green in a bid to preserve the link with the past.

In Bagshaw's 1846 Directory of Derbyshire Elmton is 'pleasantly situated, with an unenclosed common to the north and a romantic rocky ravine called Markland's Grip at one end'. In 1846 there were 37 houses and 211 inhabitants.

Unlike Clowne and nearby Cresswell, Elmton was not chosen for the development of a coalmine in the nineteenth century, and so we can get a very good idea of how it appeared in the eighteenth century, when five generations of the Adsetts family lived there.

The baptism of Robertus Adsetts, *filius* (son of) Robert, on 22 November 1663 was the first reference to the Adsetts name in the Elmton church records, and it was followed by his brother Gulielmus (William) in 1666 and sister Martha in 1669.

Twenty-seven years later, in 1690, Robert Adsetts and Mary Alsop had a son, John Adsetts; his birthplace is named in separate sources as 'Nottinghamshire' (the county boundary is close) and 'Elmton'. I have found no record of Robert marrying Mary, who died in 1690 – perhaps in childbirth – but in 1691 Robert did get married to Dorothy Holme of Beesley in Derbyshire, and brought her to live in Elmton.

In 1709 Robert Adsetts and his wife witnessed the will of John Davenport, the vicar of Elmton, with Robert making his mark (A) next to the mark of Dorothy Adsetts (X). John Davenport, who died later in the same year, left five pounds in his will to 'my son in law William Buxton', said to be the parish schoolmaster, who placed his signature as a witness to the will alongside the marks of Robert and Dorothy Adsetts.

With this act, the lives of Robert Adsetts and his wife touch that of Jedidiah Buxton, a famous product of Elmton, who was born in the village in 1707, the son of William Buxton and the grandson of the John Davenport, whose will they had witnessed. Jedidiah Buxton spent all his life, with the exception of one trip to the Royal Society in London, working as a farmhand in the village of Elmton, and he died there in 1772.

He could neither read nor write, yet he is remembered for his 'remarkable powers of calculation and a singularly retentive memory', even though as a child it is said that 'he evinced the most excessive stupidity and unwillingness to learn anything'.

Jedidiah Buxton would probably today be placed at the high-performing end of the autistic spectrum, an 'autistic savant' perhaps, but whatever you call it, many examples of his extraordinary arithmetical expertise are recorded in issues of the *Gentleman's Magazine* for 1751, 1753 and 1754. He is even said to have carried out a survey of the manor of Elmton for Sir John Rodes of Barlborough Hall 'by striding over the land' and calculating the total area, not only in acres, roods and perches but also in square inches. The memory of this remarkable son of Elmton is now preserved on a blue plaque, which was erected in his honour in the centre of the village in 2011.

Robert was clearly a man of some clout in the village at this time, bequeathing to his son John 'all my goods, battels and chattles quick and dead, with all the debts due to me by Bills or Bonds', and naming him as the executor of 'this my last Will and Testament revoking all other wills and legacies made by me heretofore'.

In the above will he described himself as a wheelwright, and it is probable that he had simply followed his father's trade, although this is not clear. The role of the wheelwright – someone who builds or repairs wagons and wooden wheels – was of crucial importance to the agricultural communities of the seventeenth and eighteenth centuries. Wheelwrights were clearly craftsmen of a very high order.

The 1722 map of the manor of Elmton and Creswell was produced for Sir John Rodes of Barlborough Hall by Joseph Dickinson, and provides a detailed survey of the central 'township' of Elmton. It clearly identifies both the cottage of Robert Adsett on the right of the Creswell Rd as it enters the village of Elmton from the north east, and the Adsett yard, a plot of land at the other end of the village where he presumably had his workshop and stored the wide range of timbers essential for his craft.

The acquired knowledge of this ancient craft was passed from father to son and from master to apprentice. It required a great knowledge of the properties of the different timbers used in the construction of wagons, and of the long process of seasoning timber for many years before it could be used.

George Sturt, who published *The Wheelwright's Shop* in 1923, describes the classic methods of the old-style wheelwright: 'every well-built farm wagon', he says, 'reflects in every curve and dimension some special need of its own countryside, or perhaps some special difficulty attending wheelwrights with the local timber'. Any piece of work had to last for years. In the traditional wheelwright's shop, he was the final judge and would, for instance, refuse to use a piece of likely looking timber if he held it to be unfit – and he *would* know.

The same meticulous approach applied to the selection of the timber stock, his vital stock in trade. The flaws in most timbers (oak, beech and ash) could only be detected under the plane, the adze or the axe, disclosing qualities not found by any other means. The job of the wheelwright was to decide the lengths and thicknesses of timber to hold in stock plus the range of curved pieces needed for shafts and other components, and then he had to watch over the stock for the long period of natural seasoning!

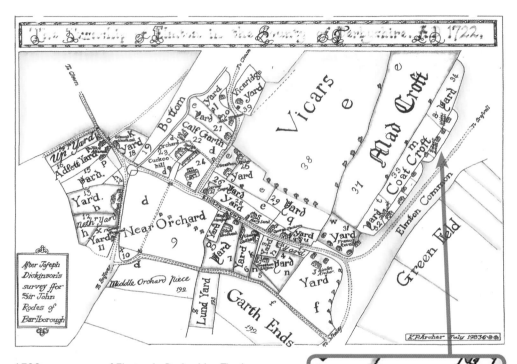

1722 survey map of Elmton in Derbyshire. The home of Robert Adsett faces Elmton Common, and the Adsett yard is at the other end of the village.

Robert's grandson John Adsetts (my great-great-great-grandfather) was born in Elmton in 1730, and he had a younger brother called Rufus, who left the village for Handsworth near Sheffield in 1756 and established himself as a wheelwright in the neighbouring hamlet of Woodhouse. Sixty years later, his son George was 'one of the

A MAN OF SHEFFIELD

three wheelwrights then living in Handsworth', and in 1841 George established a company of wheelwrights and carriage builders in the Sheffield area with his son Henry.

John, on the other hand, stayed in Elmton, where he married Mary Hunt in 1757. The emigrations continued, as his eldest son George Adsetts left Elmton for Bolsover after marrying Elizabeth Haywood there in 1787, to be followed two years later by his sister Rebecca, who also married in Bolsover.

The Bolsover connection flourished, and George's grandson, also named George, married Hannah Cook in 1860 and took over the licence of the Angel Inn in the town centre. The Adsetts family then ran the Angel for over 80 years, most of the time under the leadership of Hannah Adsetts, a matriarch and prominent citizen of Bolsover.

Finally, George's younger brother William, after his marriage to Catherine in about 1800, moved away from Elmton to the village of Scarcliffe, and began the final phase of the migration of my forebears to Sheffield.

This Elmton connection with my family line lasted for about 140 years, passing through two Roberts and two Johns to one William Adsetts, my great-great-great-grandfather, who was born in Elmton in 1777 and eventually moved a few miles south to Scarcliffe and Palterton. It seems safe to assume that the craft of wheelwright would have been handed from father to son for most of this period, giving the Adsetts family a key role in the village hierarchy.

THE PALTERTON CONNECTION

GEORGE ADSETTS
THE TREE-CUTTER IN 1806

Scarcliffe with Palterton had been the first Derbyshire parish to be subject to the Enclosure Act of 1726, which encouraged landlords and tenants to enclose mediaeval lands, manorial commons and wastes, so improving agricultural productivity to their mutual benefit. The two villages are about one mile apart, standing between Bolsover Castle and Hardwick Hall on the limestone ridge running alongside what is now the M1 motorway.

In the 1841 Kelly's Directory of Derbyshire, Scarcliffe is described as a remote village dependent on agriculture, linked to the hamlet of Palterton, with 3772 acres and 582 inhabitants – 'well-watered by the River Poulter' and a 'spring called Owlesditch which is remarkable for its greater abundance in the summer'.

Both communities were almost entirely devoted to farming, and the Duke of Portland's 1795 survey of the acreage of grain crops in the Scarsdale hundred states that 46% of the cultivated area was oats, 38% wheat, and 11% barley.

George Adsetts, my great-great-grandfather, was the second son of William and Catherine Adsetts to be born after their move from Elmton. He was born in Scarcliffe and baptised in the church of St Leonards in this small Derbyshire village in July 1806. His elder brother John was born in 1804, followed by Mary in 1809, William in 1812 and finally Thomas in 1814.

George Adsetts married Elizabeth Whiteman of Mansfield in 1827, and in 1831 they were living in Palterton with three-year-old William and baby daughter Mary. A year later, in the 1832 records of the Scarcliffe Poor Rate, he is named as the land/householder of a cottage and garden in Palterton.

In 1831 Palterton had a population of 230, with 51 inhabited houses and a total of 53 families. There were 74 men aged 20 years or over in the village, 55 of them being agricultural labourers like George. The other 19 were farmers, of whom it was said 11 'constantly employ one or more labourers or farm servants in husbandry', while the remaining eight employ 'no labourer other than their own family'.

Ten years later the family had grown to include my great-grandfather, John Adsetts, then aged 8, with four sisters and a baby son, Tom – eight children in all. They had moved to a property at the northern (Bolsover) end of the village, where they were still living in 1851, but by now all except Thomas and Mary (the latter unmarried with a baby) had left home.

Employment was beginning to fall in the depressed rural areas of Derbyshire as mining and industrial growth began to attract agricultural workers to seek better-paid employment. With the exception of his elder brother John Adsetts, who became the village butcher, all George's other male siblings left Palterton to find work elsewhere.

The first brother to leave Palterton was William, born in 1812. In 1840, while working as a farmer, he married Jane Major, the daughter of a servant to the rector of Treeton, and they subsequently lived in the parish of Aston-cum-Aughton, where by 1861 he was a farm bailiff with five children. Tragically, in 1887 two of his sons, working as miners, were killed in an underground accident at Treeton Colliery.

Then there was George's younger brother Thomas, born in Scarcliffe in 1814. In 1841 Thomas married Hannah Illingworth, a Sheffield girl, and settled in nearby Beighton, where their sons William (1841) and John (1842) were born.

By 1861 Tom and his family had left John working as a carter on a farm in Mexborough, and moved to the tiny village of Adwick-upon-Dearne near Doncaster, where Tom lived and worked for the next 30 years, first as an agricultural salesman, then as a farmer of 22 acres.

John stayed in Mexborough and had two daughters with his first wife, Ann; by 1881 he had married again, to Sarah, and had a total of five children, subsequently moving to Adwick-upon-Dearne, where his third son, George Albert Adsetts, was born in 1897.

George Albert was a 17-year-old miner with a police record when he joined the army in 1914. After serving in France and Italy he died in 1921 in Baghdad fighting insurgents in Mesopotamia. More about his eventful life later!

THE SHEFFIELD CONNECTION

JOHN ADSETTS
THE GROOM & GARDENER

The main line of my family tree then moved into the Sheffield area, as George's second son, John, my great-grandfather, born in 1833, chose to look for work outside Palterton. It seems that John Adsetts left Palterton between 1841 and 1851, but there is no indication of his whereabouts until he re-emerges in the records on 12 September 1857, to marry Mary Kitson of Broomhall Park, Sheffield, in Ecclesall church. In the register he is described as a farmer from Greenhill, and his father George Adsetts as a tree-cutter from Palterton.

At about this time George Adsetts, still living in Palterton, had moved house again. In the 1861 Census he is living next to the pub, later known as the Nag's Head, at the opposite end of the village from his earlier home. He had always been described as an agricultural labourer in earlier records, and so does this new description of him as a tree-cutter mean that he had gone up in the world at the age of 51?

John and Mary continued to live in Greenhill, where four children were born. Two daughters, Jane Elizabeth (1858) and Alice Mary (1860), came first, and were followed by two sons, George (1862) and William Tom (1864). On all the birth certificates their father John Adsetts is described as a farm labourer.

From a biographical note about my grandfather, William Tom Adsetts, published in the local press in 1910, we learn that his family moved to Sheffield when he was six months old, in about 1865.

They were certainly living in the East End of Sheffield, in Hall Car Lane, later called Carwood Lane, when Harriet Emma was born in 1866. At that time John Adsetts was described as a groom and gardener, and he was probably working at one of the big houses overlooking the Don Valley. So began the Sheffield connection.

The biographical note in the *Sheffield Daily Independent* of 14 September 1910 says that William Tom 'received his early education at All Saints School', which opened in 1871, and that he 'started work in Sheffield at the age of 11' – which would be in 1875.

We know little more about John Adsetts or his family until 1878 when his daughter Jane Elizabeth was married in Sheffield Parish Church. She was followed in 1885 by sons George and William Tom – the former in the parish church in February, the latter in Christ Church Pitsmoor in September – and in 1893 by Harriet Emma, also in Christ Church Pitsmoor. Their home addresses when they got married were respectively Coningsby Rd, Brittain St, Fox St and Spital Lane. John Adsetts is described as a gardener on every marriage certificate.

The Census of 1881 confirms that John Adsetts, then described as a groom and coachman, was the head of the household at 48 Coningsby Rd with his wife Mary and three of their children: Alice Mary aged 21, a dressmaker, George aged 18, a heater for a 'tilter' (whatever that may be), and William Tom aged 16, a railway carriage cleaner. Ten years later John and Mary were still living at the same address with their then 31-year-old daughter Alice Mary.

John Adsetts died in July 1897, when he was living at 64 Lyon St, a few doors away from 70 Lyon St where William Tom's third daughter had been born six months earlier. He was 64 years old when he died, working as a gardener at the home of William Frederick Beardshaw of Cliffe Cottage, Crabtree Lane, where he fell while mowing the grass and cut his knee on his scythe.

John Adsetts was taken directly to the Infirmary on 28 June, the day of the accident. The wound became infected and he died on 9 July 1897. There was evidence during the inquest that 'the deceased had repeatedly fallen down steps and in the street', and that 'it was thought that he fell while under a slight stroke'. The jury returned a verdict of accidental death, and he was buried at Burngreave Cemetery in plot S3 52. There is no headstone to mark his grave, where there are four other members of the family.

WILLIAM TOM ADSETTS
THE ROLLER, SHOPKEEPER
& POLITICIAN

A young man going places!

In September 1910, William Tom Adsetts was a member of a deputation of six working men sent by the *Sheffield Daily Telegraph* to report on conditions of life and labour under tariffs in Germany. His early working life is described as follows (I have inserted approximate dates).

At the age of 11 (1875) he started work in the Spring Department of Messrs Cammell and Company. He stayed there for five years (1880), and then entered the employ of Messrs Spear & Jackson, saw manufacturers, in Savile St. He commenced at the bottom of the ladder in the sheet-rolling mill, but within ten years (by 1890) he had risen to the position of foreman.

The 1881 Census return indicates that he was at that time employed as a railway carriage cleaner, presumably in the interval between leaving Cammells and joining Spear & Jackson. Spear & Jackson, the best-known of the Sheffield saw makers, was firmly established in Aetna Works on Savile St, where it employed over 600 workers by 1880 producing saws and files, edge tools and machine knives from its own steel. Market leaders, the company had a strong commitment to quality, and had pioneered the introduction of machines for circular saw grinding in the 1850s.

Spear & Jackson started rolling steel on 25 October 1881, and company records describe the make-up of the first sett, or team of four men and a boy, in the new rolling mill. Henry Lee was the first roller (at £3 pw), with a furnaceman (at £1.13.0 pw), a middleman (at £1.10.00 pw), an annealer or backer (at £1.6.0 pw), and the boy (at 11 shillings pw), working from 8.00 am to 6.30 pm, six days a week. It is possible that William Tom at the age of 17 was a member of the first sett, and was recruited for the new venture.

There are studio photographs of William Tom Adsetts, perhaps taken around the time of his twenty-first birthday, or just before his wedding in 1885, in which he appears as a very smart, slim and good-looking young man in his late 'teens or early twenties.

This young man revealed both imagination and sensitivity in a poem of 17 verses written in 1883 when he was 18 years old, which is printed later in these pages. Entitled 'The Star Lad', it is an account in dialect of a poor newspaper boy – 'his feet they wor bare/his face war wan/and his hands wor black and blue' – who attempts to return a shilling paid by mistake for a ha'penny *Star*.

His response to the narrator's subsequent generosity is to set the gift aside for his dying mother; and the clear moral message of the final verse is that we should all spare a thought for those less fortunate than ourselves.

Two years later, in Christ Church, Pitsmoor, in September 1885, William Tom married Annie Youle, the daughter of George Youle, a file hardener of Andover St West. Their first child, George William Adsetts, was born there in May 1886. George once said that he was born in Jobson St 'off Infirmary Rd opposite the church', and perhaps they lived there shortly afterwards, but by October 1888 the small family had moved to 119 Fitzalan St.

This address was the first of a number of shops that William Tom ran as a sideline while he continued to work in the rolling mill of Spear & Jackson. In the directory of 1890 he is described as a confectioner, and this confirms his son George's recollection that shortly after the wedding his father got a 'spice shop' in Fitzalan St next door to a butcher's.

The *Sheffield Telegraph* supplement in 1910 suggests that William was about 26 when he became a foreman in Spear & Jackson. The following extract from *A History of Labour in Sheffield* by Sidney Pollard describes the powerful position that he probably held as the foreman responsible for rolling-mill production in Spear & Jackson.

From the commencement of the manufacture of armour, forgings, and other heavy goods a system has prevailed of getting the work done by contract, the contractor in each department employing his own men and being responsible to his principals for…completion (of the contract). These contractors have, as is well known, held very important, and in some cases lucrative, positions, and have been able to accumulate considerable wealth.

This was very like the structure my father described, and, if it is an accurate account of the situation in Spear & Jackson, it is clear that William Tom ultimately reached a position of considerable status, and had enough earning power to set up and run trading activities of various types in the Sheffield of the 1890s.

William Tom and Annie were still living in Fitzalan St in January 1890 when their first daughter, Annie Mary, was born. In the 1891 Census, William Tom Adsetts is the 26-year-old head of a family living in Cornish St or Cornish Square (the form is difficult to read), and is described as a sheet-steel roller. George William (my Uncle George), aged five, is described as a scholar.

Then began a remarkable sequence of moves during which babies were born in a succession of different houses around Sheffield. In July 1892 Alice was born at 122 Skinnerthorpe Rd, and in November 1894 Frank was born at 39 Cavendish St, only to die nine months later at 70 Lyon St. In November 1896 Nellie was born at Lyon St, and then in June 1899 Elsie was born at 74 Cannon Hall Rd.

William Tom's elder brother George, who was born in Greenhill in 1862 and married Louisa Hibberd in the parish church in 1885, helped his brother run his shops. In 1896, when George's own son, George Arnold, was born, he and his family were living at the back of the 'spice' shop at 113 Fitzalan St, and in 1901 they were living at the back of the draper's shop at 52 Lyon St. In 1896 George is described as a labourer in a steel works, so his wife may have been working as the main shopkeeper for his brother.

In White's Directory for 1901, the home address of William Tom is

43 Harcourt Rd in Crookesmoor, indicating perhaps that the family was moving up in the world. In 1900 William Tom Adsetts is listed in the directory as a draper and furniture dealer at 50-52 Lyon St, and his eldest son, George William Adsetts, aged 15, appears in the 1901 Census as a draper's shop assistant, probably working in the Lyons St shop.

Other family occupants are listed in the 1901 Census. In addition to William Tom and his wife Annie there are the three daughters, Annie, Alice and Nellie, as well as Annie's widowed mother, Mary West – the 'Grandma West' who later lived with Ernest and his mother in Laneham.

On 29 November 1905, my father, Ernest Norman Adsetts, was born at 390 Earl Marshall Rd. His mother was 42 and the birth was a 'surprise', according to the rest of the family. The moving continued, and by early January 1906, when the birth was registered, they were living at 79 Clough Rd near Bramall Lane. Ernest also remembered living on Scott Rd 'opposite the top entrance of Burngreave Cemetery', although there is no other record of this.

Family memories recall that there were nine children in all, but that four of them died – a girl and three boys (John in 1888 and Frank in 1894 being the only ones named so far). My father, Ernest, told me that 'everyone said she lost them because of the heavy work she did lugging crates about the shop'.

In his will, signed on 25 January 1906, William Tom appointed his wife, Annie, and his brother-in-law, Ernest Hague Banks (a surveyor for George Longden's, a local building contractor), to be the joint executors, trustees and guardians of his 'infant children during their minorities'.

The name of 'Uncle Ernest Banks' returns later in these pages, both to help my father after William Tom died and to invest in his early business ventures when he returned to Sheffield in the 1930s.

An interesting point which emerges from the will is that William Tom's current shop interest in 1906 was 'a business of a clothes and boot dealer carried on by me', although it is not clear from the text where it was located.

The will also includes various references to personal bequests, including named engravings, items of furniture, a piano, an 'American Organ', a library of books, and 'my Dresden China ornaments' – a collection which appears to have contained some outstanding pieces that my father was able to describe 75 years later with wonder, a wonder which turned to some irritation when he learned that they had been left to him in his father's will, along with the books and the American organ, and that he never got any of them! The 'Bill' Adsetts of 1906 had come a long way from the boy of 11 who started work in the steel works of Chas Cammell 30 years earlier.

In White's Directory of 1909, and in the 1910 list of officers of the Anglers Association, William Tom Adsetts is said to have been living at 202 Firth Park Rd, on the corner of Andover St. However, the family had definitely moved to Brunswick Rd in 1910 before the deputation left for Germany in September.

In the Census return of April 1911 there were eight people living in 133 Brunswick Rd. William Tom Adsetts, the head of the household, aged 46, was a foreman in the steel trade, living with Annie, his wife and three children – Alice, aged 18, a draper's assistant, Nellie, aged 14, and five-year-old Ernest. There were three family boarders – his 21-year-old daughter, Annie May Bellamy, with a new baby called John William (always called Jack), and Annie May's husband, Foljambe Bellamy, aged 22, a mill underhand in the steel trade.

At this time, William Tom is described as 'well-known in local angling circles', being the vice president of the Sheffield Anglers' Association and chairman of the Finance Committee. In 1910-11 the Association was 'popular and prosperous', according to its annual entry in the directory, with 500 clubs affiliated and a membership of 20,000.

An indication of the scale of their events is provided in the Sheffield Independent of 19 September 1899, which gives details of the Sheffield Anglers' Association Annual Gala Match, for which WT Adsetts provided some prizes. 900 potential competitors paid 2/ – each to enter; they were positioned at 10-yard intervals over a distance of six miles on the Witham at Kirkstead, and their special train left Sheffield Victoria at five past seven in the morning! The winner's prize was £105 for a catch of over 10 lbs.

Ten years later in September 1909 the Sheffield and District Association (the 1908 winners) staged the Annual Team Competition of the National Federation of Anglers at Aversham Weir near Newark. Eighteen teams were competing for a Silver Cup, and the 'stayers' were to fish from 11.45 am to 4.45 pm. Stakes were drawn at the Travellers' Inn, and William Tom, as a committee member, was one of the Sheffield team of four with the responsible task of staking the competitors' positions along the river.

William Tom, vice-president from 1910 to 1912, must have been right in the middle of the fierce row splitting the Anglers' Association at this time, about a proposal to move club meetings from the Three Cranes Hotel to the Lady's Bridge Hotel.

He retired, and moved to Laneham two years later, presumably intending to continue his fishing in the Trent. It is not clear whether he remained a member of the Sheffield Anglers' Association, but my father speaks of his brother George leading weekend fishing trips from Sheffield, offering him opportunities to raise income by selling small fish for bait! I imagine that his father would have shared in these events if well enough.

A member of the Grimesthorpe Conservative and Constitutional Association, William Tom sat for some time on the committee. He is described in the newspaper profile written in 1910 as an ardent Conservative who 'for the past 30 years has assisted at all the pre-elections in Sheffield'. These 30 years were mainly years of Conservative dominance in the politics of Sheffield, with a Conservative majority on the council from 1883 to 1901.

Helen Mathers, in her article 'The City of Sheffield 1893-1926' in the 1993 *History of the City of Sheffield*, states that there were four reasons for the success of the Conservative group in the 1890s and 1900s:

Firstly, the inspired activities at crucial periods of opinion-formers like WC Leng the editor of the Sheffield Daily Telegraph, secondly the targeting of policies which appealed to Sheffield manufacturers, thirdly, the cultivation of a working-class Tory vote, and fourthly the electorally helpful connection between Conservatism and the drink interest.

The influence of WC Leng was widespread. He was a member of the Chamber of Commerce, and its president in 1895/6. Through his newspapers he was a forceful campaigner for tariff reform, and he targeted the 'skilled working class' vote by encouraging the development of Conservative clubs, not only in Ecclesall and Hallam but also in the industrial East End.

An early reference to his political activities is found in the *Sheffield Daily Telegraph* of 27 October 1890, when William Tom was 26. An open-air meeting was held opposite the New Inn in Shalesmoor in support of Mr Nixon and Mr Wright, the Conservative and Unionist candidates for St Philip's ward, at which Mr William Adsetts moved a resolution pledging the meeting to help in the return of the candidates, which was carried 'almost unanimously'.

These must have been early days in the emergence of the working-class Conservative, because the speech by the chairman of the meeting stressed the significance of the two working men, a proposer and seconder, who had ridiculed in their speeches 'the "no politics" cry of the so-called Labour party'. 'If I know anything about the intelligence of the working men of Sheffield', he said, 'they will not be deceived by the "cant" that Conservatives are against the working class'.

William Tom Adsetts was born just three years before the Second Reform Act of 1867 widened the franchise to the point at which the urban working classes became a majority of the total electorate. And just as he started work in the Don Valley, the further franchise reforms of

1884-5 expanded the electorate of the UK to include over 60% of adult males in an even more significant redistribution of single-member seats in Parliament.

For most of his adult life my grandfather William Tom Adsetts was an active supporter of the Grimesthorpe Conservative and Constitutional Association, one of the network of clubs formed 'to promote the Conservative cause primarily among the newly enfranchised electors' – i.e. to recruit working class Conservatives. This strategy was brilliantly successful, particularly after the 1885 Reform Act, which handed the political power of the vote to the working class in the great urban areas of the nation.

Karl Marx, who had anticipated an increase in revolutionary spirit as the working class received the vote, had to agree with his colleague Engels, who admitted after the election that 'the proletariat has disgraced itself terribly'. The increase in working-class voters had simply improved the relative position of the Tories, because the maintenance of a stable, tolerant and collaborative 'status quo' was preferred by the new electorate to the future of division and argument offered by the other parties.

One quotation from Lord Birkenhead, who was one of the leaders of the working-class Conservative movement, summed it up: 'All we have to ask ourselves is whether a policy of class hatred and antagonism (from either side) will profit the State'; and it was this argument that won the day, for the time being, for the Conservatives. This sentiment persuades me that I would have got on with my grandfather – it's not far from the line I put before the Image Working Party.

The Conservatives were lucky. In 1886, the Liberal party was split when Gladstone proposed to grant Home Rule to Ireland, and the most able radical politician of the time, Joseph Chamberlain, effectively worked with the Conservative party for 20 years on the issues of social unity and Empire.

But Conservative propaganda was also cleverly exploiting the situation with the argument that the party was 'uniquely qualified to run the country', and that the Liberals, Radicals and Socialists were 'uprooters' and not to be trusted. The strategy was strikingly successful, exploiting the vulnerability of their opponents to charges of unpatriotic and divisive behaviour, as the arguments for change being pressed forward by radical Liberals and the emerging voices of socialism strongly contrasted with the unifying approach of the Tory party.

The activities of William Tom for the Conservative party in Sheffield between 1890 and 1911 in Sheffield should be seen against this national background. The Conservative party in the UK had realised that once the franchise had been extended to the urban masses, the people had to accept the logic of 'market politics'; and my grandfather could credibly argue that working-class needs were best met by the responsive approach of the Tory party to the call for unity and partnership in the new cities of the North.

There is some evidence that William Tom's responsibilities in Spear & Jackson were growing, as more advertisements for extra staff appeared in the pages of the Sheffield Daily Telegraph. On 10 August 1893 he called for two first-class rollers and two sets of undermen; in January 1902 he advertised for 'six good men accustomed to sheets for railway'; and in January 1903 he was looking for a sheet roller – a good, steady man – who should apply to William Adsetts of Spear & Jackson at Etna Works.

In the *Sheffield Daily Telegraph* of 26 June 1896 he wrote to the editor about the attitude of a local magistrate (clearly a Liberal!) towards 'Blind Peter' (presumably a local character):

I have read in your columns of the ungentlemanly remark of a certain magistrate to poor Blind Peter, and my feelings have been first, of sympathy for poor Peter; and then my heart has turned in disgust towards our enlightened JP; and this is the kind of man we the toilers of Sheffield are asked to look up to! Perhaps a little board school education would be useful in his case. I have no doubt the electors will remember poor Peter, and the unfeeling remarks, when the election comes round.

Yours etc William Adsetts.

A few months later he had another opportunity to have a go at a political opponent, when supporting the candidacy of Grayson Lowood at Grimesthorpe board school in October 1896. Seconding the normal 'fit and proper' resolution, he replied to Mr Gent, the Liberal opponent, who had complained that Mr Lowood was not a 'talker' in committee; pointing out that actions speak louder than words, William Tom 'was sure that Mr Lowood's actions would do 20 times more good than all the twaddle of Mr Gent's'.

There was a Liberal meeting two days later in support of Messrs Carr and Gent, who were both standing for Brightside ward in the forthcoming municipal elections. Mr Gent, an auctioneer and furniture dealer, took the opportunity to reply to the personal attacks recently made against him in the campaign, and devoted his speech to rebutting the various 'petty accusations which the opposition have been spreading', and made special reference to the recent remarks of young William Tom Adsetts.

Mr Gent answered the heckling question, 'What do you know of the needs of the working man?' by referring to his early years as a bricklayer, before turning to the specific complaint that my grandfather had made about his own experience after buying a piano on Hire Purchase from Mr Gent in 1887. William Tom complained that when he had lost his employment and couldn't keep up the payments, he returned the piano to Mr Gent, but never received any allowance against a subsequent purchase. No one won the argument, but that wasn't really the point!

Gent.—Councillor Wm. Thompson Gent, 23, Burngreave Road, Sheffield. Son of the late Samuel Gent, of Norfolk. Born at Doddington, Cambridgeshire; educated at Trinity School, Sheffield, and Sunday Educational Institute; at the age of twenty-three commenced to practise as an auctioneer, and has gradually, in conjunction with this, developed a large house furnishing business; contested the Brightside Ward four years ago, and was returned by a majority of 500 votes; was again returned last year; sits on Technical Instruction Committee, Health, Water and Allotments Committees; as a recreation and for charitable purposes, devotes considerable part of his leisure to giving elocutionary recitals.

Councillor Gent was elected to the city council in 1896 and 1900, despite the personal attacks by William Tom Adsetts.

It seems likely that a deliberate political tension was being created, perhaps because Councillor Gent was perceived as being particularly vulnerable on the working-class issue (I wonder how his elocutionary recitals went down?).

Inevitably, a similar issue arose, or was deliberately staged, during the municipal election campaign in 1899, when Mr Gent spoke at a meeting in Neepsend National School. In the *Sheffield Independent* report of 20 October 1899, Mr Gent referred to personal attacks made by Mr Adsetts in a meeting the previous day, when he had charged Mr Gent with 'prostituting his position as a member of the city council by doing work for the council and making extortionate charges for that work'.

An earlier council decision to widen High St had called for a 'forced sale' of the stock of Mr Gent's shop, and over four days he had auctioned 700 lots for a total sale of over £200. There was disagreement over the level of compensation, and an arbitrator was appointed who questioned Mr Gent's professional auctioneer's charges as being 'heavier than usual'; this was the basis for my grandfather's accusations, which were soon obscured by further long discussion on the inclusion of 'reasonable' expenses.

While his accusations were disrupting his opponent's meeting in this way, my grandfather was happily presiding over a well-attended Conservative meeting in the Grimesthorpe board school 'to further the candidature of Mr William Grafton' for the same ward!

William Tom Adsetts was clearly earning his spurs as a highly vocal *agent provocateur*, who could be relied upon to stir up the personal issues that were an important part of the local political argument. By September 1900 he had moved up in the Conservative ranks, becoming involved with national politics when he formally seconded the nomination of James Fitzalan Hope as the Conservative candidate for the Brightside constituency, one of the two contested elections in Sheffield during the 1900 'Khaki' General Election.

The Liberal candidate was Fred Maddison, an opponent of the Boer War, and Fitzalan Hope won by nearly 1,000 votes – to give the Conservatives four out of the five Sheffield seats. This was a considerable breakthrough in Brightside, which had consistently elected a Liberal candidate from 1885 to 1900. In this election 'the Conservatives were able to play their imperialist hand to the full. It undoubtedly won them the election', says Helen Mathers in her article 'The City of Sheffield 1893-1926' from the 1993 *History of the City of Sheffield*.

This election marked the high point of Conservative support in the city, and in October 1901 a full complement of three Conservative councillors was elected to the Burngreave ward.

William Tom was particularly active in 1903 and 1904. He chaired public meetings on Gower St, Lyons Rd and Carwood Rd on 28 and 30 October 1903, and presided over an election meeting on 31 October 1903. Later, he led a crowded debate on fiscal reform in December 1903.

The Annual General Meeting of the Brightside Conservative Association was held in the Carwood Hotel on Carlisle St East on 13 February 1904, and my grandfather was elected to be its chairman and its representative to the General Council of the National Union of

Conservative and Constitutional Associations.

The newspaper report states that there was a hearty speech from Mr Adsetts supporting a resolution of thanks to the Brightside MP, Fitzalan Hope, for his services to Brightside Division. Two months later he chaired the 16 April 1904 meeting of the Grimesthorpe Conservative and Constitutional Association, also in the Carwood Hotel on Carlisle St East.

This was a busy time for William Tom. Just a week after the meeting of the Brightside Association there was an advertisement in the *Sheffield Daily Telegraph* announcing a major sale of a house furnisher's stock-in-trade, 'being a further portion of the stock removed from WT Adsetts who is giving up this department'. There were three sales notices in February, and two more in May before this substantial stockholding of household furniture, bedroom suites and household goods, including a billiard table and a 'cottage pianoforte by Collard and Collard which cost 120 pounds' had been sold. We can only assume that his furniture shops were having cash-flow problems requiring drastic action!

From 1905 onwards there was an electoral breakthrough for independent Labour with the election of three Sheffield councillors, two for Brightside and one for Darnall, and from then on there was a slow move away from the coalition of working and middle-class support which had been built up by Leng, beginning with a blatantly 'anti-labour' decision of the Conservative council education committee that the new King Edward VII School should be fee-paying and 'reserved for the sons of the middle and upper classes'.

The political scene in Sheffield in the first ten years of the twentieth century was volatile to say the least! Helen Mathers, in her article 'The City of Sheffield 1893-1926', describes the situation:

In retrospect it seems significant that WC Leng died in 1902… Thereafter the Conservative group lost its vision and took a narrow view of some possibly beneficial proposals. It became particularly resistant to ideas that would have helped working people at just the time when the Liberals had come round to greater council intervention and Labour was beginning to flex its independent political muscles.

The years following 1905 were 'notable for the rise of the Labour party and the rush to anti-socialism by the other two parties'.

In these circumstances, relationships were strained, not without cost to the unity of the Adsetts family. In a meeting with Clifford Adsetts, the 85-year-old grandson of George Adsetts, William Tom's brother, he told me that his father, Lewis (who was 18 in 1907) was so opposed to the family association with the Conservatives through William Tom Adsetts ('not a nice man'), and so disillusioned by the whole political scene, that he never would speak of it to his family again. This was serious stuff! When I first introduced myself to Clifford, and he worked out that I was one of the 'Lyon Street Adsetts', our talks were temporarily suspended while he consulted his 90-year-old sister about this association with the 'enemy'.

In 1909 and 1910 the suffragettes in Sheffield were particularly active; they were led by Adela Pankhurst, the youngest daughter of the founder of the movement, who began by disrupting the Cutlers' Feast in 1908 disguised as a waitress and went on to lead a number of demonstrations around the city.

William Tom Adsetts was still actively supporting the working-class Conservative movement in Sheffield, which we know because his son Ernest vividly recalls an incident 'in front of the Vestry Hall', probably in the 1910 election, when his father was dragged from a dray in the middle of his speech by a group of suffragettes.

The sight of this bulky man, who weighed over 18 stone, being so manhandled, made a lasting impression on a little boy of five, who was still telling the story 80 years later.

By the late 1890s the introduction of protectionist tariffs in the United States and other major importing countries had created a business environment increasingly hostile to the larger Sheffield firms. Spear & Jackson had responded with a strategy of seeking new export outlets, and this helped to compensate for the loss of the American markets, at least in part, by increasing sales in Canada, India, China and Japan. The negative impact of these tariffs was also limited by the adaptability and emphasis on quality that characterised the large number of small firms in Sheffield.

Clearly, William Tom Adsetts was still regarded as an active spokesman for the Conservative policy on tariff reform when he was named as one of the six members of the *Sheffield Daily Telegraph* deputation to Germany in September 1910. An article on the eve of their departure states that all the members of the group 'are staunch trade unionists who enjoy the confidence of their employers and are held in esteem by their fellow workers'.

I have yet to find any evidence that William Tom Adsetts had specific union affiliation, but this is not surprising, given the complex structure of trade unionism in Sheffield. Sidney Pollard states that because of the deep split among trade unionists over politics in Sheffield 'their story is an exceedingly complex one – unparalleled anywhere else in the country'.

The hierarchical structure of the steelmakers union, which was divided between the first hands or sub-contractors (like William Tom) and the other hands sometimes actually employed by them, who received much lower wages, often made it difficult to reconcile the separate interests of the workforce, particularly in firms like Spear & Jackson, which combined steelmaking with the skilled manufacture of tools. The situation was further complicated with the creation of the Labour Representation Committee in 1900, which turned into the Labour party in 1906.

In these circumstances, all I can do is accept that the *Telegraph* delegates to Germany were each in their own way staunch trade unionists. There is no evidence of any arguments to the contrary, and William Tom Adsetts was clearly able to assert his credentials as a supporter of 'one-nation' or 'popular' Conservatism in his favourable report on the working conditions for factory workers while he was in Osnabruck and Magdeburg.

William Tom was chosen for the fact-finding mission to Germany in 1910 because of his support for tariff reform. In this he was simply reflecting the policy advocated by the Conservatives, the views of his employer, and the majority view of the Chamber of Commerce forcibly expressed by Mr Beardshaw (in whose garden my great-grandfather had the accident which led to his death).

Beardshaw was clearly a very active spokesman for the steel-makers. His workaholic style of management was described in his 1957 obituary in the Chamber magazine *Quality*, stating that 'it was quite in the ordinary course of things that he should reside at the works, where he had a room for 15 years'.

Despite the strong Conservative views expressed in the editorial pages of the *Sheffield Daily Telegraph*, the delegation members were selected to provide a balance between free traders and tariff reformers. It was not expected that there would be any dramatic conversions as a result of their

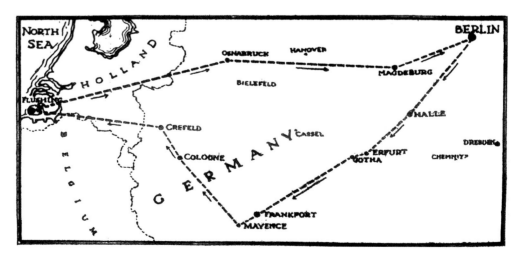

Map of the tour undertaken by the delegates.

individual experiences of life in Germany, since they were simply asked to report on the conditions of life and labour under tariffs.

Lloyd George had set the scene! Several simplistic arguments against tariffs had been put forward with his authority, stating that German workers were

Image: LSE Library

being forced by tariffs to live on horse flesh, offal and black bread, that the degrading poverty in which they had to live was due solely to their tariff system, and that tariffs crippled commerce and industry, making economic progress impossible. The *Sheffield Daily Telegraph* reckoned that the tariff reform case would be strengthened if these statements were shown to be demonstrably untrue – so they sponsored the mission to Germany.

The Sheffield group was the ninth deputation of workingmen that had been sent to Germany on behalf of the Tariff Reform League, and they were welcomed home at a formal lunch on their return to London on 26 September 1910 by Viscount Ridley, the chairman of the Tariff Reform League, and FE Smith KC MP (the future Lord Birkenhead – a champion of working-class conservatism).

A total of 478 men, from all over the country, had been sent out to investigate the actual state of the German industrial worker, and, irrespective of their individual views about the merits of free trade or protection, Viscount Ridley concluded that there was a general feeling that statements about the misery of the German workers and the conditions under which they lived were demonstrably untrue.

The individual delegates had been unanimous in finding little or no evidence undermining the case for tariff reform, thus contradicting what William Tom called, in the introduction to his personal report, 'hollow and untruthful expressions uttered for political party purposes before and during the last General Election'.

William Tom Adsetts – This was the photograph taken for the report of the Sheffield delegation to Germany in September 1910.

It seemed that no significant lessons were learned in relation to the tariff-free trade debate, but this experience of foreign travel opened the eyes of the individual delegates to better conditions of employment for workers, healthy agriculture, and low rates of unemployment in the cities they visited – let alone the attractions of the continental Sunday!

Several members of the deputation gave their views, including William Tom Adsetts, steel-roller of Sheffield, who 'spoke highly of the condition of the working classes in Germany' and gave his opinion that it was 'much better than that of the working class of this country'.

He was followed by FE Smith, who went on to say, 'If so much mischief and misery lay in Mr Chamberlain's proposals, how was it that the German working classes were today in such a prosperous and

A MAN OF SHEFFIELD

comfortable condition?' Then he made the final, clinching argument: 'Does it not show that it is possible, with a scientifically developed tariff structure, for a nation to preserve its own markets and compete in the markets of the world?'

William Tom was clearly comfortable moving in these high-level circles of political debate, and it raises a question in my mind about where his political ambitions and ability may have taken him if he had been spared an early death.

In the 20 years since the 1884 increase in the franchise, the Liberals had experienced a 'double whammy' of bad luck and bad judgement over their backing of Irish Home Rule and the subsequent departure of Joseph Chamberlain, who then picked up the imperial theme, linked it to tariff reform, and moved still further away from the Liberals.

LIFE UNDER TARIFFS.

WHAT WE SAW IN GERMANY.

"Sheffield Daily Telegraph" Tour,
SEPTEMBER, 1910.

REPORTS OF DELEGATES.

[Reprinted from the "Sheffield Daily Telegraph."]

'Without doubt we saw more poverty in London in five minutes than we saw in Germany in twelve days'.
From the final report of William Tom Adsetts.

Controversy over tariff reform and free trade raged throughout the early years of the century up to the beginning of the war in 1914, leading to heightened tension between the Liberal and Conservative parties in Sheffield and dividing opinions in the business community; but in Sheffield there was never a clear resolution of the debate, probably because of the fragmented business structure in the city.

There are some vivid tales about the life and work of 'Bill' Adsetts. He looked after his men, and this not only involved bailing them out before starting work on Monday morning, but also drinking with them most days after work. He used the same cabby-driver to travel to and from work and wherever else he wanted to go, entrusting him with his money and valuables for safekeeping before every drinking session.

He 'never came home sober', but he was a generous and spontaneous man, and there is a most engaging picture of him coming home with a chicken in one pocket and a rabbit in the other, or bringing a suit or two for little Ernest and perhaps a dress for one of his daughters, or on other occasions calling on 'Annie lass' at any time of the day to prepare a meal for one of the guests he was always bringing home without notice.

There are other recollections of his business activities, particularly of the sale of fishing prizes, which his wife and family spent hours wrapping before big competitions. He is said to have had a 'fishing prizes' shop on Earsham St, and the directories show that his brother George's widow Louisa lived at 270 Earsham St from 1905 to 1920, so she probably looked after this shop, just as she and her husband had done earlier on Fitzalan St and Lyon St for William Tom.

George William's son Ernest told me that 'grandfather's business was selling furniture on the never-never, and he would take his son George with him on the horse and cart to collect furniture from customers who didn't pay'. He also said that 'he would often borrow pieces of furniture from grandma, and he even sold the sideboard from her front room with a promise that it would be replaced next week'! He also told me that William Tom used to go often to the pictures at the Heeley Palace because he was a shareholder and probably had a pass from the owners.

He was a member of the Union Jack lodge of the Antediluvian Order of Buffalos, a friendly society of which there were over 70 local lodges in Sheffield. There is no record of a Union Jack lodge in the Grand Lodge of England website, but his son George William was in the same lodge, and we have both his silver medal and lapel badge, the first of which was awarded to him in March 1909 for 'good attendance at meetings'.

William Tom was a practical man, and he made brass working models of both the rolls and the stamping press on which he worked at Spear & Jackson. The press survives, because it was given to me by my Auntie Annie Bellamy in the late 1950s and has been a feature in every office of mine since 1960, when I was a manager at Fibreglass R&D. It bears a plaque, 'Made by William T Adsetts Sheffield', dated 1909, and its glass case contains a bronze medal, 'Awarded for Excellence' at an exhibition of 'Industrial Engineering Mining and Invention' held in the Norfolk Drill Hall on 27 April 1891. Yet my father was sure that the model was exhibited in Firth College 'before it became the university'; maybe there was a second exhibition in 1909?

Model of a Spear & Jackson stamping press made by William Tom Adsetts in 1909.

A year or two later William Tom retired from Spear & Jackson, almost certainly for health reasons, and moved to a riverside house named 'Trent View' in the Nottinghamshire village of Church Laneham. The Laneham house, which was owned in 1909 by Thomas Hill, the managing director of Sheffield Carriage and Harness Company, was still occupied by his tenant John Herring, a retired edge-tool manufacturer, in the 1911 Census return; and so it seems that William Tom could not have moved to Laneham until later in 1911.

William Tom certainly owned the property when he died in 1913, because there is a later reference to the creation of an Adsetts Trust funded by the proceeds of its sale, to be used for the benefit of his children.

The Bishop of Southwell described conditions in Laneham after his formal visit in February 1914. He referred to the massive strain on a tiny parish of preserving the fabric of the church buildings, leading to the extreme loneliness and poverty of the clergy in such parishes, the value of well-trained lay readers, and the total dependence of the area on agriculture, which 'in current conditions means that young people are leaving the villages for towns or the colonies'.

William Tom was a man of many parts, with a great zest for life; and when he retired early to live in Church Laneham in 1911 with his wife Annie, young Ernest and Grandma Youle, he hoped to play a part in village life, in addition to his first love of fishing!

William Tom apparently served on a local committee, but his time in Laneham was too short to make much impact. Did he serve on the parish council, and did he provide the village with markers made of steel rails either side of the riverside road to indicate the depth of water in the annual floods, as his son told me? Perhaps he did – the black and white painted metal posts are still there on either side of the road running past the front of Trent View to indicate the depth of the flood every year.

My father told me that William Tom Adsetts occasionally preached to the Church of England congregation in Church Laneham, and his mother helped in cleaning and decorating the church. Ernest was soon enrolled in the Sunday school and the village school in Top Laneham.

Young Ernest, meanwhile, settled into his new surroundings and enjoyed the life of a country boy under the guidance of his new friend, Arthur Leach from the neighbouring farm, who was just a few years older, and introduced him to the many unfamiliar jobs around the farm and in the fields.

Then it all came to an end. One day in July 1913, Ernest was bringing the cows in for milking with Arthur Leach when he saw the closed bedroom curtains as they passed Trent View. He ran in to learn of his father's death. His elder brother George had come from Sheffield to be with his father when he died, and so the news was probably not unexpected.

In *The Ernest Adsetts Story* he describes how he found his mother crying while she sat and picked redcurrants. She said, 'Yes, it's true – your father's dead – he's gone to heaven, so you'll be alright', and told him to 'go back to help Arthur with the cows and come straight back home'.

The death certificate says that William died of a 'bad heart and apoplexy'; he probably had a stroke, but family recollections talk of 'dropsy' brought on by heavy drinking. In these circumstances, it was inevitable that the lonely, seven-year-old Ernest would have been drawn even closer to his mother and ultimately feel responsible for her wellbeing.

As one of the executors of her husband's will, his mother became a trustee, with Ernest Banks, of a small family trust set up to use the proceeds of a sale of assets (including the Laneham house and the Lyon St shop) to support her children when required. My father may have got some help when he moved to Sheffield years later, but the main support was given to his three sisters, who were each running small shops when their mother died in 1936.

William Tom the angler, who retired in 1911 to Trent View in Laneham.

In loving memory of William Tom Adsetts, the dearly beloved husband of Annie Adsetts, who departed this life on July 9th 1913: 'A bitter grief, a shock severe to part with one we loved so dear' from his loving wife and children

(Sheffield Independent 13 July 1913)

A MAN OF SHEFFIELD

THE
ADSETTS
STORY

The Offshoots

To Handsworth and Beyond
To Bolsover and Beyond

THE ADSETTS STORY

THE OFFSHOOTS

In my genealogical research I have unearthed several interesting stories about the lives of the various Adsetts individuals who were off-shoots of the direct line, including those who left Elmton to play a part in the development of neighbouring towns and villages in the eighteenth and early nineteenth centuries, and who later left Palterton to meet the growing demand for workers in Sheffield.

Rufus, who left Elmton to become the Wheelwright of Handsworth in 1756

Rufus Adsetts left Elmton to establish himself as a joiner, wheelwright and respectable churchwarden in Handsworth near Sheffield, and his offspring played active parts in the growth of Sheffield:

George Adsetts, with his son Harry, were also wheelwrights who set up a family coachbuilding company in Sheffield.

The enterprising George Adsetts, his nephew, became an agent setting up Land Societies to help meet the growing need for houses in Sheffield and developed Adsetts Street in New Grimesthorpe.

Then there was William, an inventive toolmaker, whose son William Henry 1 followed this craft until he left his small family to follow a professional career in competitive foot racing (pedestrianism) in America.

William Henry 2, one of his two sons from a bigamous American marriage, joined the US Army, served in the Philippines, and was hanged for murder in Hong Kong in 1907.

Finally there was William Henry 3, whose father was the legitimate son of the wandering athlete in America, who left Sheffield University to become an Army officer in 1914 and was killed in the Battle of Loos a year later.

George, who left Elmton in 1787 to settle in Bolsover

Two generations after Rufus, George Adsetts left Elmton for Bolsover where his grandson George became the licensee of the Angel Inn, marrying Hannah Cook, who became the matriarch of the Adsetts Family, running the Angel for over eighty years while Bolsover was changing from a sleepy rural village to a bustling mining and manufacturing centre. Her son, John Henry, became a member of the first town council.

As part of the mid-eighteenth century drift away from Palterton, as with other depressed agricultural areas of North Derbyshire, the brothers of George, my great-great-grandfather, were also on the move to find employment.

George's brother William, who left Palterton for Aughton in 1840

His sons, the two Adsetts brothers William and George, who were cousins of my great grandfather John, died in a pit accident in the new colliery of Treeton in 1875.

George's brother Thomas, who left Palterton for Beighton in 1842

Thomas left Palterton after his marriage to Hannah in 1841 and settled in Beighton, then moved his family to the small village of Adwick–upon-Dearne.

His grandson, George Albert Adsetts, was a Doncaster miner, aged 18 when he enlisted in the York and Lancaster Regiment in 1914. In an eventful military career he survived two years as a tunneller on the Western Front, fought in Italy in 1918, and died in Baghdad in 1921 during our last colonial war, in Mesopotamia.

All these lives are just as much part of the Adsetts story as my forebears in the direct line from Clowne in 1633 to Sheffield in 1983, and their individual stories are included in this history of the family name.

From the early forebears to the modern day the Adsetts have adapted to adversity, to changing times and difficult circumstances, sometimes clinging on, sometimes making their own luck.

Sometimes they are entrepreneurs, sometimes businessmen using their nous and talents to help others as well as themselves. Sometimes there is valour, sometimes there is vice. But there's never a dull moment.

CLOWNE
RICHARD = JONY
ADSETTS
1600-

THE ADSETTS STORY
OFFSHOOT
RUFUS ADSETTS
TO
WANDSWORTH
1756.

+ BEYOND TO SHEFFIELD
NEW YORK + HONGKONG

1662 CLOWNE
ROBERT = ROSAMOND
ADSETTS   RUDDE
1633-1710 1635-1714

BEELEY
1691
2. DOROTHY = ROBERT = 1. MARY
HOLME   ADSETTS   ALLSOP
1665-1730 1665-1690

ELMTON 1730
JOHN = ANNE
ADSETTS   1700
1690-1772

ELMTON 1757   ELMTON 1756   THEN MOVED
MARY = JOHN   RUFUS = ELIZABETH   TO WANDSWORTH
HUNT   ADSETTS   ADSETTS   GLOSSOP
1735-1820 1750-1808 1734-1808 1738-1795

ECKINGTON 1729
JOHN = ANN
ADSETTS   WATHEY
1757-

1808   HANDSWORTH 1803
WANDSWORTH
LYDIA = GEORGE   ELIZABETH WILLIAM
SHEPHERD ADSETTS   TIMMONS ADSETTS
          1787-   1782

                    1826
                    DRONFIELD
MARY = HENRY   ELIZABETH = GEORGE   WILLIAM = MARIA
GILL   ADSETTS   MOSLEY   ADSETTS   ADSETTS   1806-
       1808   1807   1804   1808-1872 1866
                  -1884   -1879   KEELEY

HENRY   SHEFFIELD SAILED   WILLIAM   1. ROSANNA
ADSETTS   USM1   TO N.Y. HENRY I   HICKMAN
1838   AGENT   1867   1845-1884 1846
                                     (NY)
H. ADSETTS   2. BESSIE
& SON   HARRIS
COACH & CARRIAGE   MARY = HARRY   1855-
BUILDER   ELLEN   ADSETTS
1847   JEFFCOCK 1866
                          1866
                          (VT)

                          WILLIAM   WILLIAM
                          HENRY   HENRY
                          III   II
                          1893-1915   1878-1907
                          WW1   HANGED
                          LOOS   FOR MURDER
                          DIED   IN
                                          HONGKONG

TO HANDSWORTH & BEYOND

RUFUS ADSETTS
THE HANDSWORTH WHEELWRIGHT

A traditional wheelwrights workshop with tools and cartwheels.

The Handsworth connection began with Rufus Adsetts, who was born in Elmton in 1734. He was the younger brother of John Adsetts and the uncle of John's son William, who emigrated from Elmton to Scarcliffe with his wife Catherine shortly after they married, and who gave birth to George Adsetts, my great-great-grandfather, in 1806.

Where did the name Rufus come from? This name does not occur in any other local records. Apparently it was first used as a nickname for

King William Rufus because of his red hair. It then became a surname after the Protestant Reformation, and only appears as a popular first name in the nineteenth century, so our Rufus Adsetts was an early example. Maybe he too was born with red hair?

Rufus married Elizabeth Glossop in Elmton in 1756, and then took his new wife to Handsworth near Sheffield, where he worked as a carpenter in the nearby hamlet of Woodhouse. It has been suggested by a local historian that Rufus may originally have moved to Handsworth to work in the local nurseries. Whatever the reason, he will have taken with him the skills of the wheelwright learned from his father, Robert.

He was a solid citizen of the parish of Handsworth for the rest of his life. In 1780 he was one of the churchwardens of the parish church, and was still living in Woodhouse when his wife Elizabeth died in 1795 at the age of 66; Rufus died five years later in 1800.

John Adsetts, the first child of Rufus and Elizabeth, was born in Handsworth in 1757, and also became a carpenter living in Woodhouse. In 1779 he married Ann Wathey in the parish of Eckington, and their five children were born in Handsworth: Elizabeth in 1779, Martha in 1781, William in 1782, John in 1784 and George in 1787.

John's eldest son William initially stayed in Handsworth, where he married Elizabeth Tummons in 1803, and where their first child, George, the future Sheffield land agent, was born in 1804. Then the family moved around, and their other children were baptised in several different parishes: Charles in 1806 in Rotherham, Elizabeth in 1813 in Sheffield cathedral, and Ann in 1815, again in Rotherham. William Adsetts, the future Sheffield toolmaker, whose career is described below, is almost certainly another member of this family, born in Masbrough, Rotherham, in 1808, in the gap between Charles and Elizabeth.

William's younger brother George was married in Handsworth to Lydia Shepherd in 1808, and their son Henry was born there in the same year. George Adsetts is named in the Barnes and Parson Directory of 1822 as one of three wheelwrights then living in Handsworth; and nineteen years later, in White's Directory for 1841, he and his son Henry have joined together as 'George Adsetts & Son – Wheelwrights and Carriage Builders', still based in Handsworth.

In the *Yorkshire Gazette* of 16 September 1843 a notice of insolvency was served in the names of George and Henry Adsetts, 'carriage builders of Handsworth Woodhouse', but it seems that both men continued in this line of work. In 1845, living in Johnson St, Henry is specifically described as a railway and general carriage builder, while his 65-year-old father George was still working as a coachbuilder, according to White's Directory in 1852, living at 15 Wicker Lane.

Henry's small son Henry had died in 1838, so the rebirth of the family firm as 'H Adsetts & Son' was short-lived, and it was renamed as 'Henry Adsetts, Railway and Carriage Builder' (late H. Adsetts & Son) of Handsworth Woodhouse and Corn Exchange.

In Grace's Guide of 1847, there is an entry and advertisement in which the firm is described as a manufacturer of 'all kinds of Railway Carriages'; of 'Thatcher's Patent Break or Drag'; and as an agent of Messrs Neill and Co.'s Asphalated Roofing Felt.

And in the final line of the above advertisement, one hundred years before the formation of the Sheffield Insulating Company, Henry Adsetts has pioneered the role of insulation distributor by describing himself as an agent for:

DRY HAIR FELT FOR THE COVERING OF STEAM BOILERS

(A similar product was still being sold in 1966 for pipe insulation when I joined the Sheffield Insulating Company – although the white wool mattresses of Fibreglass were better for boilers!)

Nothing more is known of this interesting business, but fourteen years later Henry Adsetts, described as an Engineer, is listed with his wife Mary in the 1861 Census living in Merton St, Liverpool. It appears that they had for some reason started a new life away from Sheffield.

GEORGE ADSETTS
THE SHEFFIELD LAND AGENT

Adsetts St, Grimesthorpe. *Image © Harry Ainscough, copperbeechstudios.co.uk.*

George Adsetts, the eldest son of William and Elizabeth, who was born in Handsworth in 1804 and married Elizabeth Mosely in Dronfield in 1826, had a varied career before he became seriously involved in the Sheffield land and building boom as a developer and full-time agent in the second half of the nineteenth century.

A George Adsetts appears in both Pigot's Directory of 1834 and White's Directory of 1837 as a boot and shoemaker on Bramall Lane, at the foot of Porter St. I am not sure whether this was the George Adsetts born in Handsworth. He is more likely to be the George Adsetts named in the Rodgers Directory of 1841 as a type-founder living at 77 Daisy Bank, Daisy Walk, off St Philip's Rd.

This is confirmed in the 1841 Census, which includes an Elizabeth Adsetts (30-35) living on Daisy Walk. There is a notice in the 18 March issue of the *London Daily News* in 1846 naming a George Adsetts with eight others in the formal dissolving of a type-founding partnership.

In 1849 George Adsetts reappears in White's Directory for Sheffield as a manufacturer of scythes, living in Milton St. He appears to be a partner in Garfitt and Adsetts, manufacturers of hay, straw, rag and paper machine knives, scythes and sickles at 48 Thomas St. His partner, Thomas Garfitt, seems to have been a substantial man, a saw and file manufacturer in his own name, living at Wellfield House, Little Common Lane, in Ecclesall Brierlow.

The partnership was short-lived, and on 29 September 1849 announcements in the *Yorkshire Gazette* and the *York Herald* state that 'the partnership of DT Garfitt and G Adsetts scythe makers' had been dissolved. It was replaced in White's Directory of 1852 by Thos Garfitt and Son, a scythe sickle and machine knives manufacturer, at 48 Broomhall St.

In 1853 George Adsetts, now described as a commercial traveller, entered into an agreement to buy land in Walkley with two partners – Edward Cooper, a file maker of 31 Norfolk Lane, and John Gatley, a filesmith, probably associated with Gatley and Wortley, the ironmongers of 121 West Bar. He is said to have formed Fir View Land Society and Steel Bank Society to develop land in Walkley with the same two partners.

There is a reference to such activities in the Pawson and Brailsford *Illustrated Guide to Sheffield* of 1862. Describing the outskirts of the city, the writer goes on to say:

"Even more pleasing…is the spectacle presented by Walkley and other of the out-districts. There are several localities where

estates have been purchased and partitioned out by means of the Freehold Land Societies. The hillsides are dotted in every direction with houses, almost all of them obtained by working men through the instrumentality of the Freehold Land and Building Societies."

A description of the process leading to this explosion of building enterprise has been provided in an article by Donald J. Olsen, 'House upon House – Estate Development in London and Sheffield', which appears in Volume 1 of *The Victorian City: Images and Reality*, published in 1973, as follows.

> *"Building land on the outskirts of Victorian cities was plentiful, cheap, and not subject to significant fluctuations in price... landowners consciously kept both freehold prices and ground rents low in order to attract purchasers and builders to their estates.*
>
> *The practice of charging peppercorn rents for the first years of a lease, or accepting payment in instalments, meant that the speculator himself often paid little or nothing for the land.*
>
> *Nor was there any shortage of speculative builders. Entry into the business required no specialised skills and little or no capital, so the smallest of firms was able to coexist perfectly satisfactorily with the largest.*
>
> *To an abundance of landowners eager to participate in the unearned increment that urban growth offered to them, and an abundance of builders ready to risk their all in covering their land with houses, there was added a complementary abundance of investors, virtually forcing their money on the builders and developers. The buoyant supply of capital for house building matched the supply of land and labour."*

There are less complimentary descriptions of this process. G. Calvert Holland, for example, writing in 1843 in *The Vital Statistics of Sheffield*, attributed the over-production of houses in Sheffield to 'the petty capitalist desirous of realizing a handsome percentage' as much as to the landowner 'naturally anxious to appropriate his land to building purposes' and the 'penniless speculative builder'.

The Hammonds also wrote with passion of the new industrial cities of the Midlands and the North: 'They were not so much towns as the barracks of an industry, and they reflected the single passion that had thrown street on street in a frantic monotony of disorder; these shapeless improvisations represented nothing but the avarice of the jerry-builder catering for the avarice of the capitalist'.

George Adsetts certainly seemed to prosper in this environment. In White's Directory of 1856 he appears as an agent to Land Societies, living at 38 William St. In 1859, now a secretary to building societies, he has an office in Barkers Pool and lives in Oak View Cottages, Brightside.

In the 1861, 1862 and 1863 directories he is described as a land building agent, with an office at 16 Bank St. Then in the Burgess Rolls for 1864-65 he is listed with offices at George St in Brightside and Cambridge St in the city centre. Later on, in 1865, his office is at 60 Snig Hill, and he finally appears in 1871 as a land surveyor and agent with offices on Change Alley.

Peter Harvey, the late feature writer of the *Star*, has provided further information about the involvement of George Adsetts with land and building societies in Sheffield. He was president of the Sheffield and Grimesthorpe Freehold Land Society that was established in 1861, and built Adsetts St between 1864 and 1866 as part of the development called New Grimesthorpe. The neighbouring terraces of Botham St, Howsley St and Moss St were named after his partners in the venture.

Peter Harvey, who did his original research on George Adsetts for a feature on Adsetts St, says that he was also president of the Fourth

Borough Benefit Society in 1872, and a director of the Seventh Borough Benefit Society in the same period.

In fact, his responsibilities extended further than this, and the regular reports in the *Sheffield Independent* include the annual meetings of the Second Borough Building Society in 1859 and the 'highly successful and flourishing' Fifth Borough Building Society in 1869, at which George Adsetts, in his speech as president, congratulated members on the high position attained by all the 'Borough' societies, viewing them with pardonable pride, and remarking on the advantages of such societies to the working man.

In the 1871 Census he has moved from Brightside to Penrith Villa, located between Brocco Bank and Wilson Rd near Hunters' Bar. At this address he appears with his wife Elizabeth, and the Census data records confirm that he was born in Handsworth Woodhouse in 1805 (actually 1804 from the church baptism records), and his wife in Dore in 1807 (incidentally making her roughly the same age as the Elizabeth Adsetts who lived on Daisy Bank in 1841).

The list of subscribers to the 'new and enlarged edition' of Joseph Hunter's 'Hallamshire', reissued by Alfred Gatty in 1869, includes the name of George Adsetts. He died, recognised as a solid citizen of Sheffield, at the age of 74, on 23 January 1879 in 6 Wilson Rd, after six years' 'paralysis'. It was an interesting career, but more enquiries are needed to make sense of the earlier years. His widow, Elizabeth, died four years later, in February 1884, at 'her residence in 19 Redhill'.

WILLIAM ADSETTS
THE SHEFFIELD TOOLMAKER

W illiam Adsetts was born in Masbrough, Rotherham, in 1808. I have found no record of his birth, although there will presumably be some trace in Rotherham parish registers, but he was probably a son of William and Elizabeth Adsetts, originally from Handsworth,

W. ADSETTS,
MANUFACTURER OF
TURNSCREWS,
BRACE HEADS, BRAD AWL & HAND PADS,
SAW PADS,
Hammer Shafts, Turnscrew Handles,
BRAD-AWL HANDLES,
DRAWING KNIFE HANDLES,
And every Article Suitable for the Edge and Joiner Tool Trades;
POOL WORKS, TOP OF BURGESS STREET.

and would have been born between Charles in 1806 (in Rotherham) and Elizabeth in 1813 (in Sheffield).

William senior first appears in the 1851 Census of Sheffield living at 204 South St Park with his wife Maria (born 1806 in Sheffield), their five daughters Mary, Sarah, Betsy, Ellen and Martha (born between 1832 and 1845), plus son William Henry (born in 1845). On William Henry's birth certificate his father is described as a bookkeeper.

In 1852, however, he is described in White's Directory of Sheffield as an ivory, wood and brass turner, working in Pool Works, 3 Burgess St, near Barkers Pool in the city centre.

Pool Works, in 1854, was the address of a number of 'little mesters' in addition to William Adsetts – Chas Burkenshaw, William Marsden, manufacturer of table cutlery, James Taylor, horn and bone merchant, and Henry Wilder, knife manufacturer.

In 1852 William Adsetts had taken over the lathe of John Cartwright at Pool Works. John Cartwright was described as a commercial traveller in 1841, but by 1845 had changed his trade to become a turner and hardwood merchant working from Soho Wheel, and in 1848 was operating as a manufacturer of 'brace and bit and joiner's tools'.

The invention of the metal-framed carpenter's brace was a major event in the history of the Sheffield tool trade. Described in *The Ultimate Brace – A Unique Product of Victorian Sheffield* (Reg Eaton, 1989), the first patent for a 'revolutionary metallic-framed brace' was filed by John Cartwright in 1848, and Royal Letters Patent 12,377 was granted on 16 June 1849. William Adsetts may have been an associate of Cartwright during this period, and he appears to have carried on Cartwright's work on the brace, being granted in 1856 a registered design No 3839 for a 'Double or Single Action Rotary Carpenters' Brace'.

An advertisement by William Adsetts appears in the *Sheffield Daily Telegraph* of July 1857 for a French polisher, a female accustomed to polishing wood handles etc by steam power, 'who should apply to Pool Works in Burgess St'.

Subsequently, William Adsetts appears in various directories up to 1865. He is usually referred to as a turner, but also as a manufacturer of joiners' tools, the fullest description being provided in 1859 when he is said to be 'the inventor and manufacturer of the improved double or single action rotary carpenter's brace heads, and wood turner of every description of handles'.

In Drake's Directory of 1863 a new home address appears, and the family is seen to be living in Shirebrook, Heeley. But William himself certainly reappears in the 1871 Census, living in South St, by which time he is, at the age of 63, a 'retired' manufacturer of joiners' tools; he died in the South St house on 17 June 1872 after several years' illness.

His son William Henry had married Rosanna Hickman in Heeley, Christ Church on 22 April 1866, and on the birth certificate of their son Harry, born later in the same year, William Henry is described as a master wood turner, clearly trained to follow his father in the family business – but it did not happen.

On 11 March 1867, a few months after the birth of his son, the new father, William Henry, landed in New York after sailing from Liverpool on SS *Helvetia*, leaving his new wife and baby son behind. Eleven days later, the whole of the finished and unfinished stock, lathes and working tools of his father in Pool Works, Burgess St were sold by auction.

Sale by Mr. Geo. Eadon.

THIS DAY.

TO JOINERS TOOLMAKERS, &c.
POOL WORKS, BURGESS STREET.
Mr. GEORGE EADON has received instructions to SELL by AUCTION, on FRIDAY, March 22d, the whole of the Finished and Unfinished STOCK, LATHES, and WORKING TOOLS, and also a quantity of Dry Beech and Box WOOD, the property of Mr. W. Adsetts, Pool Works, Burgess street.
Sale to commence at Eleven o'Clock.

Sheffield & Rotherham Independent March – 22nd 1867.

The young bride, with her new-born son, Harry, went to live with her parents, Rose and Thomas Hickman, and was still living with them in Hackenthorpe at the time of the 1871 Census; by 1881 the small family had moved to 211 Gleadless Rd, by which time Rose Hickman had died, and Harry Adsetts, now aged 15, was working as a hammer forger.

Ten years later Rosanna's father had died, Harry was married, and Rosanna, now described as a widow working as a silver burnisher, was effectively the sole occupier of 211 Gleadless Rd.

Harry Adsetts had married Mary Ellen Jeffcock in Sheffield in 1888. The Jeffcocks settled in Handsworth in the 17th century, and by the end of the eighteenth century John Jeffcock had placed the family in an influential position as local coalmasters, and the new town council elected his son William the first mayor of Sheffield in 1843.

She was born in July 1866 to Osmond Jeffcock and Catherine Blythe in Andover Massachusetts. Osmond Jeffcock, born in 1827 , was probably a member of the well-known Sheffield family originally based in Handsworth. He eventually returned from the States with Mary Ellen to Sheffield, where he died in 1880.

WILLIAM HENRY ADSETTS No.1
THE USA PEDESTRIANIST

William Henry Adsetts was born in 1845, and first appears in the 1851 Census of Sheffield living at 204 South St Park with his parents, William and Maria, and five sisters, Mary, Sarah, Betsy, Ellen and Martha.

On William Henry's birth certificate his father is described as a book-keeper, but in 1852 he appears in *White's Directory of Sheffield* as a turner of ivory, bone and

THE TURF.

MYSTIC PARK.

THURSDAY, OCT. 10.

Great Match Foot Race of 300 yards for $200 and the Championship of the United States, between JOSEPH A. STRATTON, of Fall River, Mass., and W. H. ADSETTS. of Philadelphia, Pa. There will also be a quarter of a mile dash between two well-known runners for $250.

Same Day, Sweepstakes $150.

Owners.		
"	"	..............b. m. Rosa Temple
"	"	...............g. g. Doctor
"	"	...............m. g. Romeo
"	"	...............s. m. Blackstone Maid
"	"	...............blk. m. Gypsy
"	"	..............b. g. Hindoo

Mile heats, best 3 in 5, to wagon.

These parties are considered the fastest and best runners, for a short distance, in the country, and as there is a large amount of money, as well as the honors of the championship at stake, it may be expected to see a very fast and close race. Horse cars leave Scollay's square every 30 minutes, and steam cars leave Lowell depot.

Admission 50 cts.

o7   4t   **B. S. WRIGHT & CO.,**
Proprietors.

Notice of a great Foot Race for $2,000 and Championship of the United States – *Boston Globe* of 9 October 1872.

wood handles for knives and joiners' tools, working in Pool Works, 3 Burgess St, near Barkers Pool in the city centre.

On 22 April 1866, at the age of 22, William Henry married Rosanna Hickman in Christ Church, Heeley, and on the birth certificate of their son Harry, born later in the same year, he is described as a master wood turner, a qualified craftsman who appears to have been trained to follow his father in the family business – but it was not going to happen!

In March 1867 William Henry sailed to New York, leaving his new wife and baby son behind. A few days later all of his father's stock, lathe and tools were sold by auction – clearly William Henry was not destined for the family business.

We now know that he sought a new career in the United States, but why did he abandon his family so abruptly? We will probably never know, but we can guess why he went – to increase his earnings by pursuing a career as a professional athlete. He went on to compete in a succession of sprint races over the next twenty years across America, gambling on his ability to win over distances of 100, 200 and 300 yards.

'Pedestrianism', as it was known – the staging of competitive races over both short distances and long 'endurance' events, mainly held for professionals and funded by wagering – had become a very popular spectator sport in both England and America in the second half of the nineteenth century.

Maybe William Henry had an earlier experience of pedestrianism in Sheffield?

My guess was correct. Sheffield was one of the great centres of professional athletics in Victorian times, and from the 1850s major handicaps for professional sprinters were being staged annually at grounds around the city, one of the more popular being the Queen's Ground in Hillsborough, behind the pub directly opposite my office in the barracks.

'Pedestrian' competitors from home or abroad who had the necessary turn of speed for races between 100 and 400 yards would dream of winning one of the Sheffield Handicaps.

From the pages of *Bell's Life in London*, a sporting paper which covered the events and records of many sports in England and America, I have learned that William Henry Adsetts was competing in pedestrianism events in Sheffield for several years before he decided to leave his wife and son to seek his fortune in this booming professional sport in America.

The possible reason for this dramatic shift in his life may lie in the impact of the American Civil War. American demand for all kinds of Sheffield products remained high until the outbreak of the Civil War, but many of the local steel cutlery and tool firms 'began to experience a shrinking order book towards the end of 1861' and 'the economic repercussions of the American Civil War hit Sheffield's metal industries with full force in 1862', according to David Hey in his *History of Sheffield*.

In his 2017 book *Running for Money*, Tom Carruthers makes the point that the 1861 foot-racing season in Sheffield was 'one of the most successful on record. During the year 20 major handicaps were run, 15 at Hyde Park and 5 at the new Queen's Hotel Grounds'.

The situation was, however, worse in 1862, when there were only 17 races with prize money of 20 pounds or more, while 'the quality and integrity of the contests took a dive'; and in 1863 the number of such races in Sheffield fell to 12, the lowest since 1857.

This wasn't all. Promotions were cancelled, ground attendances fell, few runners and bookmakers turned up for races, and criminal influences and physical violence began to 'destroy the integrity of the sport'. Corruption and thuggery 'drove away spectators, bookmakers and talented runners from the running grounds'.

And the young William Henry was indeed a talented runner! The first record of his running career is of a meeting in the Athletic Sports of Christ Church, Heeley, on 5 April 1863, when he was aged 18. William came first in the 100-yard flat race, the 120-yard handicap (competing off scratch), the running high jump and the running wide jump, but only came second in the blindfold wheelbarrow race!

A year later he competed at Bramall Lane in the Athletic Sports of the Mackenzie Football Club; he came second in a 120-yard flat race, won a run-off for second place in a 200-yard steeplechase, and came first at 4-1 in a 'remarkably well-run' 150-yard handicap race, with 42 entries. 'Adsetts winning cleverly' was the reporter's final judgement!

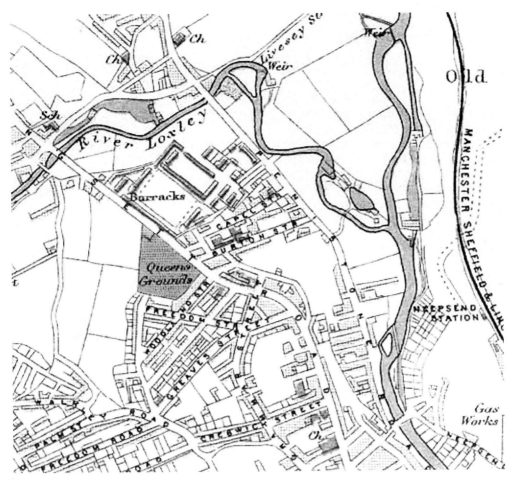

1890s Ordnance Survey map showing the Queen's Grounds.

In November 1864 he entered the Great All England Handicap 125-yard pedestrian race at the Queen's Ground; and, in what was probably his first senior pedestrianist outing, he was backed at 10-1, but without getting any further than third in the first heat.

On 3 May 1865 he was again at Bramall Lane, for the 3rd Annual Sports Day of the Norfolk Football Club, in front of a crowd of 2,000, entertained by the band of the Hallamshire Rifles, when he came second in a handicap 170-yard flat race, the running high jump, and the main event of the 120-yard handicap race, in which he started 'scratch' in a large field of runners.

Later in the year, in the two-day November meeting for Mr G Mellor's 150-yard Novice Handicap at the Queen's Ground, he was the outright winner by 1 yard in the final at odds of 2-1.

His subsequent record in the few months before he left for the States in 1867 was impressive. In September 1866, in a Great All England 3-day Handicap over 200 yards in Hyde Park, Sheffield, the betting odds on William Henry fell from 15-1 in the first round to 3-1 in the final, when he came third.

Two months later, the 1866/7 winter campaign was inaugurated in the Queen's Ground, when 6,000 spectators witnessed a successful, fast and well-run handicap, while again in Hyde Park, Sheffield, William Henry competed in the Great All-England 250-yard Novice Handicap and came first in the final, beating his more experienced opponent by six inches in the best time of the day.

No more than three months later, at the peak of his form, William Henry sailed for New York on the SS *Helvetia* from Liverpool, arriving in New York on 11 March 1867.

A MAN OF SHEFFIELD

Corruption was still prevalent in the sport in Sheffield, and a few weeks after he sailed there was a riot in the Hyde Park Grounds when the All England Easter Handicap was staged there before a crowd of 7,000. Tait of Carlisle had obviously been 'squared' to lose the running off heat and received 'a severe beating at the hands of the crowd'.

His 'backer' in the States a few years later was Fred Norley, who had played cricket for Kent in 1864 and 1865, and who had coincidentally retired as professional of the West of Scotland Cricket Club a few months before William Henry left for the States. He may have provided the initial advice and funds to persuade William Henry to head for the lucrative, and safer, 'pedestrianism' scene in the boom years after the American Civil War. There are other possibilities – perhaps the family firm had collapsed in the depression, or perhaps he had been threatened and left just in time?

The first mention of William Henry's record in the States is in a *PA Times* report on a foot race in Reading Fair Ground on Christmas Eve 1867, nine months after his arrival in America, which was won by 'Adsetts of New York', beating Bollman of Sinking Spring 'who gave out before the outcome owing to the heavy track'. Presumably William Henry had not yet based himself in Philadelphia.

The *New York Herald* reported on him in September 1869 in the second session of the Pedestrian Congress of 'Pedestrianism, Running and Velocipede Racing' at the Capitoline Grounds in Brooklyn, when William Adsetts won the third race of the day.

Then something went wrong: on 23 October 1869 the *New York Clipper* reported that Adsetts, 'winner of the recent unsatisfactory 160-yard race with Wm Young, decamped after receiving the stakes, and it is believed that he is now on the way across the Atlantic'. The race had created intense dissatisfaction, and Young's backers accused Adsetts of 'throwing' the race, to which he replied that he had not worked to get fit because he understood he was going to win anyway. It all sounds a bit fishy!

Despite the report of his imminent departure he then appears in a press notice of a race in Providence, Rhode Island, in the *Fort Wayne Gazette* of 22 December 1869, reporting that Forbes of Canada beat Adsetts of Philadelphia in the international foot race at the Washington Driving Park.

Bell's Life was reporting on pedestrianism on both sides of the Atlantic at that time, noting that the results of his first two years in America (two wins, two seconds and one dead heat) were most impressive.

Whatever the reason, there is no doubt that his American career was resumed successfully, because William Henry Adsetts then appears in the notice from the *Boston Globe* of 9 October 1872 about a race in Mystic Park for the Championship of the United States.

Far from disappearing from the pedestrianism scene, he must have established an impressive record in 1871 and 1872 to be a credible contender at this level.

In August 1873, in Wilmington, Delaware, William Tom appears in a 100-yard race, in contention with a Mr Moulton. The report in *The News Journal* goes on to say that 'the crowning feature in the afternoon's sport was the 100-yard race between Mr and Mrs Moulton, this being the first opportunity of witnessing female pedestrianism'. It is not clear whether William Henry was in the same race!

A few days later, on 26 August, *The Philadelphia Enquirer* reported that in the Irish Nationalists Games in Oakdale Park, William Tom demonstrated his versatility by coming second in the Running Jump of 16ft 10 ins and the Hurdle Race which followed it.

His racing career continued, with the *Boston Daily Globe* of 29 November 1873 reporting on a meeting in Providence, when William Adsetts of Philadelphia defeated Tom Gallagher of Boston in a 200-yard foot race.

In October 1874 in Pittsburgh William Henry of Steubenville, Ohio (another change of home base?) faced James Wheat, 'a coloured man from the oil regions', in a 200-yard road race for $250. In an exciting trial of pedestrian skill, Wheat was given a three-yard start and won by six yards.

In 1875, *Bell's Life* delivered an appraisal of his impact on the American scene: 'Adsetts is a Sheffielder and has run for the Championship of the United States and Canada; in the final of the 150-yard race he was second to Forbes of Canada by 6", and in the final of the 300-yard race he was second to Stratton of Fall River by 2 feet; he is now open to run against anyone in America for $600 a side!'

William Henry appears in December 1874 in Fort Wayne, and then in December 1875 in Steubenville, Ohio, as the newspapers continued to report on the popular pedestrianism events across America.

Between June 1875 and January 1876 William Henry was based in Bucyrus, Ohio when the *Stark County Democrat* announced that 'an article of agreement has been signed between Wm H Adsetts "The Western Champion" and OC Kent, student of the Mount Union College"' for a race over 100 or 110 yards on 17 July. The report on this meeting said there was 'quite a crowd to see Kent and Adsetts "trot" for $250', in a race which Kent won by 4 yards after receiving a 3-yard start.

They met again in September in an even-start race for $200 a side, which the reporter said had been 'thrown', and which confirmed his view that the 'mania for foot-racing had about exhausted itself'. Presumably William Adsetts won, because a month later, in a 200-yard foot race, Kent was forced into third place by three men who obstructed him 'because he had sold the Adsetts race'.

William stayed in Ohio, because there is a news item in December 1875 reporting that Bill Adsetts of Philadelphia and Fred Hart of Pittsburgh were in Steubenville, Ohio to work out details of a foot race there. In January the *Stark County Democrat* announced that Scott and Adsetts were to run a 75-yard foot race at Bucyrus on 25th January for $500.

William Henry reappears in New York on 5 July 1877 for a Professional Athletics Display in the grounds of the New York Athletic Club, which included professional races offering prizes of $25, $10 and $5 for 1st, 2nd and 3rd respectively – he won $5 in the final of the 100-yard run!

There are two further references to his involvement in active racing in 1877: firstly in the *Boston Daily Globe* of 14 December, which reported on an exciting foot race between William Adsetts of Philadelphia and William Kendricks of Chicago over 200 yards for $500 – 'after an even start they stayed closely together for a dead-heat finish in a magnificent race' – and then on New Year's Eve the paper announced that W Adsetts of Providence would meet John Manning of Boston over 150 yards on New Year's Day 1878 in Philadelphia for $250 a side.

In the *New York Clipper* of 3 August 1878 there is a 'Challenge from Carter' via Noah Makinson, presumably Joseph Carter's 'backer' from Philadelphia. William accepted a challenge from Jack Alison to 'run 125 yards, 15 feet scratch start, for $100 or $250 a side'; and he was offered 'alternative wagers', including 'giving old Bill Adsetts 3 yards start in 100 yards: to run on any enclosed ground, giving and taking expenses, for $100 or $250 a side'.

This is, so far, the last reference in newspaper records to his racing career in the States; naming him 'old Bill Adsetts' may suggest that he was reaching the end of his first-class career in 'speed' pedestrianism. Maybe he retired to a quiet life in Philadelphia? There are entries in the City directory for 1879 and 1880 in which he is described as a bartender and a button-maker respectively at his home address.

Certainly, there is no evidence that he ever went back to Sheffield, and in the 1880 US Census he is listed as living in Philadelphia, described as a 'Pearl Button Cutter', with an English 'wife', Bessie Adsetts, and two sons, Benjamin, aged 7, and William Henry, aged 2.

I have not yet found any evidence of a bigamous marriage with Bessie in the US. He lived in a 'tavern' in Philadelphia run by an English widow called Elizabeth Harris, Bessie's mother. Originally named Elizabeth Smiley, she had married Bessie's father, William Hall, in Manchester, where Bessie was born in 1855.

In April and June 1881, William Henry appears as 'marker' in two footrace events in Philadelphia. His racing days appear to have been over, and his extra-mural activities are described in *The Wilkes-Barre Record* of 23 July 1883:

> *"The pool selling (for foot races) was done by WJ Rhoades and WH Adsetts of Ashland, Schuylkill County, well-known pool sellers who do a regular licensed business and are special correspondents of The Clipper and the Police Gazette."*

This was his role in October 1883 at the Mahonay City Grounds in Pennsylvania, when Bill Adsetts appears in an entry in the *National Police Gazette* that describes a 125-yard running race between Charles Price and Patrick Herron before a large crowd of sporting men of the Schuylkill and Luzerne counties. The 'betting was heavy, and Adsetts the poolseller [printed 'poolsetter'] alone was holding between $1200 and $1400'.

The end came in January 1886, when both the *Sheffield Daily Telegraph* and the *Independent* recorded the death of 'William Henry son of the late William Adsetts of Sheffield in New York USA at the age of 39'.

My son Philip, who lives in New York, has now traced William Henry's death in the Health Department records of the City of New York. William Henry died on 17 November 1885, and the death certificate states that he died of tubercular meningitis and that syphilis was a contributing factor. Described in the certificate as a button maker, he had been three weeks in New York, died at 159 Elm St in 14th Ward, and was buried in Lutheran Cemetery in Queens (now called All Faiths Cemetery) two days later, on 19 November. The original spelling of his surname was wrong and had to be corrected by the doctor. It seems to have been a lonely death.

WILLIAM HENRY ADSETTS No.2
THE HONG KONG MURDERER

In the Census of 1900, William Henry's widow, Bessie, was still in Philadelphia with her sons Benjamin Adsetts (27) and William Henry Adsetts (22), who had married May Maher in Philadelphia in September 1899.

William Henry Adsetts, the 22-year old son of the father of the same name who came from Sheffield, England to follow a professional career as a pedestrianist in America, is recorded twice in the US Census of 1900.

As well as being recorded in the Adsetts household in Philadelphia, he is listed as Corporal William Henry Adsetts, a member of the field staff band of the US 28th Infantry stationed in the Philippines.

MISS GERTRUDE McKELVEY –
(SITTING)
MRS. J. C. WHITFORD –
(STANDING)

He and Mary had two children: Elizabeth, born in 1902, and Catherine Pauche, who was baptised in the Roman Catholic cathedral of Saints

Peter and Paul in Philadelphia in July 1902. However, by 1905 Mary had left William Henry for John Kilcullen, with whom she had two more children by 1907, when her first husband was hanged in Hong Kong.

In January 1907, William Henry 2 appears on a muster of members of the US Marine Corps stationed as a Marine detachment at the American Legation in Peking, China. Now Sergeant Adsetts, he appears under a sub-heading 'Discharged', on the expiration of his enlistment. Described as of 'excellent' character, and in 'excellent' physical condition, he was recommended for a good conduct medal should he re-enlist.

Subsequently, after a short and unsuccessful career as a prizefighter, he owned or managed the *Bohemian* nightclub in Cafoo (now Yantai) in China, and was ultimately tried in Hong Kong in November 1907 for the murder of an American actress and opera singer named Gertrude McKelvey (or Dayton) from Youngstown, Ohio.

There are suggestions in the massive press coverage of this dreadful crime that his earlier career in the Orient had been colourful to say the least, and there may well be more to tell. He was a young man with a record as a juvenile delinquent, who had been committed in January 1895 to the Huntington Reformatory in Philadelphia for stealing a suit of clothing, a watch charm, and a pair of skates valued at $13.

It was initially reported that Gertrude McKelvey had hired him as a tourist guide to show her round Hong Kong for a day, and that he strangled her in Youngs Hotel, where she was staying. The motive was apparently robbery, and the press reports referred to thousands of dollars in cash and money orders, with a considerable amount of jewellery, which were found in his possession when he was finally caught in Cafoo.

Following the murder he had fled Hong Kong by boat, after trying to divert attention away from the crime by placing her body in a trunk onboard another ship, due to sail from Hong Kong harbour to Canada. When its departure was delayed, the body was discovered, and William Henry was immediately a suspect.

He was detained in Cafoo, and, after a failed attempt to escape, he was finally shipped in an American warship to Manila in the Philippines, which had an extradition treaty with Britain; he was then sent back to Hong Kong for trial. He pleaded guilty, and asked for clemency in sympathy for his first wife, and for his sick mother in Philadelphia. His plea was ignored, and he was hanged on November 13 1907 in Hong Kong.

A photograph of WH Adsetts appeared in the *New York Herald* of Tuesday, 1 October 1907 alongside a very full account of the events leading up to the murder; and this, together with reports of the court proceedings, tells an even more extraordinary story.

Also, a report in the *Victoria Daily Colonist* in September 1907, after the RMS *Monteagle* docked in Victoria British Columbia, describes the events in Hong Kong before and after William Henry Adsetts left a Saratoga trunk in the ship's baggage room, saying that he intended to be a passenger.

It seems that his career as a boxer had come to an end earlier in 1907, when he was knocked out in the third round of a bout in Tientsin, China, and that he married Hatty Dale shortly afterwards – emulating his father as a bigamist.

Here is where the press report departs from the earlier report that Gertrude Dayton had hired Adsetts as a tourist guide, because it states that 'the couple came from Manila by steamer *Eastern* and registered in the Hong Kong hotel as Mr and Mrs WH Davis'.

In a fuller account, on 3 November, which declares that Gertrude Dayton 'belonged to the unfortunate class in Manila', it appears that Adsetts had made her acquaintance in Manila at least two months before the crime.

Family sources indicate that she was on a tour of the Orient with a female companion, and the *NY Dramatic Mirror* says she was travelling with a concert company; but the trial record and her behaviour with Adsetts in Manila and Hong Kong suggest, at the very least, that she was a 'woman of pleasure'.

AMERICAN HELD IN CHINA FOR STRANGLING AND ROBBING WOMAN

Body Was Found Packed in a Trunk on a Steamship at Hong Kong.

MYSTERY SHROUDS THE CRIME

Prisoner, Formerly a Sergeant in American Legation Guard at Pekin, Arrested After a Long Chase.

[SPECIAL CORRESPONDENCE OF THE HERALD.]

HONG KONG, Aug. 15, 1907.—The body of a woman, later identified as Gertrude Dayton, was found in a trunk on board the Royal Mail steamer Monteagle and H. Adsetts, formerly a sergeant in the American Legation guard at Peking, has been arrested charged with murder. The circumstances of the killing are shrouded in mystery and the forthcoming trial of the suspect is expected to be one of the most sensational cases brought before the criminal tribunal here in recent years.

The woman apparently was strangled. The trunk was taken on board the vessel by an American who represented himself as a passenger. The circumstances surrounding the case will not be disclosed before the opening of the preliminary trial of Adsetts, but it is believed that robbery was the motive. Adsetts when arrested at Chefoo had $2,400 in gold and several valuable jewels.

When the body was discovered suspicion at once centred on Adsetts. He had resigned from the United States Marine Corps and became a professional pugilist, but his aspirations in that line ended at Tientsin early this year, when he was knocked out by "Mike" Paton in the third round of a contest.

While training for this contest Adsetts married a woman known as Hattie Dale, who had some money and much jewelry. She was at that time living with a girl friend. She told her husband, according to the police, the combination of an American safe in which both girls kept their money and jewelry. One evening when the girls were out the safe was robbed and the Chinese boy of the house insisted that the robbery was done by "the man with the golden teeth." The jewelry found its way back to the house, but the money was never returned.

The seven golden teeth of Adsetts brought the police first on the track of the alleged murderer.

At Shanghai Adsetts went on board the steamer Hsinming. On the trip to Chefoo, where he is well known by every European, he showed not the least sign of excitement on board the steamer. He played whist with the passengers to whom he spoke about his many wanderings and adventures. He showed his fellow passengers also his military papers, bearing the name of Adsetts. The passengers did not know that after their departure from Shanghai a reward of $500 had been offered for the arrest of H. Adsetts, alias Jones, alias Anderson, who is wanted on the charge of having murdered Gertrude Dayton.

Adsetts left the steamer on August 13 at Chefoo. The police appeared on board at noon to seek a passenger with seven golden teeth. Adsetts was later on arrested in a public house by the British authorities, but broke from the consular jail after severely injuring the jailer.

When rearrested in the native city of Chefoo he was taken on board the United States cruiser Galveston, on which he was locked up.

The British authorities at Hong Kong ask for the extradition of Adsetts, who will be tried at Hong Kong.

H. ADSETTS.

RELATIVES HEAR OF MISS DAYTON'S DEATH

Consul General at Hong Kong Reports That the Opera Singer Died in a Hotel There.

[SPECIAL DESPATCH TO THE HERALD.]

DENVER, Col., Monday.—Worn with fear over the fate of his sister, Gertrude Dayton, an opera singer, J. F. McKelvey, manager of the Star Electric Theatre of this city, has at last received news of her death from A. P. Wilder, American Consul General at Hong Kong. He wrote to Mrs. Margaret Hupfer, of Youngstown, Ohio, a sister of the singer, and she forwarded the letter, dated August 21 to Mr. McKelvey, who received it yesterday.

Miss Dayton, with Mrs. J. C. Whitford, of New York, was travelling about the Orient and was last heard from on August 3.

As to how the young woman met death the communication gives no word. Mr. McKelvey is at a loss to account for the silence of his sister's friend, Mrs. Whitford, unless she, too, has been murdered. The letter written by Consul General Wilder to Miss Hupfer reads:—

"It is my painful duty to inform you of the death of Gertrude Dayton, whom I understand is your sister, the event occurring on August 4 in her room, No. 194 Hong Kong Hotel. She arrived the previous day from Manila. The body was buried in the Colonial Cemetery at Hong Kong. Such personal possessions as were left are in the hands of the authorities, this being a British colony, and later the Public Administrator will make an accounting to me, who will in turn communicate with the relatives."

On arrival in Hong Kong, and after booking into their hotel, the pair 'went to a notorious house where they drank considerable wine and returned intoxicated to their hotel room...[and on] the night of their arrival the woman, who had considerable jewellery which was taken by the murderer, plus 14 postal money orders for $100 each, was strangled, placed in the trunk, and Chinese coolies were brought to carry the box out of the hotel'.

After an initial attempt to ship the trunk to Australia had raised too many questions, William Henry hired a sampan to row him, along with the casket, to the bamboo wharf known as the Murray, where the steamer *Monteagle* was berthed. Saying that he was due to follow on as a passenger, he asked for the trunk to be placed in the hold, but it was instead stacked in an area for passengers' luggage.

Three days later, a bad smell was noticed and blood was seen coming from the trunk; the police were called, and, when the trunk was opened, it was found to contain the doubled-up body of a woman, very decomposed, strangled with a piece of calico, and clad only in a chemise and nightgown. His very obvious possession of a mouthful of golden teeth had helped to identify William Henry as the murderer, and led to an immediate manhunt once the body had been found.

William Henry had converted some of the woman's jewellery to money, and, under the false name of Mr Jackson, now sailed on the steamer *Tara Maru* bound for Shanghai. On hearing that detectives were waiting for him in Shanghai, he disembarked at Woosung and went to Chefoo, from where he had planned to follow his 'wife', who had sailed for Italy the day before he arrived (Presumably this was not the wife he had left in Philadelphia!).

In Chefoo he was arrested 'after a desperate fight' with Mr Millbank, the British consulate constable, and a local boxer, Billy Below. Henry was well known in Chefoo as the former proprietor of a local saloon, and had been drinking heavily before his arrest.

A Man of Sheffield

He then escaped from the British consular jail by squeezing through a window barely 18 inches square. He was a tall, muscular man and former boxer, and 'there was general alarm that this desperado was at large'. Hunted by marines from the US warship *Galveston*, he was eventually caught 'hiding in a native house'; he was handcuffed and then detained on board the *Galveston* and taken to Manila for extradition to Hong Kong, where he was put on trial and hanged.

In the *Vancouver Daily World* of 14 December 2007 there is a press report from Hong Kong stating that since his incarceration 'Adsetts has behaved well and eaten well and even yesterday morning, the morning of his death he ate a hearty meal'. He walked calmly to the scaffold, and as one observer put it, he appeared to be in 'a sort of stupor'.

There was enormous coverage of this gruesome tale in newspapers across the United States, and so far I have counted forty accounts of this murderous monster called Adsetts in the American press between August 1907 and February 1908.

The final item appeared in the *Elyria Chronicle* of 19 February 1908, when Ben Fell, the former US Consul in Chafoo, was interviewed on his return from China. The interview contained one new 'fact' that I had not seen in any earlier report. Ben Fell, who had 'assisted in the arrest and extradition of the murderer', gave more details of the murder of the Youngstown Ohio girl who was 'known in the Philippines as Gertrude Dayton, but whose real name is said to have been Heffner'.

The story is even more complicated than I thought!

AMERICAN GIRL MURDERED.

Cruel Tragedy Which Occurred in China—The Story

(Special Correspondence.)

Youngstown, Oh. Oct 8.—Mrs. Margaret Hupfer has written to Consul General Wilder at Hongkong, China, for further information regarding the death of her sister, Gertrude McKelvey, known on the stage as Gertrude Dayton, who was reported by the consul general to have been found dead in Hongkong last August.

The body of a woman, later identified as Gertrude Dayton, was found in a trunk on board the steamship Monteagle at Hongkong. and indications pointed to murder by strangulation. When the body was discovered the suspicions of the Hongkong police centered on H. Adsetts, formerly a member of the American legation guard at Peking, who was arrested later at Chefoo after considerable difficulty and now awaits trial charged with the murder.

Miss Dayton with Mrs. J. C. Whitford of New York, was traveling about the Orient and was last heard from on Augiust 3. Mrs Hupfer and her brother, J. F. McKelvey, a thatre manager of Denver Col. sought in vain for information as to the fate of their sister until Mrs. Hupfer received notifications from Consul General Wilder of Miss Dayton's death. Further information as to the death of Miss Dayton is now being sought.

WILLIAM HENRY ADSETTS No.3
SHEFFIELD UNIVERSITY TO LOOS

The Royal Army Medical Corps marching past the Somme Barracks in Glossop Rd, Sheffield in 1914.

When Karl Noble of the York & Lancaster Regimental Archive in Rotherham was searching for background information about Corporal George Albert Adsetts, he also found the record of a 2nd Lieutenant William Henry Adsetts, who completed a degree course at Sheffield University in 1914 and joined the army immediately after war was declared. He was commissioned as 2nd lieutenant, and served with the 3rd (Reserve) Battalion, and then C Company 1 Battalion of the York & Lancaster Regiment.

Not to be confused with his grandfather of the same name, who had such an eventful life in America after leaving his new wife and baby son Harry in 1867, nor yet with the other William Henry, whom his grandfather had sired in 1878 in a relationship in Philadelphia, and who died in Hong Kong in 1907, this William Henry was born in Sheffield in 1893 to Harry and his wife, and should perhaps be referred to as WHA 3 to avoid confusion.

According to his service record, WHA 3 went to Sheffield Central Secondary School and then to Sheffield University, from where he matriculated in July 1910 and July 1911 respectively. In 1912 he was awarded a Town Trustees' Scholarship. In June 1913 he took the intermediate examination for a BSc degree, and he got a Pass in his final examination in Chemistry in June 1914.

His university record also indicates that he was a training college student, so he may have been planning a career as a teacher, and his enlistment form gives his occupation as a lecturer in Chemistry. For his three years as a student he lived at 33 Wentworth St, Upperthorpe, not in the family home. In the Census of 1911 he is recorded as a 'visitor' at this address, the home of Mr Samuel Marshall, a 61-year-old printer, and his wife Elizabeth.

Physically, he was 5ft 7.75ins, with a fair complexion, grey-blue eyes and light-brown hair. He was also very active in the university Officers Training Corps, his commanding officer reporting that he was 'very keen and likely to make a good officer'.

He passed his army medical in Sheffield on 7 September 1914, enlisting three days before the recruitment of the Sheffield 'Pals' Battalion, and his attestation as a worthy recruit was signed on the same day. He became No34301 Private WH Adsetts, trained locally with the Royal Army Medical Corps, and was appointed a 3rd class medical orderly on 1 December 1914.

The photograph from a 1993 history of Sheffield shows the Sheffield

RAMC marching past the Somme Barracks on Glossop Rd in 1914; William Henry is probably in this smart group of men.

However, William Henry Adsetts was destined to be an infantry officer. Apart from the OTC commendation, he had support from Rev JW Merryweather, the vicar of Fulwood, who said that he had known William Henry for eight years and confirmed his good moral character.

In addition, the vice-chancellor of Sheffield University, Herbert Fisher, confirmed the positive endorsement of the university, saying that he had known the student from October 1912 to October 1914.

HAL Fisher, who had been a prime mover in the creation of the Sheffield City Battalion, became MP for Sheffield Hallam in December 1916, and immediately became president of the Board of Education as a member of Lloyd George's wartime coalition.

William Henry's service file contains a letter of 21 December 1914 from the War Office confirming his commission as a 2nd lieutenant in the Special Reserve of Officers, and approving his transfer to the 3rd Battalion of the York & Lancaster Regiment. A letter from the OC 45th Field Ambulance confirms his discharge from RAMC on receipt of His Majesty's Commission.

He embarked for France on 25 May 1915, and joined 1 Battalion on 29 May with two other 2nd lieutenants, Gowing and Ellison. After a 10-day respite away from the front and a relatively quiet spell in the trenches around Locre, the fighting resumed, and William Henry got his first experiences under fire. There were seven deaths from wounds in June, including 2nd Lieutenant Gowing.

In the early weeks of September, 1 Battalion was out of the line, resting in Scherpenberg, and during this period it was inspected by Lieut-General Sir H Plumer, now commanding the 2nd Army. On 23 September it moved forward to billets near Meteren, and finally was ordered to take part in the Battle of Loos as part of the 28th Division, 'which had been held back in readiness to meet unexpected eventualities'.

First day of Battle of Loos 25 September 1915 – British troops advancing through clouds of poison gas.

Hence the Battle of Loos had already been in progress for two days before 1 Battalion took part. They began to move up to the front on 26 September, but, delayed by confused directions and congested trenches, A and B companies did not enter the very fierce fighting around the Hohenzollern Redoubt until early on the morning of 29 September.

A Company suffered 'very great losses' from a German attack with bombs just as they were relieving the Buffs, and the historian of the York & Lancaster Regiment states simply: 'Of what happened in the next few minutes there are few left to tell the story'. Five officers were killed, and the other new arrival, 2nd Lieutenant Ellison, was wounded.

Later in the day C Company was brought forward to reinforce the East Surrey Regiment, repelling an enemy attack with heavy losses, and 2nd Lieutenant William Henry Adsetts received the wounds from which he later died. He was taken to No 1 Casualty Clearing Station in Chocques and died of Gun Shot Wounds (GWI) to the abdomen on 1 October 1915.

His death was notified to his father, Harry Adsetts, at 12 Watery Lane, Sheffield in a cable beginning 'Lord Kitchener desires to express his sympathy…'. He was buried in the new cemetery in Chocques (now a military cemetery maintained by the Commonwealth War Graves Commission), and this was confirmed to his father in a formal letter of 9 November 1915.

The file also contains a sad letter from Harry Adsetts to the War Office on 4 May 1917. Essentially he was complaining that he did not get back all his son's property – particularly his pistol and his binoculars – and asking for more support. 'I have lost a son, an officer, not a private like my other two sons, and I am left with three younger children to support, without a mother'. There is no copy of a reply. In referring to his other two sons, Harry Adsetts was speaking of Harry Osman Adsetts and Frank Adsetts (respectively Regimental Nos 20229 and 41152) of the Kings Own Yorkshire Light Infantry, both of whom returned safely from the war.

William Henry had written a will on 3 August in which he asked his former landlord, Samuel Marshall, to manage his estate, distributing the cash from the sale of his effects and his bank accounts between his brothers and sisters, with his father receiving his silver watch and chain, his sword and revolver. Samuel Marshall, the printer with whom he had stayed in Wentworth St while he was in university, was to take 'anything he desires from my personal effects'.

Army records indicate that his father received William Henry's sword, watch and chain, and a long list of other effects, which were sent to him via Cox & Co Shipping Agency: 17 shillings and 8 pence (on body), plus 2 cigarette cases, 1 whistle, 2 compasses, 3 packets of tobacco, 1 set of false teeth, letters, 1 pocket knife, 8 pencils, 1 pocket book, 1 cigarette holder (broken), 1 charm, 1 cheque book, 1 card case, and snapshots.

The Battle of Loos was a disaster, and within a few months it cost Field-Marshall Sir John French his job, to be replaced as Commander-in-Chief by General Sir Douglas Haig. Lessons were learned from the delay in bringing forward the reserves from distant locations, the absence of clear orders for individual units, the lack of effective traffic control, as well as the inadequate training of the individual soldier. But most sources stress the appalling casualty rate of officers. In the slagheaps around Loos, battalions had sometimes suffered the loss in action of all their officers, just as A Company did in the action described above.

The statistics prove the point. In the period from October 1914 to end-September 1915 the percentage of officers killed in action was 14.1%, and for other ranks it was 5.8%. In the rest of the war to end-September 1918 the comparable percentages were 8% for officers and 4.5% for other ranks. Something had obviously been done about it.

In producing this account of the life and death of William Henry Adsetts I had great help and support from both the Development Office of the University of Sheffield and the members of its very active OTC; and at my request the 1914-1918 Memorial Roll of Honour was opened to reveal the full list, including 2nd Lieutenant WH Adsetts, of those who died from this one institution in the Great War.

It contains the names of 'seven members and former members of the academic staff, one hundred and sixty-nine students and former students, twenty members of the University contingent of the Officers Training Corps not included above, and three library and laboratory assistants'.

THE ADSETTS STORY
OFFSHOOT
GEORGE ADSETTS
TO
BOLSOVER 1787
& BEYOND TO TREETON
ADWICK-UPON-DEARNE
NWI - FRANCE & ITALY
TO MESOPOTAMIA

CLOWNE
RICHARD = JONY
ADSETTS
1600-

1662 CLOWNE
ROBERT = ROSAMOND
ADSETTS   RUDD
1635-1720 1655-1734

DOROTHY = ROBERT   1. MARY
HOLME   ADSETTS = ALLSOP
M 1691   1663-1730 1665-1690

JOHN = ANNE
ADSETTS 1700
1690-1772

1757
ELATON
JOHN = MARY
ADSETTS HUNT
1730-1808 1735-1820

BOLSOVER 1787
WILLIAM = CATHERINE   GEORGE = ELIZABETH
ADSETTS   BUTLER   ADSETTS   HEYWOOD
1727   1784   1764   1768-
-1858   -1861   BOLSOVER 1834

THOMAS = HANNAH   TREETON-1840   JOHN = MARY
ADSETTS ILLINGWORTH JANE = WILLIAM   ADSETTS EATSON
1814   1818   MAJOR   ADSETTS   1807
-1900   -1887   1815   1812
                    -1843   1886
SARAH = JOHN   HANNAH   GEORGE
1857   ADSETTS   COOK   ADSETTS
        1842   WILLIAM   GEORGE   1855-1928 1855-1890
                  ADSETTS   ADSETTS   'MATRIARCH'
                  1850   1855
TOM   -1887   -1887
ADSETTS
1894-   BOTH DIED IN   JOHN   FREDERICK   ELIZA
M   COLLIERY 1887   HENRY   ADSETTS   COOK
MABEL   GEORGE   ACCIDENT   ADSETTS   1871-1943   1865
PICKERING ALBERT TREETON   1870-1945   M
         ADSETTS   REV HILLS
         1898-   1885
         1921   JACK   USA-TRIAL
         WWI   ADSETTS   FOR BIGAMY
         DIED IN   619 SQUADRON
         BAGHDAD   RAF
         AFTER WWI   SHOT DOWN
         IN FRANCE   ON COLOGNE
         + ITALY   RAID
                                        1943

TO BOLSOVER & BEYOND

HANNAH ADSETTS
THE BOLSOVER MATRIARCH

We have already identified one connection between Bolsover and the earliest forebear of my Adsetts line, Robert Adsetts of Clowne. The manors of Bolsover and Clowne had been linked since 1485 in the Bolsover Court Leet, a manorial court, and on 12 April 1658 he appears under the name of Rob Adsotes in a list of 32 men from Clowne who had been fined 2d each for failure to attend a meeting of the court.

Robert Adsetts moved to Elmton after he married in 1663 to work as the village wheelwright, and it was his great-grandson George Adsetts who in 1787 moved to Bolsover to marry Elizabeth Haywood, closely followed by his sister Rebecca, who left Elmton in 1789 and married Richard Harrison in Bolsover church.

George and Elizabeth settled in Bolsover and raised four children, beginning with Mary in 1788, followed by William, Sarah, and finally John in 1807. In 1834 John Adsetts married Mary Eaton in Bolsover, and their first son, George, was born in 1835. By 1851 John, with his wife Mary and son William, was living in High St, Bolsover, next door to his grandmother, Elizabeth Adsetts, now aged 84 – the Bolsover girl who had married George Adsetts from Elmton in 1787.

In 1851 their eldest son George, aged 15, was living in the Swan Hotel in Market Place, Bolsover, apprenticed to Joseph Cree, who is recorded as both the innkeeper of the Swan and a boot and shoe maker. But within a few years, George Adsetts was making a name for himself in Bolsover, becoming an officer of the Portland Lodge of the Society of Oddfellows, who gave an impressive address at the funeral of one of its members, a local surgeon, in May 1859.

In 1860 Hannah Cook married George Adsetts, who had apparently given up the idea of making boots and shoes, and she joined him in running the Angel Hotel when the Bolsover magistrates approved the transfer of its alehouse license from Thomas Stubbins on 13 July 1861 'in the days when the law permitted public houses to be open all night'; and this was the start of an unbroken spell of 80 years in which this branch of the Adsetts family were licensees of the Angel.

Hannah Cook was born at Woolley Moor near Clay Cross, one of a family of 13, and worked with her father on the cultivation of camomile and other herbs for sale to local chemists. She remembered the construction of the Derby to Chesterfield section of the Midland railway

A Man of Sheffield

near her home. But her proudest recollection was that she had known Florence Nightingale, and would have gone with her to the Crimea if she had been older – 'she was 18, and there were home ties'.

In the street view of the Angel (bottom left) taken from a collection of old photographs of Bolsover, 'it is highly likely that the woman outside the door of the pub is Hannah who also worked as a linen maid to Mrs Hamilton-Grey at the castle'. Perhaps this is how George met her?

In the 2008 website of the Chesterfield and District branch of the Campaign for Real Ale, the Angel, described as an old coaching inn constructed of stone with casement windows and a red pan-tiled roof, is said to have been in the hands of the Adsetts family for 300 years! This statement was probably taken from an earlier publication, 'Bolsover Remembered', where it appears alongside a pre-1890 photograph of the Angel on Castle St.

Two questions arise. How did George Adsetts, a 15-year-old apprentice in 1851 who was the son of an agricultural labourer, manage to become the licensee of the Angel nine years later? Perhaps it was the influence or the training of Joseph Cree. And what evidence is there to support the claim of a 300-year connection with the Adsetts family? Perhaps it was just a promotional gimmick to stress a long-term family link. I asked these questions of one of the surviving Bolsover clan. 'It's quite clear', she said, 'he had the gift of the gab'.

George Adsetts was described on an early birth certificate as a farmer and innkeeper of Bolsover, and he and Hannah had four sons and two daughters; their first son, George Henry, was born in 1868 and died in 1872, and one of his brothers, Charles Edward, also died young in 1874. The two other brothers, Fred W Adsetts (1871 to 1943) and John Henry Adsetts (1870 to 1940), were each in their turn licensees of the Angel.

One of the two daughters, Eliza-Cook Adsetts, born in 1863, married the curate of Bolsover, Rev RP Hills, in 1885, but he left her a few years later and fled to America, where he settled in Nebraska and married again, before moving on to become a teacher and later a professor at Puget Sound University.

The family traced him, and he was found guilty of bigamy in 1900 after a trial in Blair, Washington County, in Omaha, which was attended by Fred Adsetts in support of his sister. The 4 November 1900 issue of *New York World* tells the story under the headline: 'Bigamist pursued o'er land and sea by deserted wife'.

Eliza-Cook Hills initially planned to remain in Blair as governess to the children of a local matron who had befriended her during the trial, but she eventually returned to her Derbyshire roots, living in Smedley's Hydro in Matlock – a little old lady who looked like Queen Victoria in full mourning dress as she hosted afternoon tea for her nephews and nieces in the Palm Court with dainty, crustless 'Matlock sandwiches'.

George Adsetts was a leading figure in Bolsover. He presided over meetings of local societies such as the Bolsover Pig Society, which held annual drinking suppers in the Angel with 'numerous speeches and good songs'. In 1871, moreover, he wrote to the editor of the *Sheffield Daily Telegraph* with a fierce condemnation of the new Government Licensing bill, calling it 'this blundering unjust senseless piece of legislation', and asking all licensees in the region to join together in acting against it.

He died in a Nottingham asylum in 1890 at the age of 54, and his widow succeeded him as licensee. She was quick to place a notice in the *Derbyshire Times* early in December 1890, headed 'Christmas', stating that 'Mrs Adsetts desires to thank her numerous customers for their patronage and…notify that she intends to carry on the business both wholesale and retail'.

She promised 'special efforts to supply goods of best quality at low prices'. George's regular adverts in the local press for 'Hay, Thatch, Wheat or Oat Straw in small or large quantities' indicate that this was a diversified business, and she clearly took control of the lot!

In the 1891 Kelly's Directory for Bolsover, 'Mrs Hannah Adsets' is described both as a farmer-farm bailiff and as the innkeeper of the Angel in Bolsover. Four years later, in the 1895 Bulmer's Directory for Derbyshire, Mrs Hannah Adsetts is again described as a farmer, as an innkeeper of the Angel Inn, and as a brewer's agent.

These were to be the 'boom' years. Bolsover had slept for well over one hundred years until 1889 when the Bolsover Colliery Company sank its shafts on the side of the river Doe Lea and proceeded to transform the town. The population grew tenfold to ten thousand people, importing labour from Wales, Durham, Lancashire and Staffordshire.

In about 1895, when John Henry was 25, he became licensee of the Golden Ball in Renishaw. It seems likely, although the record is not clear, that his brother Fred took over from his mother as licensee of the Angel in Bolsover at this time. Certainly, by 1901 Hannah Adsetts, aged 66, was living with her son John Henry Adsetts, who was earning a reputation for the 'excellent repasts' provided in the Golden Ball.

John Henry Adsetts eventually moved back to Bolsover to run the Angel Inn in 1907, to take over from Fred Adsetts who retired through ill health, and Kelly's Directory for 1922 names John H Adsetts 'of the Angel public house'. He remained licensee of the Angel until his retirement in 1940.

When Hannah died in 1928, at the age of 93, she was the oldest woman in Bolsover, described in the local press as a most 'remarkable personality'. It is clear that both Hannah and her son John Henry were well-known 'characters' in Bolsover as it grew from a sleepy market village to busy colliery town.

A woman of many parts, Hannah Adsetts, from the time of taking up residence in Bolsover, was the village dentist, with a practice extending throughout the surrounding villages. The obituary in the local paper goes into detail on the mechanics of extraction – a good, strong straightforward pull. She charged one shilling per tooth, and in all adult cases gave the patient a warm drink at the hotel as a stimulant and steadier before leaving her 'surgery'.

John Henry Adsetts had grown up in the shadow of this remarkable woman. He was born in the Angel Inn in 1874 and spent his early years in Bolsover; he was then apprenticed to a butcher in Pleasley before returning to Bolsover to work on the farm next to the inn.

He is described as a 'useful boxer and a good horseman in his younger days', with a successful record in trotting races and a string of ponies. He was a member of Bolsover Council for many years and sat on numerous committees.

Following a serious accident to one of his farm employees, Joseph Neep, whose arm was caught in a threshing machine, John Henry insisted on him receiving treatment in Chesterfield Hospital, and in memory of this incident he ran the fund-raising event of Bolsover Hospital Sunday for well over twenty years.

John Henry seems to have had a finger in almost every pie. He was said to be rather 'dressier' than most men in Bolsover at the time, and the photograph below illustrates this – a workaholic and dandy as well!

In front of the old Angel pub in Castle St – John Henry Adsetts in knee breeches.

In 1938 the Angel hotel was rebuilt 'to become one of the finest licensed houses in the district', but John Henry never returned to it. Early in the war he became a member of the local Food Control Committee and was also an ARP ambulance driver, but he was finally advised to retire in 1940 after having been in poor health for some time.

Fred Adsetts died in 1943. His obituary in the *Derbyshire Times* described him as a former Bolsover licensee and chorister, a member of the District Council for some years, the local representative of the *Derbyshire Times*, and active in Bolsover amateur dramatics. He had travelled a great deal, and 'only returned to Bolsover 4 to 5 years ago', i.e. in 1939.

John Henry Adsetts died in 1945 after learning of the death of his second son, Sergeant Jack Adsetts of 619 Squadron in RAF Bomber Command, in operations over Germany. Jack Adsetts was the flight mechanic of an Avro Lancaster ED979 on a bombing mission to Cologne on 29 June 1943, shot down 7km south of Eindhoven in Holland; he is buried in the Eindhoven (Woensel) General Cemetery with other members of his crew.

An artificer in the pre-war RAF, Jack Adsetts had transferred to flying duties, and had trained in what was then Southern Rhodesia. He was a sociable and active young man and a prize-winning middleweight boxer; 'Uncle Jack' holds a very special place in the hearts of his nephews and nieces in Bolsover today.

The Adsetts family is still strongly established in the Bolsover area. David Adsetts, the grandson of John Henry Adsetts, lives in Sutherland Farm in Bolsover, named in memory of his grandmother Annie Sutherland, who married John Henry in Owlerton, and was the daughter of a Scot who had built up a large bread and confectionery business in Sheffield.

David's brother, John Adsetts PhD, has pursued a very successful career in local industry and in research. He has been chairman of the Trustees of the Nuffield Orthopaedic Centre in Oxford, and is a Research

Supervisor of The Open University. He is a director, with his brother Ian, of Elmleaze Ltd, a stud in Gloucestershire, while their sister Wendy lives in Cornwall. I met them all at a large gathering for the christening of a new addition to the family in Bolsover.

The former Angel Inn is now a large and busy antique centre!

WILLIAM & GEORGE ADSETTS
DEATH IN TREETON COLLIERY

In a small, overgrown cemetery at Aston outside Sheffield there is a headstone marking the grave of two brothers, William and George Adsetts, who died on the same day in 1887. It bears the epitaph:

You may be summoned on a breath
Though not like us be burned to death
You know not what before you lies
Prepare to reign above the skies
No prayer nor tears its flight could stay
It was Jesus that called our souls away

These men were first cousins of John Adsetts, my great-grandfather. Their father, William Adsetts, was born in Scarcliffe, the son of William and Catherine Adsetts, and christened in the parish church in August 1812.

In 1840, William Adsetts, described as a farmer, married Jane Major, the daughter of the servant of the rector at Treeton Church. William and Jane subsequently lived in the parish of Aston-cum-Aughton, where their first child, Elizabeth, was born in 1842. By 1861 William was a farm bailiff with five children. Elizabeth was a dairy maid in the household of William Holdsworth, a silver and metal roller of Sheffield, and the other four children were living at home – Jonathan (born 1847), William (born 1850), Sarah (born 1852) and George (born 1855).

Ten years later, in 1871, William Adsetts and his wife Jane were still living in Aughton at Grange Cottage with only William and Sarah still living at home, described in the Census as servants.

Nearby, in the household of Charles Longden, their brother, George Adsetts, aged 16, was working as a farm servant, while his elder brother Jonathan, a farm labourer, was also living in Aughton with his wife Sarah Ann Brashaw and two children.

In 1868, when his son George was born, Jonathan is named on the birth certificate as a coal miner, and in due course his two younger brothers followed his example. In 1887 both William and George were fatally injured in an underground accident when working together in Treeton Colliery.

In giving evidence to the inquest, Mary Adsetts, the widow of William, said that her husband had been working in Treeton colliery for three years and had previously been a farm labourer. Similarly, Martha Ann Adsetts, the widow of George, said that George had been a miner 'almost two years, and previously a farm labourer'.

Until the 1870s, Treeton was a quiet village community that had stayed more or less the same for hundreds of years. Then it all changed. Treeton colliery was one of the local mines operated by Rother Vale Collieries Ltd. The company was formed in 1874 with a nominal capital of £300,000, and the cutting of the first sod for the new colliery at Treeton took place on 13 October 1875. After financial problems, and a special meeting of shareholders, work was suspended in 1878, and development of the colliery did not resume until March 1882.

On the day of the accident on 22 April 1887 the two brothers, both employed as rippers, were in No 1 District at the far end of the north level, putting shots in for firing. The deputy, George Bonsall, reported that after firing three shots at the head end he was in the 'act of shouting to the deceased to tell them to get out of the way' when one of the shots blew out, and in his words 'the blowing out of the shot made a report like a cannon'. He went on to say that a small flash 'enlarged and spread out – he believed from igniting dust' and that 'it could not be gas because he had not found any that day'.

George Adsetts and his brother were both badly burned. They were carried out of the pit and taken home, where both died the following morning. Apparently William never spoke, but his brother George told Mr Bonsall that 'if he should live to get better from this, he would never go down the pit again'.

At the time, there was some confusion about the cause of the accident. The early report of the *Sheffield and Rotherham Independent* on Monday 25 April indicated that there had been a gas explosion. Subsequently Mr Wardell, Her Majesty's Inspector of Mines, made clear at the inquest that this was not the case. Mr Wardell said that he had no doubt as to how the accident occurred:

> *"This blown-out shot had been badly planted, and been the means of igniting coal dust, which had carried the flame on and burned the deceased men. The place was very dusty and like a chimney. The sides top and bottom were covered in coal-dust. The shot was badly drilled and planted and no doubt the blown-out shot had carried the light and fired the dust like a 'trail of gunpowder'."*

After considering the evidence, the Coroner concluded that while there may have been an error of judgement on the part of the men responsible for drilling the holes, he could not see how the jury could bring in a verdict making them responsible for the deaths. In the Coroner's opinion, no one was criminally responsible. The jury's verdict was that the deceased had been 'accidentally burned by the blowing out of a shot', and this is recorded on the death certificates of the two brothers.

Martha Ann, the 30-year-old widow of George Adsetts, was still living at 76 Wood Lane, Treeton four years after the accident, working as the caretaker of a local board school, with three children, 3-year-old George William, 5-year-old Albert and 7-year-old Lucy.

By the time of the next Census in 1901 she had remarried, and was now Mrs Martha Ann Cope, the wife of 33-year-old William Cope, a lamp-keeper at the colliery, living a few doors away from her former home at 91 Wood Lane, Treeton; George's two sons were both working at Treeton colliery, Albert as a colliery fitting shop apprentice, and his younger brother, George William, as a coke breaker at the colliery. Two other boys still at home were named Edwin Adsetts, aged six, and James T Adsetts, aged four, both born years after George Adsetts had died in the accident.

Mary Adsetts, the 38-year-old widow of William Adsetts, was left with four young children, and was the first to remarry after the accident. In 1889 she married Charles Longbottom, another coalminer, and two years later the new family was living in Main Rd, Aston-in-Aughton.

By 1891 the four children of William Adsetts were all working. Thomas William was a 16-year-old engine driver, presumably in a local colliery, the next oldest, Arthur, was a colliery trammer who was born in Beighton in 1877; his sister Jane, a 14-year-old machinist, was also born in Beighton; and the youngest son, Henry, who was born in 1879 after the family had returned to Aughton, was already working as a colliery boy.

Twenty years later, in 1901, the situation had changed, and Mary was now a farmer's wife, helping Charles run Thackage Farm in Brampton-en-le Morthern. Two of the children from her marriage to William Adsetts were also working on the farm – her widowed son Arthur and his sister Jane, with her husband, Charles Nunwick.

Henry, who was now a coalminer hewer, had married in 1900, and in 1901 was living in Brinsworth Rd, Catcliffe; ten years later, now named Harry on the Census form, he and his wife, Mary Jane, were still living in Catcliffe with three children, Hilda (born 1901), Harry (born 1904) and John (born 1907).

William Edgar Adsetts, born in 1921, was a late addition to this extended family, and though he died in 1995 at the age of 74 I have talked to his 90-year-old widow, Joyce, who gave me useful information about family connections. Henry, after retirement from the mines, forged a respectable career as a licensee in Rotherham, but although Joyce knew that he held shares in Treeton colliery, she was never told anything about his father's death in the mine.

TO BOLSOVER & BEYOND

THOMAS ADSETTS AND THE ADWICK CONNECTION

Browsing through a computer list of references to the Adsetts name, I noticed a number of items concerning a Corporal Adsetts of the York & Lancaster Regiment who was buried in Baghdad. The source was an article in the *Independent* of 1 April 2003, written by its Middle East correspondent, Robert Fisk, after watching the bombing of Baghdad from the North Gate Military Cemetery surrounded by the graves of British soldiers and airmen who died in the first Mesopotamian campaign between 1914 and 1917, and in the Arab rebellion and insurgency of 1920 and 1921.

Robert Fisk later included this experience in his book *The Great War for Civilisation – the Conquest of the Middle East*, which was published in 2005:

> "At dusk, the ground around the Baghdad North Gate Cemetery shook with the vibration of the bombs. The oil-grey sky was peppered with anti-aircraft fire. And below the clouds of smoke and the tiny star-like explosion of the shells, Sergeant Frederick William Price of the Royal Garrison Artillery, Corporal AD Adsetts of the York and Lancaster Regiment and Aircraftman First Class P. Magee of the Royal Air Force slept on.

An eerie place to visit, perhaps, as the first of the night's raids closed in on the capital of Iraq. Not so. For Iraqi Foreign Minister Naji Sabri had spoken earlier of these graves of colonisers past. For No. 1401979 Sergeant Price and No. 4736364 Corporal Adsetts and No. 210493 Aircraftman Magee all died in Britain's first colonial war in Iraq, in 1921."

I searched the website of the Commonwealth War Graves Commission to learn more about this corporal, whose name was actually GA Adsetts of No 2 Battalion, the York & Lancaster Regiment, who died on 5 August 1921.

His war service record card in the National Archive showed that 4736364 George A Adsetts (York & Lancaster Regt No 13788) entered the French theatre of war on 27 August 1915, and that he was eventually awarded three medals – Victory, British, and the '1914-15 Star'.

The York & Lancaster Regimental Archive in Rotherham provided more background information on the role of 2 Battalion in Iraq and Iran between 1919 and 1921, plus an entry in the regimental journal reporting the 1921 death in Baghdad of Corporal GA Adsetts, 'much to the regret of all ranks'.

At first I thought that his full name was George Arnold Adsetts, and that he was my father's cousin, one of the sons of George Adsetts, the elder brother of my grandfather, William Tom Adsetts. I applied to the Army Personnel Centre in Glasgow for the service record of Corporal George A Adsetts, which revealed that the soldier buried in Baghdad was not George Arnold but a man from Doncaster called George Albert Adsetts.

According to the attestation he signed on his enlistment in the army on 2 September 1914, George Albert Adsetts was born in Doncaster, in the parish of Adwick upon Dearne, on 21 April 1897, the son of John and Sarah Adsetts. At the time of his enlistment he was 18 years and four months old, and he describes himself as a pony driver; almost certainly, he was a coal miner who worked with the pit ponies. He was 5ft, 2.5 ins tall, with a fresh complexion, blue eyes and mid-brown hair; and it is recorded that he was a Primitive Methodist. He was unmarried on enlistment, and in response to the question, 'Have you ever been sentenced to imprisonment by the Civil Power?' he answered, 'Yes'.

His father, John Adsetts, was born in 1842 in Beighton in Derbyshire. In 1891 John was working as a dairyman with five children – three sons and two daughters – and two other sons were born later, George Albert being the youngest. In the 1901 Census John Adsetts, then 59, was living in Billingley and working as a farm labourer. There were four children living at home, Maria (13), Ernest (10), Tom (7) and George Albert (3).

George Albert's grandfather, Thomas Adsetts, who was born in Scarcliffe in 1815, the younger brother of my great-great-grandfather George Adsetts, was by 1871 an agricultural salesman and farmer of 22 acres, probably living in Addsett's Cottage, still clearly identified in the centre of Adwick upon Dearne, with his wife Hannah, who died in 1877 and is buried next to the parish church of St John Baptist, bearing a moving epitaph on her tombstone:

> To Hannah, the beloved wife of Thomas Adsetts
> Weep not for me , I'm free from pain
> My earthly sufferings o'er
> I hope to meet you all again
> On a bright and happier shore

Thomas had a son, William, a railway engine driver who was born in Beighton in 1843, and he was also the father of John Adsetts, born in Beighton in 1842, and George Albert's grandfather. There is a clear family link between George Albert and my own line of the Adsetts clan!

Three siblings were named by George Albert as his next of kin on the military history sheet prepared in 1914: his sister Maria Smith, by then 26 and married, was living at 22 Holmes Yard, Green Lane, Rawmarsh,

Rotherham; and Ernest and Arthur were also married. In 1911 Ernest was working as a colliery labourer and living in Swinton, while Arthur was a haulage man working underground, living in Barnsley.

So far, I have no idea where George Albert was living in the years before 1914, and his address at the date of enlistment was not recorded. His brother Tom, a miner who married Mabel Pickering on Boxing Day 1914, was living at 65 Barnsley Rd, Highgate, and this could be a clue to George Albert's whereabouts before he joined the army, or perhaps he had just come out of prison? There may be more information available from the records of local magistrates' courts, or the 1911 Census returns from local prisons.

GEORGE ALBERT ADSETTS GOES TO WAR – TUNNELLING IN FRANCE

He signed a Short Service contract, committing himself to serve for seven years with the Colours and five years with the Reserve. After his initial medical on 2 September 1914 in Rotherham he was enlisted into 3 (Special Reserve) Battalion of the York & Lancaster Regiment in Pontefract on 7 September 1914.

It was the role of the (Special Reserve) Battalion to provide trained recruits to make up the losses in the battalions on active service, and George Albert Adsetts was posted to Aldershot on 1 December 1914 for intensive training before he embarked for France from Folkestone on 27 August 1915. His active service in the field began inauspiciously. In his service record there is a simple entry noting that on 4 November 1915, on the authority of the O/C Battalion, he was awarded 21 days Field Punishment Number 2, with the further comment that these 21 days 'were to be deducted from his pension entitlement'.

After the abolition of flogging in the army, it was thought that there was still a need for some form of exemplary punishment, and this led to the introduction of Field Punishment No 1, in which the convicted man was shackled in irons and secured to a fixed object, often a gun wheel or similar, for a period of up to two hours in 24, for no more than three days in four, up to a maximum of 21 days. Field Punishment No 2 was basically the same, in that the prisoner was shackled, but the punishment did not include the daily attachment to a fixed object.

Common to both were the forfeiture of pay, some form of hard labour or 'unpleasant sanitary duties', and rations reduced to bully and biscuits with no cigarettes and rum. The application of such sanctions varied widely across the different units of the army in France because many officers thought the whole business degrading and out of place in a citizen army. George Albert avoided the more severe punishment, but Field Punishment No 2 was bad enough. It is unlikely that we will ever find out what he was punished for, whether it was administered by the office of the Provost-Marshal or by his own unit officially on the move – either way, it is unlikely that detailed records were kept.

The onset of trench warfare by the end of 1914 had taken everyone by surprise, and it took some time for the reassessment of this move back to traditional siege warfare to result in a decision to introduce underground warfare and mining as a tactical option that could help break the stalemate on the Western Front.

A 1st Corps memorandum of 18 February 1915 ordered immediate action 'to organise special tunnelling companies'. The memorandum went on to state that authority would be given to raise eight companies and that:

1. These companies will be built up locally from the following:
   (i) Expert mining engineers, gangers and tunnellers (kickers).
   (ii) Miners that may be available in units now at the front.

2. You are to ascertain and report with the least possible delay the number of miners available in the units under your command, and

3. In order to make an immediate start, Major Norton Griffiths …has proceeded to England and will, it is hoped, return in a few days with a certain number of expert tunnellers for work at GEVINCHY and GUINCHY.

The first eight tunnelling companies in the British army were created in February 1915. Later in the year, twelve more were formed, including the 181st Tunnelling Company, to which George Albert Adsetts was attached on 22 February 1916, just four months after his arrival in France.

There are no details of the selection process, but it was probably his mining background and size that led to his selection for the tunnelling operations that had now become a vital part of trench warfare in France.

As a hint of the priority given to this strategy the 'experienced clay-kickers' recruited for the new tunnelling companies were paid more than a regimental sergeant major in the infantry. These pay differentials, both within the tunnelling companies and outside them, caused ripples of disruption so long as they existed. George Albert received a substantial pay increase to a higher grade shortly after joining the 181st Tunnelling Company.

The requirements for a good tunneller are described in the following extract from *The Western Front* by Richard Holmes, and it is clear that the underground experience of George Albert Adsetts and other miners would make them ideally suited for such work.

> "*Sapper Jack Lyon of 171st Tunnelling Company Royal Engineers described how he worked as part of a twelve-man shift under a corporal. Three men worked at the tunnel face, one 'clay-kicking', lying on his back on a plank inclined between floor and roof, using both feet to jab a short spade into the clay. One of his mates put the clay into a sandbag, and the third dragged the bag back to the start of the trolley rails. Three men worked the trolleys, another operated the air pump and the remainder helped get the sandbags up to the surface. All were volunteers, either Royal Engineers, or 'permanently attached' infantry, usually miners who had joined the infantry at the start of the war.*"

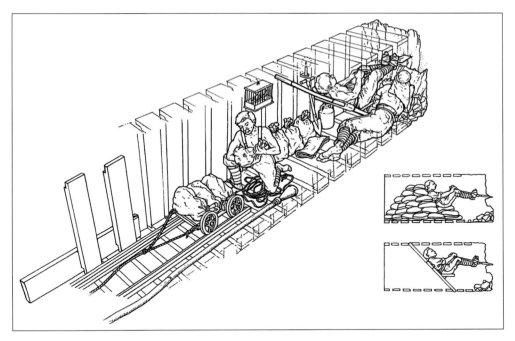

Tunnelling: A clay-kicking team at work, with kicker, bagger and trammer.

The 181st Tunnelling Company had been formed at Steenwerck in the autumn of 1915 and was in the Rue du Bois sector when he joined. The company moved south a few weeks later to face Vimy Ridge in response to an urgent call for more tunnelling activity from the controller of mines for the 3rd Army.

By May there were eight tunnelling companies along the length of Vimy Ridge, and the 181st was in the heart of N sector, right in the middle of the 'Labyrinth', so called because the trenches were so numerous and maze-like in an area of such total devastation that, in the words of Captain Trounce, the American mining engineer commanding the 181st, 'it was a puzzle to get in and out'.

According to Captain Trounce, the period from April to June 1916 was one of intense activity for the 181st as the tunnelling companies sought to wrest the initiative from the enemy. Twice in May 1916 the

181st broke into German tunnels without the enemy being aware of the fact, and set mines which caused considerable damage and casualties to the enemy front line.

This marked a turning point in the underground war, and they were able to seize the initiative, laying more mines in June and July.

The 181st Tunnelling Company took heavy losses during their time in the Labyrinth, with nineteen ORs killed, and two officers and thirteen ORs wounded or gassed. In the Maroeuil British Cemetery nearby, which is regarded as a tunnellers' cemetery, twenty-five tunnellers are buried, including ten from the 181st who died between 16 April and 2 July 1916, the last-named being Sapper Charles Hopkinson from Sheffield.

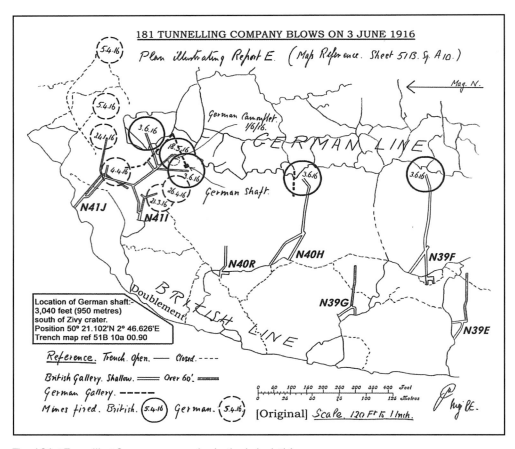

The 181st Tunnelling Company – one day in the Labyrinth!

A MAN OF SHEFFIELD

The company was then moved to Foncqevilliers on the Somme, and was set to work building a number of galleries under No Man's Land to be used for housing ammunition carriers, and for receiving casualties from the coming offensive. Later, based in Albert, part of the company was consolidating enemy trenches when they were taken over by the infantry. Captain Trounce confirms that 'We had said good-bye to underground mining for a while!'

They moved in January 1917 to Ronville near Arras, where their mining skills were not needed for offensive purposes. They were now directed towards the protection of the infantry, working in the caves and tunnels of that area to construct subterranean accommodation and subways giving safe passage to the front.

The offensive use of tunnelling, and indeed of all mining warfare on the Western Front, came to an end with the attack on Messines Ridge on June 7 1917, when one of the most strongly fortified German positions on the front was shattered by the massive explosion of nineteen mines with a blast so savage that it was heard in London and detected by a seismograph on the Isle of Wight.

There was great loss of life, and several thousand German troops were vaporised or buried under tons of earth. Two days later on 9 June 1917 George Albert Adsetts began 10 days' leave in the UK. From his subsequent service record it is difficult to see where he was until 6 September, when he arrived in Etaples en-route to his unit.

Etaples was a notorious British army base camp about 15 miles south of Boulogne to where soldiers on the way to the front, whether raw recruits from England or battle-weary veterans, were sent for intensive training. Three days after his arrival at the camp, trouble broke out. In the afternoon of Sunday 9 September a New Zealand gunner was arrested, and, despite his subsequent release, a large angry crowd of soldiers gathered and would not disperse.

The arrival of the military police made matters worse because one of them fired into the crowd, killing a corporal and wounding a Frenchwoman. News spread, and a thousand men broke out of camp and chased all the military police into the town. Similar demonstrations continued throughout the following day, and the troubles only ended when troops of the Honourable Artillery Company were brought in to bring about a peaceful truce.

George Albert Adsetts was in the camp during these events and the enquiries that led to the court-martial of Corporal Jesse Short of the Northumberland Fusiliers, who was found guilty of attempted mutiny and executed by firing squad in Boulogne on 4 October. He was the only man to be executed for taking part in the Etaples mutiny, although another forty-three soldiers were given sentences ranging from a few months to ten years.

George Albert remained in Etaples until 21 September 1917, when he returned to his unit in the field. He went on leave again to the UK on 18 October, and was admitted to the 3rd Northern General Hospital in Sheffield, finally re-joining his outfit in France on 13 November 1917 when his two-year spell in the 181st Tunnelling Company came to an end.

The life of a tunneller is described in the novel *Birdsong* by Sebastian Faulks, written in 1992. It became the central theme of his account of the horrors of the First World War after reading in 1988 of tunnelling operations on the Western Front: 'I had previously had no idea that beneath no-man's-land, in tunnels so low you could not stand up, another war had been fought: a hell within a hell'.

Captain Harry Davis Trounce, the American who was commanding officer for most of the life of the 181st, wrote a detailed personal account of his war experiences entitled *Fighting the Boche Underground*. In the introductory chapter he provides an insight into the nature of the underground war and the soldiers who fought in it:

"*The men engaged in this work [of tunnelling] do not receive that inspiration and access of courage which comes from above-ground activity and which enkindles and stimulates enthusiasm, as in a blood-stirring charge. This trench tunnelling and mine-laying requires a different form of bravery: that unemotional courage which results from strong self-control, determination, and perseverance of purpose.*"

His final tribute to the men of the 181st is also worth recording:

"*They were a tough crowd, no doubt, but certainly some of the finest fellows under the sun, and they would follow their officers through hell itself.*

Back in our rest billets we had our troubles with them but never anything serious. As long as I live I'll take off my hat to those lads of the 181st R.E."

GEORGE ALBERT ADSETTS IN ITALY
THE FORGOTTEN FRONT

George returned to the York & Lancaster Regiment in November, and was almost immediately moved on to a field posting in Italy. He joined the 9th (Service) Battalion of the York & Lancaster Regiment, which, with the 8th, was being transferred to the Italian theatre of war as part of 23 Division.

Italy had joined the Allies in May 1915 in the hope of making territorial gains at Austria's expense. In a bitter series of eleven battles in the mountains along the Isonzo river on the north-eastern frontier between Italy and Austria, the Italian army had made little progress, and in late October 1917 the Austrian army, substantially strengthened by German reinforcements released from the Russian front, broke through the Italian line at Caporetto. Lt Erwin Rommel, who was leading a company of the Wurttemberg Mountain Battalion, came to prominence in the final battle, where he won the Blue Max.

With the Italians in full retreat, five British and six French divisions were ordered to Italy in support of their ally. The British generals had reluctantly agreed to this under pressure from Lloyd George, who had for some time been arguing for more troops to be sent to the Italian front. By the time they arrived at the end of the year the new Italian commander, Diaz, had formed a more compact and easily defensible line on the Piave river just in front of Venice, and the 23rd Division had moved into place

British troops marching from the railway station past an Italian welcoming party in December 1917.

by 4 December, relieving the Italian 1st Corps in the Montello, a pivotal spot in the Piave defence.

Coincidentally, Bernard Minnitt, a newly commissioned officer attached to the 18th Battalion of the King's Royal Rifles Regiment, whose family ran the village shop in Laneham and for whom my father had run errands during his first stay there, was also on the way to Italy. My father's copy of Bernard Minnitt's 1978 memoir describes the delights of a five-and-a-half-day train journey via Paris and Marseilles, through Cannes, Nice and Monaco, to the Italian border and beyond, followed by rail escort duties to Milan and Verona, before taking position on the lower part of the Montello slopes south of the River Po.

On their arrival in Italy after a long train journey, the British soldiers had been astounded by their warm welcome. 'We were showered with carnations, and barrels of wine were waiting for us at the official opening ceremony', said one soldier on arrival in Ventimiglia.

Many years later, in 2005, the longest-lived veteran of this Italian campaign spoke of the absolute joy of seeing the Mediterranean and enjoying the December sun; he said that when they moved to the front the contrast with the mud and perpetual gunfire in Flanders was immense – all exactly as described by Bernard Minnitt!

In February 1918, however, fears about the increase in enemy forces on the Western Front led to the withdrawal from Italy of two British divisions, to be followed in March by three of the French divisions, so 2nd Lt Minnitt was soon back in France, where he won the Military Cross in fierce fighting around Bapaume to add to the Military Medal he had earned in 1916 serving with the 11th Bn Sherwood Foresters in Le Sars.

The 23rd Division, including the 8th and 9th York & Lancaster Battalions, had not been recalled, and was still in the centre of the front line on the Asiago plateau when the calm was shattered by the Austrian guns, which opened fire at 3.00 am on 15 June 1918, marking the beginning of the Battle of Asiago.

After a barrage of gas bombs on the British front, the Austrian ground attack began, and was repelled by a hail of rifle and machine-gun fire along the front of the 23rd Division, with the 9th Battalion holding firm in the

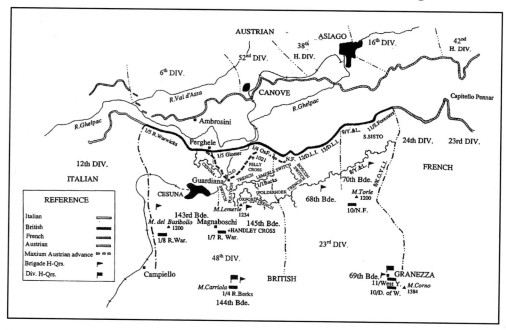

The Battle of Asiago, 15-16 June 1918.

A MAN OF SHEFFIELD

centre. The battle continued, and some ground was lost in fierce fighting, but a counter-attack was eventually mounted, and by 7.30 am on 17 June the British forces had regained the whole front line with minimal opposition.

For a few months, there was calm, and Diaz prepared for an offensive against increasingly demoralised Austrians, who could expect no further support from their German allies, whose forces were collapsing on the Western Front.

The end came with the battle of Vittorio Veneto, launched on 24 October. After six days of hard fighting, the Austrians crumbled under an offensive which was launched all along the Trent and Piave front. The performance of the British 10th Army under Lt-General Lord Cavan, consisting of the 7, 23 and 48 Divisions which spearheaded the main offensive across the Piave towards Vittorio Veneto, was a crucial factor in the ultimate outcome of the battle, although this was rarely acknowledged after the war.

The War Diary of the 9th Battalion, covering the left flank of the 10th Army, written and signed by the Commanding Officer Lieutenant Colonel

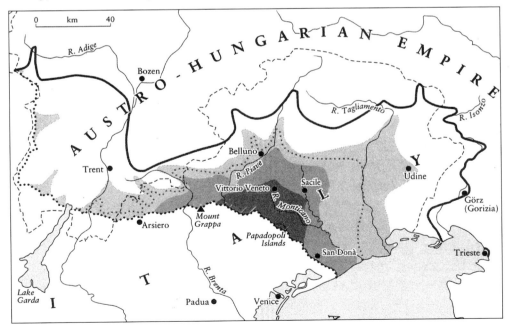

The Battle of Vittorio Veneto 24 - 31 October 1918.

SD Rumbold DSO MC, covers the period from 25 October, when the battalion returned to billets in San Giuseppe, to 31 October, when the daily report ended with the words: 'by 1900 hours our objective had been gained'.

The battalion had remained near Catena for two days, under orders to move at half an hour's notice, and crossed the River Piave at 0700 on the 29th, advancing to support the 8th Battalion Yorkshire Regiment 'who were held up by hostile shelling and machine gun fire'.

Later on the 29th, having taken the village of Cimetta and established a line of forward posts, the battalion captured 150 prisoners, 10 machine guns, and 2 small field guns, at a cost of only 31 casualties. The next day, the 30th, the objective was the town of Sacile, but the cavalry already there warned of an enemy counter-attack and 'we set up a defensive position for the night and sent out patrols'. The counter-attack did not materialise, but 7 prisoners, 2 small field guns and 8 machine guns were captured at no cost in casualties.

The advance towards Sacile was resumed on the morning of the 31st, and by midday the battalion lined the western bank of the River Licenza, unable to cross because the bridges had been destroyed, and pinned down by incessant fire from snipers in houses and from machine guns mounted on the church steeple. Bombardment of the houses by mortars and machine guns cleared the snipers, and the section of 18-pounder field guns made direct hits on the steeple, which silenced the hostile machine guns. The river crossing was completed in near-darkness, and Sacile was taken.

The War Diary states: 'An outpost line was immediately established on the whole front, touch being obtained on either flank'. 298 able-bodied prisoners were taken, plus a further 239 wounded or sick in hospital, and 42 field guns, 53 machine guns, 44 French mortars and over 3,000 rifles were also captured. The casualties suffered by the battalion were 8 killed and 33 wounded.

While talks over an armistice began in Padua, attacks on the enemy rearguard continued, and the road from Sacile to Pordenone was packed with Austrian troops in headlong retreat, 'bombarded, bombed and machine-gunned from the air'.

The Austrians sued for peace, the armistice was signed on 3 November 1918, and hostilities were formally concluded on the 4th. The defeat at Vittoria Veneto signalled the dissolution of the Austro-Hungarian empire, and contributed to the end of the First World War less than two weeks later.

The York & Lancaster Regiment had been heavily involved on the battlefields of Asiago and Vittorio Veneto in the Piave campaign, and battle honours were awarded to the regiment after the war. George Albert Adsetts was almost certainly involved in the heart of the action during both battles.

He was in hospital for about two weeks in December 1918. He then remained in the Italian sector in San Giovanni until he returned to the UK via Cherbourg in January 1919, along with 219 other ranks sent home from 9 Battalion. Elements of 8 Battalion were also demobilised.

Reporting to the UK Dispersal Unit in Clipstone, he was granted 28 days' furlough 'under the Demobilisation Scheme' from 21 January 1919 to 19 February 1919. He returned to the regiment in Bordon on 28 February 1919, and then joined the 2nd Battalion of the York & Lancaster Regiment when it was reformed as a regular army unit at Clipstone in April 1919. Where would George Albert be going next?

One thing which makes this Italian campaign of real interest to my wife Eve is that the town of Maniago, only about 25 miles from Sacile, was the home of the Stefanuti family, and her grandfather had emigrated to Sheffield from there only 20 years earlier. The battle map seems to indicate that the C-in-C of Austrian Forces was based nearby, and one of Eve's nieces is checking with the Maniago library to see if there are any local or family memories.

GEORGE ALBERT ADSETTS
DEATH IN MESOPOTAMIA

Then the next phase of an eventful career opened up for George Albert Adsetts. Quoting from the regimental history:

> *"It was now the turn of this Battalion to proceed overseas on a foreign service tour and it remained at Clipstone till it embarked for Mesopotamia (now called Iraq) in September; with just one break when a large detachment was sent to Sheffield on 20 May for the ceremonies for a Royal visit."*

In an earlier visit to Sheffield in 1915, King George V had visited the major steel-makers and praised the workers of the city for producing munitions 'to their greatest capacity'. In the 1920 visit, the Queen came with him, so that they could together acknowledge the contribution made by all its citizens, men and women, to the final victory. A public holiday was declared, and there was a tour of the city and a civic reception, but the main event was a march-past of 8,000 soldiers and ex-soldiers in front of the town hall.

In the *Sheffield Independent* the following day it was reported that the 'applause rose to its highest pitch when the remnants of the City Battalion, officially known as the Sheffield City 12th (Service) Battalion, marched past in the ranks of the 2nd Battalion of the York & Lancaster Regiment together with the local demobilised men'.

George Albert Adsetts was almost certainly one of the large detachment of the York & Lancaster Regiment from Clipstone which marched with fixed bayonets past the King in what one onlooker called 'the most inspiring spectacle of the day'.

George Albert Adsetts was promoted from paid lance corporal to temporary corporal on 19 September 1919, the day that the battalion sailed from Tilbury on HSS *Khyber*. On reaching Malta, Field Marshall Viscount Plumer, governor of the island, an 'old boy' of the regiment, who had been mentioned in despatches in 1902 when serving with the 2nd Battalion Mounted Infantry in South Africa, visited the 2nd Battalion on board and inspected a guard of honour. Over the course of a distinguished career, Plumer had led the 2nd Army in France between 1915 and 1917, and had commanded British troops, including the 8th and 9th Service Battalions of the York & Lancaster (with George Albert Adsetts) in the Allied force sent to strengthen the Italian front after Caporetto.

Arriving in Bombay around the middle of October, the battalion stayed at a rest camp there for about a fortnight. On 17 October, George Albert signed a will stating that 'In the event of my death I give the whole of my property and effects to my friend Miss A Pickering, 65 Barnsley Rd, Highgate, Nr Rotherham, Yorkshire, England'.

Ada Pickering was the younger sister of Mabel Pickering, who had married George's brother Tom in December 1914. Over five years, his relationship with Ada had developed to the point where, as sole legatee of his will, she had replaced his sister Maria, formerly recognised as next of kin, in the service record.

He then embarked on another ship, the HG *Elephanta*, and reached Basra on 29 October. The battalion then sailed up the Tigris to Baghdad on two paddle steamers and settled in Daura Camp, about 7 miles outside the town. On 1 January 1920 Lieutenants Proctor and Tennent left with 43 other ranks, including George Albert Adsetts, to join A Company of the 17th Machine Gun Battalion, based initially in

Karradah and then sent to Baghdad for training.

In May, the remainder of the battalion began to move to the British summer camp established at Karind in the Persian hills to the north east of Baghdad, 50 miles beyond the railhead in Quaritsu. The wives and children, already suffering in the heat, were taken by motor transport while the troops marched.

When the battalion had arrived in the country five months earlier, everything in Mesopotamia had seemed quite peaceful, but this was the quiet before the storm. There were two possible dangers: the danger that Arab impatience could erupt into action in the Euphrates valley; and the danger of Bolshevik penetration into northern Persia from the Caspian Sea. The civil and military governments in both London and Baghdad were aware of the risks, but were divided and slow to react. Then both dangers became real at the same time!

The Arabs had been promised self-determination after the war, but the end result was a British mandate until the new state of Iraq was ready for independence – an arrangement confirmed in April 1920 at the San Remo Conference – and this was seen as patronising imperial rule by another name.

Beginning in May 1920, Arab frustration at the lack of serious attention to their nationalist aims led to scattered uprisings both north and south of Baghdad, the general pattern of the insurgency being to attack isolated outposts, taxation offices, railways and telegraph lines, creating communication problems and transport disruption which made an effective military response very difficult.

Meanwhile, the Russian threat to northern Persia, driven to some extent by the prospect of securing future oil supplies, also became real in May 1920 when Bolshevik forces landed at Enzali on the Caspian coast. A British force named 'Norperforce' had for a long time been stationed in the area, but its two Indian Regiments with one small mountain battery were now all that stood between the Bolsheviks and British interests in both Iran and Iraq!

Reinforcements were needed quickly, and barely had the soldiers of the 2nd Battalion marched to their summer camp in Karind than they were ordered to travel immediately to Kasvin in northern Persia to reinforce 'Norperforce'. Motor transport was used to take A, B and C Companies of the 2nd Battalion the 318 miles from Karind to Kasvin, and they were soon in action to regain a bridge after the withdrawal of one of the Indian battalions following attack by Bolshevik forces.

Later, A and D Companies joined the mobile column 'Strawcol' and, alongside the Guides Cavalry, the guns of the Royal Horse Artillery and two armoured cars, they mounted a dawn attack on an enemy force at Yuz-Bashi-Chai, capturing three officers, forty-five ORs, six machine-guns, one female nurse and eight ponies (plus thirty killed and wounded).

The remaining soldiers of the York & Lancaster Regiment, including George Albert Adsetts, attached to the 17th Machine Gun Battalion in Baghdad, were divided into two platoons, one of which, under Lt Tennent, remained on guard duties in Baghdad, while the other, under Lt Proctor, was called on to deal with separate Arab attacks occurring with increasing regularity in the valley of the Euphrates.

At the beginning of July 1920 there was an Arab attack on Rumaytha (Ramaitha in the Y & L history), one of the stations on the new railway line just completed between Basra and Baghdad, and the railway line was torn up in several places. 2,500 insurgents attacked the town, and by 5 July all troops and civilians had been surrounded in a walled rectangle of 150 by 75 yards around the local headquarters, which was now completely under siege.

A relief column was quickly formed, but was repelled by a large force of insurgents that was only driven off by air support, enabling the relief column to withdraw northwards.

A second, considerably stronger, relief column was then assembled, to be joined by 1st Battalion 10th Gurkha Rifles after a forced march from the upper Euphrates. Lt Proctor's machine-gun section, including

Corporal George Adsetts, was also ordered to join the Gurkhas at Hillah on the mid-Euphrates on 13 July, but after 'a brush with the rebels at Ibualli' on 15 July, they had to meet the 1/10th Gurkha Rifles further down the line.

According to *Bugles & Kukri*, the history of the 10th Princess Mary's Own Gurkha Rifles, they were ordered to wait at Imim Hanza for the late arrival by train of one section of artillery guns and the Y & L section of machine guns under Lt Proctor before advancing to Ramaitha.

When the reinforcements arrived, the weather conditions were appalling, and the combined support force of Gurkhas and gunners which left Imam Hanza at 11.00 am on 19 July did not reach the main relief column at Ramaitha until 17.00 hours, after covering barely sixteen miles in a blinding sandstorm during the heat of the day.

Within an hour they were ordered to support the relief column,

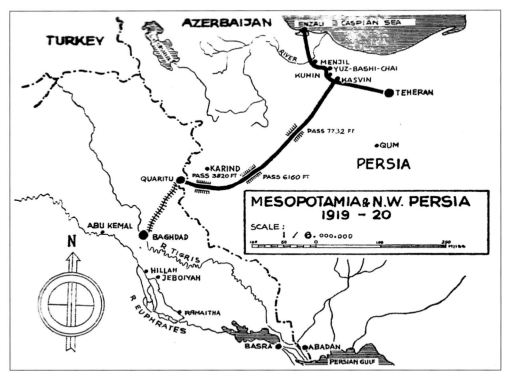

Movements of York & Lancaster Troops in 1920 and 1921.

A Man of Sheffield

exhausted after a day-long attack on a strong Arab position in the intense heat and scorching dry wind of the Mesopotamian summer. Most of the British troops had collapsed from heat and lack of water and the Indians were also at the end of their tether.

Sensing imminent disaster, the commander of 'Rumcol' immediately ordered A and C Companies of the newly arrived 10th battalion of the Gurkha Rifles to break through the Arab shield, to gain the riverbank and access to precious water. The artillery and Lt Procter's machine gun section were to provide covering fire, but only one sub-section of the machine gunners came into action, the rest of the gun-crews having collapsed from the heat.

The machine-gun section remained at best partially operational, and took some part in the direct assault of A and C Companies across the river at 5.00 am the following morning, successfully driving the Arabs from two village strongholds and clearing the way for Indian troops to enter Rumaitha later in the day.

The planned withdrawal from Ramaitha was still hampered by the weather – heat and sandstorms – and was subjected to fierce Arab attacks, but the column finally reached relative safety after further fighting on the way to Hillah, after which the Arab insurgents finally dispersed.

Lt Proctor's machine-gun section had covered the flanks of the column during the withdrawal from Rumaitha, and was then based at Hillah until it returned to Baghdad at the end of the rebellion, having seen a good deal of fighting in the Euphrates Valley.

Ramaitha was just the beginning. Within a month the Arab rebellion had broken out in earnest, spreading beyond the mid-Euphrates to other areas, and the number of insurgents rose to well over 100,000. It began to look and feel like a nationwide revolt, and there was serious threat to the British presence in Mesopotamia before it was finally put down, after months of heavy fighting, with thousands of soldiers needing to be brought in quickly as reinforcements from India.

For most of this period George Albert Adsetts was an active member of the machine-gun battalion. He had been promoted to corporal on 1 May 1920, and, apart from a short period in June with sand-fly fever in hospital in Baghdad and Karind, he was actively engaged with the military response to the Arab rebellion.

The rebellion was slowly brought under control, and the two machine-gun sections under Lieutenants Proctor and Tennent were released in November 1920 from active duties in Baghdad and the Euphrates valley. They marched from the railhead at Quaritsu to re-join the rest of the 2nd Battalion that had returned to barracks in Kasvin after 'Norperforce' had finally recaptured Enzali and the Bolshevik incursion had melted away.

At the end of 1920 the War Office withdrew all troops from northwest Persia as part of a general withdrawal from Iraq, driven mainly by the British need to cut overseas military expenditure. The 2nd Battalion began its withdrawal in January 1921, but wintry conditions of ice and snow caused delays, and the whole battalion did not reach Baghdad until the beginning of May. The battalion finally left on 17 November 1921 for their first station in Karachi.

On 25 April 1921, George Albert was re-admitted to the military hospital in Karind. He was moved to the railhead at Quaritsu, and then to Baghdad for treatment before rejoining the 2nd Battalion in Hinaidi on 14 May. He was finally admitted on 25 July 1921 to the 23rd British Stationary Hospital in Baghdad and died there of heart failure, 'one of seven other ranks who died in Baghdad in that summer'.

The length of his army service since he was recruited in Rotherham on 2 September 1914 was a total of six years and 319 days, including two years, 78 days in France, one year, 68 days in Italy and one year, 321 days in Mesopotamia. He was born on 21 April 1897, and died at the age of 24 years and 107 days, thousands of miles from home.

The *York & Lancaster Journal* of October 1921 reported his death on 5 August 1921 with the comment that it was 'much to the regret of all ranks'. A simple epitaph, but it says a lot about this young man. A sum of £20 9s 5d was sent to his sole legatee, Miss Ada Pickering, on 20 December 1921.

From the electoral registers of South Yorkshire I traced David Adsetts, a retired miner living in Bolton-on-Dearne, who is the surviving grandson of Tom Adsetts, George Albert's brother. He and his younger sister Jackie Benner nee Adsetts told me of Addsett's cottage in Adwick-upon-Dearne, and referred me to an elderly Aunt Hazel in the Midlands, George Albert's niece. Regrettably I found no family record or recollection of his exploits in the Great War, but I will keep on looking.

THE ADSETTS STORY

Ernest & Norman Get to Work

THE SHEFFIELD CONNECTION

ERNEST ADSETTS IN LANEHAM & SHEFFIELD

Shortly after the death of his father in Laneham in July 1913, Ernest and his mother moved back to Sheffield to live at 52 Sedan St, next door to the shop that his brother George ran with his first wife, Mabel. These were the familiar surroundings of his mother's youth, with memories of her early married life on the hillside overlooking the industrial valley of the lower Don, and within easy walking distance of the factories where his family members worked.

Ernest Adsetts was the fifth and last surviving child of William and Annie Adsetts, who were both in their forties when he arrived, somewhat to everyone's surprise. His brother George was twenty years older than the newest member of the family. Ernest was well loved, and his eldest sister Annie, at eighteen, was like a second mother – then and in later years. But in his memoir eighty years later, my father acknowledged that 'the difference in our ages created a generation gap which was impossible to bridge'.

Back in Sheffield, with her only income coming from her mother's pension and the rent from the few cottages in Laneham, things were very difficult for Annie Adsetts. The other children helped where they could, and Ernest decided to play his part. So began the money-raising ventures based on his knack for recognising 'what might be called commercial opportunities', that stayed with him for the rest of his life.

In his days at Laneham he had discovered that there were always odd jobs people wanted doing, and there were many ways of earning a few pence. In the hilly streets of the Don Valley he delivered coal and groceries on behalf of local merchants and shopkeepers, graduating from small to larger barrows and go-karts as he got older and stronger. He also remembered doing occasional Saturday shopping for his father's older sister, Aunt Jane, 'a very fat lady' who also lived on Carwood Lane.

Ernest's favourite sister, Annie, lived nearby with her husband Foljambe Bellamy, and he recalled staying at her house on Carwood Lane at the time of the Zeppelin raid on Sheffield on the night of September 25-26 1916, which resulted in the deaths of 29 people. He remembered the crowds rushing past the Hall Car Tavern at the end of Annie's road while the family all stood at the window watching the people running away from the works towards the open country.

The L-22 Zeppelin was one of seven airships that left Germany on the afternoon of Monday 25 September, targeted to attack London and the South, the North East, and two industrial cities in the North. The Sheffield air-raid alarm was sounded just before 11 o'clock, and the Zeppelin circled around before it dropped its first bombs over Burngreave shortly after midnight.

People in the city therefore had time to find shelter, but many 'ran to the woods and parks believing that only buildings would be targeted', and this mass exodus led indirectly to the tragic death of Mabel, the pregnant wife of Ernest's brother George. She had heard the factory buzzers sounding the warning of an air raid, and with her children joined the crowds of people running through the blackout to the safety of the woodland along Grimesthorpe Rd. She fell, had a miscarriage, and within eleven days she died, at the age of 29, leaving George a widower with three young children, Billy, Alf and Zena.

The *Sheffield Evening Telegraph* of 7 October 1918, two years after the Zeppelin raid, reflects the awareness of a great loss: 'In loving memory of Mabel, the dearly beloved wife of George William Adsetts who passed away October 7 1916…Thy purpose Lord we cannot see, but all is well that's done by Thee – From her affectionate Husband and Children'. My own recollection is that the loss of Mabel, 'a lovely woman', was still felt deeply by my father twenty years later.

The Zeppelin hovered over Sheffield for a time, causing the panic described by my father, and then dropped its bombs in a swathe across the East End. Presumably, the attack was aimed at the factories and railways, but the bombs all landed on houses, according to a later newspaper account. At the time, wartime restrictions limited reports to a raid on a 'North Midlands' town.

The mother of Annie's husband Foljambe Bellamy was killed in the raid by a piece of shrapnel from a bomb that fell near her home. The official report of her death states that 'Elizabeth Bellamy, wife of William Bellamy, a fitter of 43 Writtle St, died in the Royal Hospital from the shock of injuries (wounds in her back and shoulder exposing the spinal column) sustained through the explosion of a bomb dropped from an enemy aircraft'. An inquest was held on 12 October 1916. I have been told that Foljambe had the piece of shrapnel put in a tiepin, which he later lost in a motorcycle accident.

In Ernest's word's, 'these tragedies numbed the family', and shortly afterwards it was decided that Ernest and his mother, along with one of George's now motherless children Billy, should return to Laneham.

So began his second spell in Laneham, a blissful period in which he resumed the happy village life he had enjoyed in the final years of his father's life – but this time he had a companion. Ernest and Billy, his six-year-old nephew, were more like brothers than uncle and nephew, and my father's autobiography, *The Ernest Adsetts Story*, devotes a whole chapter to his recollections of their two years together as country boys in Laneham.

These two lonely boys, each with a recent memory of suddenly losing a parent, were partners in a series of escapades that my father, for the rest of his life, would frequently recall for the entertainment of his family, always with the preface, 'When I was a boy in Laneham …'. They were outsiders, 'city boys' who had to fight to maintain their independence in the face of open aggression from their schoolmates, but I get the impression that they rose above such difficulties.

My father's notes on his time with Billy in Laneham take up more space than those on any other period of his life, and there are many short references which we have yet to interpret, but here goes! The two boys were paid to take cows, bullocks and pigs to Retford market on most Saturdays; my father saved the local postman time and effort by delivering the post to Church Laneham; and their other paid tasks included milking, butter-making, thrashing, baling, hay-making, the thinning of swedes and turnips, and the delivery of groceries from Mr Minnitt's general store in Top Laneham.

He and Billy would also bring in the shire horses after their work in the fields, and when his brother George came to Laneham with fishing parties at the weekend, the big 'earner' was to catch five-inch willow-blades during the week and sell them for use as live bait to catch pike at the weekend. It all added up to three or four shillings a week, a valuable addition to the family budget! I also learned from Uncle George's son Ernest of yet another fishing technique, which was to catch eels on a line with 20/30 hooks cast across the Trent.

The two boys were also armed with catapults by local farmers to deal with rooks and magpies, a tactic which back-fired on one occasion when Billy, the real marksman, turned his catapult on my father and others who wanted to take him back to school after one of his escapades.

The church also played a big part in their lives, as they were both in the church choir and attended Sunday school. The Bishop of Southwell, in his report on parishes in the diocese between 1911 and 1915, while stressing the sterling efforts of the clergy in most parishes to maintain Sunday attendances, still had strong words on the weakening of Sunday observance, saying, 'On the borders of Sheffield and Manchester, where Derbyshire provides a playground for the city dweller, this freedom effectually destroys the quietness of Sunday in our border parishes!'

The bishop went on to say in his report that 'Sunday labour robs the labouring man of the opportunity which God gave for the refreshment of body and soul'. I observed the lasting impact of such words on the young Ernest many years later, when my father agonised for weeks over a decision whether or not to employ people selling ice cream on Sunday. Eventually he went ahead, but I don't think he was ever very happy about it!

Memories of the two-roomed school in Top Laneham, a walk of one and a quarter miles from their home in Church Laneham, are always linked with Billy's addiction to truancy. Miss Blake and Miss Harrison had a lot to contend with, and usually solved the situation by sending Ernest out to find Billy and bring him back; and it did not get any better when Miss Black joined up, and Ernest, at the age of 12, was called on to teach the infants, listing his teaching aids as sand-trays, coloured sticks and raffia work!

There are other references which defy explanation: 'Mr Golding and the Ferry Boat', 'Leach's farm and Old Harry', 'Barges and Packet Steamers', 'Mrs Rawson chased by own Bull', and finally 'Jarve and his Wrist' – a clear reference to Jarvis Binge, the son of a Laneham farmer who married Ernest's sister Nellie a few years later!

'Bottles in the cellar' is easier to understand, since it refers to the dramatic effect of severe flooding one year, probably during my father's first stay in Laneham, when all the contents of my grandfather's wine racks were floating around under the house.

My father described Mr Coldron the blacksmith as 'one of the great characters of my boyhood'. He was a huge man, a jolly, friendly fellow who entertained the village children in his smithy on Main St in Top Laneham. He was also a man of some influence, owning a farm and fields in the village; he was a churchwarden, and perhaps a member of the parish council.

Trent View, the riverside home 'with four cottages at the rear' that had been bought by William Tom several years earlier, now housed Ernest and his mother Annie, her grandson Billy, her mother, and two lodgers.

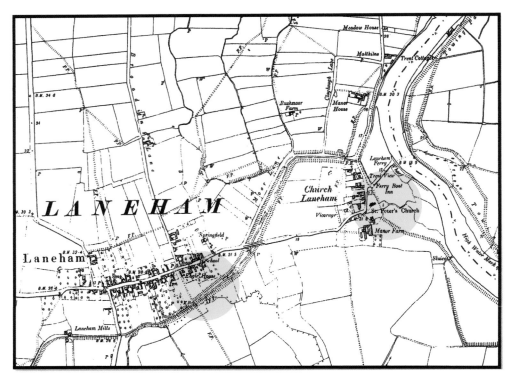

1905 map of Laneham showing Top Laneham, where they went to school, and Church Laneham, where they lived in Trent View next to the Ferry Boat Inn.

A MAN OF SHEFFIELD

One lodger was Sergeant Major Durrant from Sheffield, who was in charge of the camp for German prisoners of war in the old Malt Kilns, and who had arranged for one of the prisoners, Hans from Düsseldorf, to carry out general duties around the house. The second lodger was a Western Front veteran called Todd, a future director of the Sheffield estate agents Ellis Willis and Beckett, who had a 'Blighty' wound – a bullet right through his foot. Ernest's mother once asked him to show her the hole in his foot, at which sight her son fainted on his way to bed and fell downstairs with a lighted candle in his hand!

There were thirty or forty prisoners of war in the Malt Kilns, and they were marched out daily to the local farms where they worked; it is clear from my father's memoir that he and Billy, with the wooden rifles and bayonets carved for them by the prisoners, shared in this daily escort duty.

This happy period came to an early end, which my father always regretted. While he and his mother were enjoying their lives in Laneham, the other guardian and trustee under William Tom's will, Uncle Ernest Banks, who was married to Annie's sister Nelly, had reached the conclusion that young Ernest should return to Sheffield to get a proper education. Ernest was very reluctant to do so, but the family pressure was strong, and his mother begged him to give it a try.

Ernest Banks was born in 1873, the son of a cabinet-case maker, and by 1891, aged 18, he was working as a builder's clerk and draughtsman. He married Ellen (or Nelly) Youle in 1897, becoming the brother-in-law of William Tom and Annie Adsetts, and appears to have qualified as a builder's surveyor some time before he was granted one share on the incorporation of George Longden's building company in 1901.

The managing director of Longden's, James Longden, died in 1907 and Ernest Banks was appointed director in his place. By 1911 aged 38 he had become managing director, taking over the reins just as Longden's began building cinemas in Sheffield to meet the growing demand for large, purpose-built theatres to stage this new form of entertainment.

Longden's led the way with the Palace Union St in 1910, the Electra Fitzalan Square in 1911, and the Cinema House Barkers Pool in 1913, creating a city centre hub to rival such suburban giants as the Heeley Electric Palace, which was built by Longden's in 1911. 600 Heeley Cinema shares, originally owned by William Tom Adsetts, were still part of the Adsetts Trust in 1936, showing a dividend of £267 11s 3d in the accounts.

When young Ernest was brought back to Sheffield, he stayed with Uncle Ernest and Aunty Nelly Banks in their large new home at 76 Carsick Hill Crescent in Sandygate, sharing the extensive family accommodation with his cousins Elsie (six years older) and Sidney (a year older). After a short period at Hunters Bar School, he went to King Edward VII School with his cousin, Sidney Banks. I have not confirmed this in the school records, but it clearly did not work out very well for either boy, and he recalled the next eighteen months as the most miserable of his life.

It is not clear when Ernest left Uncle Ernest Banks's house in Fulwood, but he was still there at the end of the war in 1918, because he remembered his uncle throwing back the curtains to mark the end of the black-out and hearing all the factory buzzers sounding at once to celebrate victory.

My father told me once that he ran away from the Banks's house in Fulwood, but it does seem from his autobiographical notes that there was, either before or after he left, a reluctant agreement with Uncle Ernest that a move was inevitable, and so he went to live with his sister Annie, then living at Primrose Avenue on the Flower Estate.

The final escape from this unhappy period came in 1918 after this move, when a family friend called Mr Hinde gave him a pair of callipers and recommended him for a job at Arthur Lees on Bessemer Rd. At the age of 13 he was put to work on a lathe, with a labourer to work with him!

He was unwittingly drawn into industrial action taken in protest at the delay in releasing women workers in favour of soldiers returning at the end of the war; Ernest was told to increase the 'cut' on his lathe at the same time as everyone else in the workshop – overloading the power supply and bringing all work to a stop!

The wage of 7s 6d a week, which rose shortly to 17s 6d with overtime, was helpful, but Ernest soon began looking for new opportunities. With permission from the foreman he began to charge one and a half pennies a week to 'mash' the tea for the twenty men in the fitting shop, and when others joined in the scheme he had to employ two lads to help him meet the demand. After diversifying into sweets, he started a very profitable weekly raffle, and the income continued to grow to the benefit of his mother in Laneham.

This all happened in 1919, when Ernest was or was near fourteen. The house on Primrose Avenue was very crowded when Ernest first lived there, because apart from Annie's family and the young Ernest, there was his recently widowed brother George, with sons Alf, Billy and their sister Zena, all crammed into the same small space.

About half a mile from Annie, at 48 Primrose Ave, lived 'Jack' Adsetts and his wife; this is John William Adsetts, who appears at this address from 1923 to 1932, and is the son of George, my grandfather's brother, who helped William Tom with his shop ventures.

'Jack' Adsetts was born in July 1885 at Carlisle St, and is recorded in the Census of 1901, aged 15, as a saw-maker's apprentice. He was eventually to become foreman, then assistant manager, of the handsaw department of Spear & Jackson. According to the late Stephen de Bartolomé, a future chairman of the company and Master Cutler, who knew him from 1936, Jack Adsetts was a remarkable man – 'he knew everything, he was highly intelligent, a bit short tempered but a very fine chap'.

The Spear & Jackson connection continued, therefore, long after the death of William Tom. It is probable that William Tom helped to bring his nephew Jack Adsetts into the company before he died, just as he had helped his own son, George (the same age as Jack), who finally took over his father's position in the rolling mill. George's son Alf was also brought into Spear & Jackson at a later date.

Alf's friend Ellis 'Joe' Goodhead, who joined Spear & Jackson in 1926, named the 'Big Five' of the rolling mill at that date – 'they did all the big stuff' he said. They were George Smith – odd lad; Hubert Mosely – backer; Fred Thorpe – middler; Albert Charles – furnaceman; and finally, George Adsetts – roller. Joe told me that Fred Thorpe knew all about the man who 'cut his head off on the machine which Bill Adsetts made a model of'.

Joe, who later joined Ernest Norman Adsetts in the ice cream business, was a great storyteller, and the horror of his simple description of the man who turned a stamping press into a guillotine lay in the final sentence – 'and his head fell into t'scrap bucket'. There has to be a record of this in the local press, but I have not found it yet.

George married again, in 1920, to Ruth Annie Senior, and they had two children. His daughter Doreen was born in 1923 and his son Ernest on Boxing Day 1926. My cousin Ernest told me of some of his memories from weekly visits to his father – he spoke of an impressive 20ft flywheel driving the rolls, of the sight of the backer catching the red-hot steel as it flew from the roller, and of the key role of the beer boy, who was regularly sent with two buckets to bring back beer to the mill from a local pub.

My father returned to Laneham for another short spell with his mother, while he recovered from an accident in Arthur Lees when he ran a drill through his thumb and got 'compensation' leave. He was able to look up old friends, and there was now a new family link with Laneham following his sister Nellie's marriage in 1916 to Jarve Binge, the son of a local farmer.

Main St, Top Laneham, with Minnitt's General Store on the right.

Things were changing in Laneham too. In Bernard Minnitt's memoir of 1978 he describes the situation on his return from the war in March 1920: 'I arrived home and re-joined father in the family business, which was now in a parlous state with practically no stock left and very badly overdrawn at the bank. My total energy was used in making the business into a going concern again…money was short and prices were all one way – downwards. Farmers, our main customers, were having a bad time, many going bankrupt, and for some years we had a real tussle on our hands'.

The future of Binge Farm, the home of Jarvis Binge, who married my father's sister Nelly in 1916, may have been threatened by the post-war conditions described by Bernard Minnitt in his war memoir.

As far as my father was concerned, when May and I managed to get him to take us to Laneham in the 1950s the changes in the village had gone much too far for his liking. In particular, he hated the caravan parks covering some of the fields around, and he never went again.

In my own recent visit, some of the caravans had been replaced by holiday homes, and good landscaping had made them all less obtrusive. It is a pleasant area, a weekend resort with nice views over the river, and it still has the feeling of the small and friendly village that comes over so clearly from my father's memories.

THE MANCHESTER CONNECTION

ERNEST ADSETTS
THE BIRTH OF A SALESMAN

Ernest Norman Adsetts, aged 16, working in the Shakespeare garage.

The family link with Laneham began to weaken. Ernest returned to Sheffield to stay with his sister Annie, and eventually his mother left Laneham to move to Manchester to live with her daughter Alice, who had married William Elliott, a warehouseman working in the Manchester depot of Stephenson Blake, the Sheffield type-founders, in October 1913. Their first child, May, was born in Sheffield in 1914, followed in 1917 by son Billy (christened Charles William Ernest).

Ernest's stay with Annie did not last long. She was pregnant with twins and could no longer cope with the number of family members living in her small house, and so Ernest had to move on. He followed his mother and joined her to live with Alice, who had moved, probably with help from the small trust created on the sale of Trent View, to a house and shop in Heaton Chapel, Stockport, selling stationery, confectionery and tobacco, to which a small selection of books for a two-penny library was added later. May was seven and Billy was four when Ernest came to stay in 1921, and he must have become a sort of elder brother to both of them.

Many things happened in Manchester: he met a girl called Hilda Rachel Wheeler soon after he arrived; he married her in 1928; and I was born there in 1931, but that's a later story. Manchester was the vibrant city of business in which Ernest began to realise his potential as a salesman, and it shaped his future career.

His first job was in the primitive conditions of the Shakespeare garage, where he was taught how to maintain and drive motor cars for the princely sum of twenty-five shillings a week, an improvement on his wage at Arthur Lees. He was then sixteen, made an impression on the owner, got a driving license for five shillings, and became his chauffeur.

His notes include a brief reference to a weekend outing when he borrowed a Cadillac from his boss to take his new girlfriend, Hilda, and her brother, Bob, along with Bob's girlfriend, Madge, over the Pennines to visit Sheffield and Laneham. I vaguely remember his account of the journey – a hair-raising tale of numerous breakdowns and punctures in bad weather, with a thrilling climax of an exploding manhole cover – all we can assume is that these young people had a thoroughly enjoyable and memorable experience.

Then the garage closed, and the unemployed Ernest immediately got a job with Halfords in Albert Square as a bicycle-wheel builder. He had assured the shop manager that he had the necessary experience, and so he spent the next weekend taking his sister's bicycle apart and putting it together again until he knew how to build a wheel. The 'wheelwright' genes inherited from Robert Adsetts of Elmton presumably came in useful.

Every now and then he helped in the shop and discovered that he enjoyed dealing with customers. He had already worked out what he wanted to do next, and continued the search for income-generating opportunities that had been tried with promising results in Laneham and Sheffield.

My father never really saw why the word 'marketing' entered into the simple concept of making a sale, but his next venture was a perfect example of market research identifying an opportunity to create a new and profitable product.

He recognised that during the imminent General Election, the deliverers of party leaflets needed to find letterboxes in the dark – and all the parts were available in Halfords for making the battery flash-lamps to meet this need! He talked to all the party agents, confirmed the usefulness of such a product, and got a lot of orders. The size of the demand led to a series of problems – opening a bank account, finding a bulk supplier who would open a credit account, and enlisting and paying family members as assembly and packaging 'staff'. He felt that he was now a real businessman!

And so he moved on again and got a job as the manager of the Baby Car and Cycle Company shop in Salford, where at £3 a week plus commission he got his first experience of opening and running a shop, with impressive results. He focussed on developing the sales of gramophones and records, which he demonstrated and sold in a new and imaginative way by playing the music outside the shop to attract passers-by! Perhaps the resulting sales growth outstripped the resources of the owners, because after two years they decided to close, and once again Ernest was looking for a job.

This time he became a 'proper' salesman – a commercial traveller, no less! In the centre of Manchester he saw a sign for Caribonum Ltd over a shop. On a sudden impulse, he went in, and learned they were looking for a traveller. After being interviewed by a manager from the London office, he was engaged at £3 a week plus commission. After three weeks' training in London he went back to Manchester with a bag of samples and a territory.

Ernest was 21 in 1926 when he began to work for Caribonum, launching a company career in which he would enjoy remarkable success as a salesman and manager of salesmen, and would gain commercial experience of massive benefit to his future.

Caribonum Ltd had been formed in 1908 to make and sell high-quality typewriter ribbons and carbons from a factory in Leyton. It was a subsidiary of Lamson Paragon, a leading supplier of office equipment, and the invented name was a combination of CARBON RIBBON and BONUM. A local history website describes the company as follows:

> "In 1908 Caribonum Ltd, a carbon paper manufacturer, set up new premises off Church Rd, Leyton. It had to improve its product to equal that coming from the United States. Under the leadership first of Robert Clark and then of the unrelated CF Clark, it operated in markedly American ways. Instead of selling through intermediaries, it had salesmen calling on potential customers every four weeks to obtain orders, using centrally devised methods calculated to optimise efficiency."

At the time of Ernest's appointment the leading light in Caribonum was Mr CF Clark, who was the first home sales manager in 1909 and was promoted to managing director in 1916.

He was described by Frank Muir, the future writer of radio comedies, whose father had worked for Caribonum and who had himself been a Caribonum salesman for a brief spell in the late 1930s, as 'a Yorkshireman, stocky with an under-slung Habsburg jaw, who ran Caribonum according to modern American business methods, but with a strong Yorkshire paternalism'.

Before joining Caribonum, CF Clark had had a remarkable career. He was born in 1876 near Harrogate, where his father was a railway signalman, and started work at the age of 12. Apprenticed to a hatter in Hull, he specialised in window dressing, and studied American advertising techniques.

Apparently, he had a very good memory, based on years of studying the Loisettes Memory System, and had built up a reputation as an advertising expert before he moved to London in 1906. After a short period as advertising manager of a trade paper he moved on to become a copywriter for SH Benson's advertising agency in Kingsway.

He was a copywriter of prodigious energy, and in his final period at Benson's he handled the accounts of Colman's Mustard, Waring, and Bovril, moving to Caribonum after designing the first catalogue and advertising campaign for the UK launch of their products.

When CF Clark took over as managing director in 1915 the new company was struggling. The policy of selling through stationers was not working, and so he made the fundamental decision to sell direct to the users of the goods, bypassing the stationers, who rarely had stock, and providing immediate delivery. He then set up more branch offices around the country and increased the number of commercial travellers – all still wearing frock coats and silk hats!

In *The Ernest Adsetts Story*, Ernest tells a number of anecdotes about his early times with Caribonum in Manchester. They all stem from the need to adopt Mr Clark's 'intensive selling' principles, which put a lot of emphasis on the efficient planning of the territory and of the interview – there should be no wasted time in travelling between contacts, or in conversation with the potential customer. Everything has to be directed towards achieving maximum results with minimum wasted effort.

There was, however, one incident that he remembered all his life – the pretty girl who stopped him in the street one Saturday morning and asked him to call into the office for an order – an order that never got delivered because he couldn't remember her name or where she worked.

Meanwhile, family life continued in School Lane, Heaton Chapel, and his courtship with Hilda Wheeler became more serious, as he put his name down for a council house – the only condition being that when he reached the top of the waiting list he wouldn't get a house unless he was married!

Hilda finished her studies at a secretarial college and combined her work as a qualified secretary/book-keeper with an active sporting career playing hockey for a local club. Her mother died, and after a short and unhappy stay in the Elliott household she got lodgings next door.

Ernest Adsetts was a real believer in the 'Caribonum Ideals', a collection of twelve commandments written by CF Clark to guide his sales force, and he moved rapidly through the ranks because he was determined to succeed. He worked very hard, and he got the results the system called for. He learned that selling was a tough business, that it was a battle of wits, and that you needed to be single-minded.

Ernest's personal copy of the 'Caribonum Ideals', published by the company in 1918, has been well used, with many pencil markings to indicate the most valuable advice for the career salesman. They include a number of themes that were still central to his thinking fifty years later.

Ideal No. 11: 'To beat our competitors by ways they do not try', was the one he quoted most, together with Ideal No. 10: 'To use every

The Twelve
Caribonum Ideals.

No. 1.—To Build our own Business in our own way, irrespective of prevailing customs.

No. 2.—To have a policy that is fair, square and sound, and then to have the courage to pursue that policy—to stick to it through thick and thin.

No. 3.—To sell goods at a profit and not to cut prices to meet competition.

No. 4.—To raise the status of the trade generally by our honourable and straightforward dealing.

No. 5.—To secure the maximum degree of prosperity in its widest sense for the Company and its employees.

No. 6.—To build up the individuality of our business by value, service and originality, so that Caribonum becomes a *Faith* with each of our customers.

No. 7.—To prove, not how cheaply Carbons and Ribbons can be sold, but how well they can be made.

No. 8.—To maintain our standard rate of progress and improvement in time of War as well as in time of peace.

No. 9.—To raise the standard of excellence in type-writing, by force of example and strength of precept, in the business world generally.

No. 10.—To use every incident—wars included—as a positive occasion for improving the business world's acquaintance with Caribonum Carbons and Ribbons.

No. 11.—To beat our competitors by ways they do not try.

No. 12.—To do the maximum profitable business with the minimum unprofitable effort.

incident…as a positive occasion for improving the business', which CF Clark called a 'doctrine of opportunism'. Ideal No. 6: 'To build up the individuality [we would now say image] of our business by value, service and originality so that Caribonum becomes a *Faith* [a first port of call] with each of our customers', was also a favourite.

Fully aware of his own very limited education in Laneham and at Hunter's Bar School in Sheffield, this must have been the first occasion when Ernest was provided with a textbook to guide the development of his career, and he made the most of it. It was not all about selling; there is a short paragraph in the article accompanying Ideal No. 12 which was his future guide:

> "*Do the things that matter. Leave undone everything that does not matter. And do not deceive yourself that certain things matter when they do not. Think incisively. Analyse your work.*"

But he went further, and taught himself the art of making friends, even with customers 'whose manner irked me'. It didn't take my father long to discover that you won't sell a man anything if he doesn't like you.

He also realised that the real secret of selling was to get the interview, and to achieve this he developed a range of stratagems to provide second chances. For example, leaving behind his coat, hat, bag, umbrella or gloves in every office where an interview had been refused, giving him an excuse to go back. These were dangerous tactics, which at times had him thrown out and once nearly sacked, but the orders kept on coming.

Three years after joining Caribonum, my father learned that he had risen to the top of the housing list, and within a week had arranged his wedding, on 1 September 1928, at Robey Congregational Church. As they left the church in a car, slowly weaving its way through the Manchester City crowds, one of the cloth-capped fans put his head through the open window and said feelingly, 'God 'elp thee lad!'

After this heart-felt blessing, and a weekend honeymoon in Blackpool, when he introduced his wife to the landlady as his 'young lady', everything seemed to happen at once. Ernest's Caribonum career began to take off after he was given more responsibilities as a special representative.

The young couple began to settle into their new life together in Meltham Ave, Withington. Shortly after I arrived on 6 April 1931, my father was promoted again, this time to become manager of the Hammersmith Sales Office in London.

It must have been a difficult time for my mother, who was leaving her new home, her family, and her friends in Manchester, and her recently widowed father. I imagine also that my father was sad to leave his mother behind in Manchester, nearly twenty years since his father died, during which time he had felt personally responsible for her welfare.

His nephew and protégé Billy Elliott, now 14, had just left school, and was beginning to train as a typographer for Stephenson Blake, so it was a painful break all round. But it was exciting too, as my father took over his new role, and he soon found a new rented home for his little family in Hounslow, determined to address this great challenge and succeed.

He began as the manager of the Caribonum branch office in Hammersmith with three travellers reporting to him; later he was promoted to the St Martin Le Grand branch in the City of London with 11 travellers, and finally moved to Tottenham Court Rd, where he had 13 travellers and three girls in the office.

He then became one of the two national sales supervisors, choosing to take responsibility for all sales in the North, including Scotland. This led to a period of much travelling, away from home for weeks at a time.

He became a regular user of the London to Glasgow sleeper, and I still have a small booklet called 'Weekday Walking Sticks – Thoughts for Daily Meditation' that was given to him by a fellow traveller on one trip, after a rather prayerful night in which, according to my father, he had very little sleep! There is a handwritten note inside the front cover: 'In memory of a very happy train journey. A pilgrimage to work', signed by J Sholto-Douglas on 1 May 1934.

My father, after opening new offices in Aberdeen and Middlesbrough, decided to provide a practical example of intensive selling in a difficult territory in Scotland. His report appeared in Caribonum Way in June 1934 under the headline, 'How many men REALLY DO a full day's work every day?'. The introduction by CF Clark was typical, 'Representatives who do not do a full day's work', he said, 'little realise how much of the real joy of life they are missing'.

On a rainy day in Glasgow, my father clearly enjoyed himself. He made forty calls and brought in fifteen new prospects, obtaining fifteen orders and eight new accounts, compared with the local man whose daily average was twenty-two calls with three new prospects, six orders and one new account; he also doubled the value of daily sales to £11. Mr Clark summed it up: 'in the face of all the conditions it is a first-class proof of my contention'.

The end was coming, however: my mother, seriously affected by rheumatism, was advised that she should move from Hounslow, and my father was pressing for a move back north, but for some reason the head office was not in favour. Reluctantly, my father confirmed his decision to leave Caribonum, worked a month's notice, and moved his small family back to Sheffield in the late summer of 1934. The family now numbered four, since my sister May had arrived on 21 May 1934, and by the late summer of the same year we had moved to Derbyshire Lane, Sheffield, where my father was going to run a small shop.

Ernest's mother Annie was still living in Stockport with his elder sister Alice, and I have copies of two letters she sent to Hilda and Ernest in the first few months of their arrival in Sheffield. The first letter is mainly concerned with the condition of May and myself, who were both 'down with measles'. The words of advice are the voice of experience – 'keep them warm Hilda and let them drink plenty of Saffron tea' and 'I am sorry but with cair they will pull through all right', and 'it is bad for our little baby cutting her teeth at the same time'.

But even in this expression of concern for her little ones Annie cannot dissociate it from the 'business', noting that they were down with the measles 'just at the busiest time' and hoping that 'you have help for it is very awkward in business – I know, Hilda – I have gone through it love'. And the letter closes, 'how is business Ernest – Nellie says your library is doing fine' with a final afterthought, 'Alice is doing well, hear they are nearly sold out of eggs – Nellie as well'.

Clearly my grandmother, a Trustee of the Adsetts Trust, had an active interest in the shops being run by her three daughters with support from the Trust – Annie in Sheffield, Nellie in Mansfield and Alice in Stockport.

In her second letter there is little about May and me. She notes simply that 'Aunty Banks 'as been over and she says they was alright' and goes on to say, 'I have been very upset with regards our Annie [her eldest daughter] and her affairs – it 'as very much upset me. I have not been myself since I got to know all about it...if Annie had looked after the business more herself it would have been better'. (The Adsetts Trust accounts for 1935 indicate that the Sheffield shop had done very badly).

Grandma Annie Adsetts with Norman.

Having delivered judgement on her eldest daughter, she turned to Ernest and Hilda. 'Well my dears I wish you every success but you will be like your poor old dad and me, it will mean a lot of hard work – more so with having the little ones. But we did not mind so long as they was well looked after – the dear little souls'.

And finally, 'Anyway we struggled along for 15 years together and then to be taken away and leave us all in the middle of life bless him'. I am not sure where the 15 years come from – they married in 1885, started the first shop in 1888, and he wrote his will in 1906 before he died in 1913 – but what seems to emerge from this revealing letter is that she was, if not the driving force, then an active partner in their 'business', and still regrets what they missed out on by his illness and early death. She died suddenly in early November 1936.

Uncle Ernest Banks once again stepped in to help his nephew Ernest, as he had done more than twenty years earlier when he brought him back to Sheffield from Laneham to try unsuccessfully to get him a better education. Clearly there was mutual respect. Ernest Banks had started as a lad in an architects' office and had risen to become managing director of the company selected to build the Sheffield City Hall, originally planned as a memorial to the Sheffield men and women who died in the Great War.

My father believed that Uncle Ernest, a self-made man who had climbed to this top job in the construction industry, admired the energy and determination of his namesake nephew whose eye for new and viable business projects reminded him of William Tom.

He had been a friend and brother-in-law of William Tom Adsetts and an executor of his will, and was clearly impressed with the successful career young Ernest had built for himself after his move from Sheffield to Manchester. And so he lent him the money to buy the Derbyshire Lane property – a small shop with living quarters for the family – perhaps from the small Adsetts Trust established by the executors of William Tom's will for his children.

My father was soon selling sweets and tobacco with his usual flair, and to increase the turnover he added a popular 'two-penny' library stocked with a selection of books from WH Smith. Such libraries had first appeared in North London in 1930, and they were spreading rapidly throughout urban Britain. Mainly serving a working-class clientele, most of them were side-lines to existing businesses such as tobacconists, newsagents and sweetshops, and their main value to the shop-keeper was that they brought customers into the shop more regularly – each transaction requiring two visits!

In the 1930s the traditional business of WH Smith, running railway bookstalls and shops, had been overwhelmed by the phenomenal growth of their Provincial Wholesale Houses, which served independent retail news agencies and shops, most of them small. Over the years these wholesalers had claimed the right to buy their supplies wherever they chose, and when run by men of initiative, like Mr EC Scott in Sheffield, they were able to provide a full range of services to the small independent retailer.

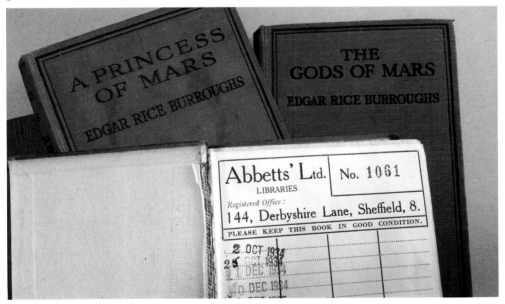

The Princess of Mars, The Gods of Mars and *The Warlord of Mars*: the Martian tales of Edgar Rice Burroughs – in the Derbyshire Lane shop twopenny library.

The showrooms on every floor of their warehouse in the centre of Sheffield were an Aladdin's cave of delights, with toys, stationery, books and magazines on display for me to explore whenever I went with my father to place the next order for our shop. Clearly Mr Scott recognised my father's enterprising drive and encouraged him to set up a two-penny lending library of modern popular fiction on the shelves in a corner of his little shop.

I had begun to teach myself to read at the age of five, and I certainly took an early opportunity to sample this treasure trove. I read all kinds of fiction, from the romantic novels of Ethel Boileau to the adventure stories of John Buchan, and my taste for the Martian stories of Edgar Rice Burroughs, the Westerns of Zane Grey, and the novels of Sir Philip Gibbs was established for good. I still have a few books on my library shelves with the lending label of 'Abbetts Ltd Libraries of 144 Derbyshire Lane Sheffield 8' stuck to the inside front cover.

'Abbetts' was a combination of the Adsetts and Banks names, used in a number of the projects my father suggested to his uncle, who decided to invest in a site on Ridgeway Rd that was ready for shop development. Two more shops, a sweetshop and a greengrocer's, were subsequently added to my father's responsibilities in partnership with his cousin Sidney Banks.

I believe that Ernest Banks at this time was planning to set up a secure and profitable investment for his immediate family with the help of his nephew Ernest, knowing that his health was failing. In March 1937 his solicitor had already advised the board of Longden's that 'the serious state of Mr Banks' health was such as to preclude him from taking any part in the management of any business in the future'. Ernest Banks sold his shares to one of the Longden family members and took no further part in the company.

Sidney was a brilliant amateur golfer, the captain of Hallamshire Golf Club in 1936, whose sporting activities meant that he had little time for working in the business; it is evident from the local press that he still played regular competitive golf, and inevitably the partnership between him and Ernest did not survive. My father became increasingly frustrated; but I imagine that the problem was to some extent made worse by his own ambitious plans for growth, which had included conversion of the large basement of the shops into an ice cream factory.

When the split came in 1938, Uncle Ernest, who was the principal investor in the partnership, decided to divide the business into two parts. Sidney took the shops and my father the ice cream business. Relations clearly remained good, because my father continued to drive his uncle to the board meetings of the Worksop and Retford Brewery, of which he was chairman.

This coincided with the peak of Sydney's golfing career: aged 32 he won the Yorkshire Amateur Championship at Moortown in July 1939 to earn the *Yorkshire Post* headline 'First Sheffield Success for 15 Years!' Even after the war started Uncle Sidney continued his high-profile golfing career as one of the finest amateur golfers in the country; and I remember my father telling me about a match in April 1940 when he caddied for Sidney, who partnered Henry Cotton in a local match against the British amateur champion.

Having set up the Ridgeway Rd investment in such a way that there was secure income for his family while providing his nephew Ernest with the starting point for a new enterprise, Ernest Banks could withdraw from active business.

On his doctor's advice, he and his wife took several cruise holidays, the last one in March-April 1939 on the MS *Sibajak* of The Rotterdam Lloyd Royal Dutch Mail from Southampton to Tangier.

Ernest Hague Banks died aged 68 in Sheffield on 28 November 1941, the day before my father's 36th birthday; probate on his estate of £56,142 19 6d was granted on 27 April 1942 to Sidney Ernest Banks, then a flight lieutenant in the RAF, and to Hyman Stone, the family solicitor. Sydney took over his father's position as a board member of the Mansfield Brewery, and from this base he invented and promoted a new machine for bottle labelling which was eventually licensed successfully to Morgan Fairest. His sister Elsie, meanwhile, ran the shops with considerable support and advice from my father.

So began the ice cream years!

THE SHEFFIELD CONNECTION

ERNEST ADSETTS
THE ICE CREAM YEARS

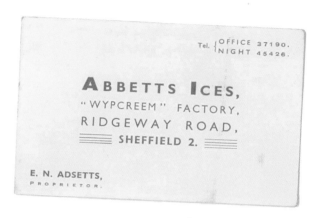

When describing his feelings on taking over Abbetts Ice Cream in 1938 my father said, in *The Ernest Adsetts Story*:

> *"I became a businessman. At the outset I was a businessman in a small way – a shopkeeper. But once a salesman always a salesman, and I made use of my selling experience in setting out to develop the business."*

Apart from the necessary business cards to make clear his new independent status, my father began to use the intensive selling skills acquired in Caribonum to very good effect. He created a good team, persuading his nephew Alf, who was working with his father George in Spear & Jackson, to join him in running the factory. Ernest Norman Adsetts was already following the example of his father, William Tom, by employing the family, and his nephew, Alf Adsetts, from Spear & Jackson was only the first!

The new company of Abbetts Ices began to take shape in the space below the shops on Ridgeway Rd. These were now managed by Elsie Banks, who was at first dependent on the advice of her cousin Ernest and on the shop staff he had recruited and trained.

His main task, however, was to increase the number of shop and cinema outlets, and this depended entirely on his own efforts, on his personal contacts with shopkeepers and cinema managers, and on the provision of a first-class service.

My father began quite quickly to involve his family, as can be seen from the following report in my Norton Free School exercise book in 1938 describing a selling trip when I was seven with my father to Fox House, a beauty spot in Derbyshire, where we had a stall selling ice cream every weekend in the summer.

June 16th. A Nice Day. One day when I was playing my little sister May went inside the house; and my daddy sent her out again. He took me in the van and we went into the country selling ice-cream. We went to a hill which had some rocks on it, A pipe

True to his training in Caribonum, he also took steps to launch his new venture and plant a positive image in the market place. The slogan 'For Children up to 90' was used for the first time on a leaflet featuring my 4-year old sister May offering an ice cream cornet to a cuddly dog.

In a brilliant and imaginative move my father also arranged for the British child star Binkie Stuart, six years old in 1938, to open the new ice cream factory of this tiny company in Sheffield. In the 1930s she enjoyed brief fame as Britain's answer to Shirley Temple, appearing in six films between 1936 and 1938, and the visit must have had real publicity value!

At some point in this hectic period my father resorted to the calming process of writing poetry, just as his father had done in 1883. 'The Friend of the Music Man' is a poem of 24 typed verses dated 24 November 1938 and signed EN Adsetts, which tells the story of a blind traveller, a hurdy gurdy man, who plays his musical box in fairgrounds, and the tragic death of his 'Old Pal', a dancing monkey, as 'fate played its hand in our friendship' when some equipment breaks and falls. The final verse ends: 'At dusk I sit by his graveside – and I play

FOR CHILDREN UP TO 90
ABBETTS ICE CREAM.

My sister May, aged four, promotes Abbetts Ices 'For Children Up To 90'.

whilst I know he is with me – the friend of the Music Man'.

A lorry was bought to provide the new shop customers with a daily delivery of the heavy steel panels, chilled in brine, which maintained the freezing temperature of the shopkeepers' insulated cabinets. In the case of the cinemas and theatres, where the real potential for growth existed, there was a need for more electric refrigerators, and my father's first big achievement was to forge a relationship with a local supplier, Mr Payne of British Automatic Refrigerators, who supplied a dozen on hire purchase.

Ellis, or 'Joe', Goodhead, a friend of Alf, also joined Abbetts from Spear & Jackson, and he took over the important job of maintaining the refrigerators which were vital to the cinema business, combining it with driving the lorry which delivered the 'eutectic' panels to the shops.

Joe and I got on well, and during weekly trips in my father's Ford 10, taking me to tap-dancing class, he taught me to tell the time on the dashboard clock. This wasn't all he taught me – he introduced me to the wide range of colourful swear words which were part of his normal vocabulary. Much later, during my National Service in the RAF, they came in very useful!

On occasional visits to the factory with my father I would sometimes be allowed to work the tub machine, 'help' the girls hand-wrapping the small briquettes cut from large blocks of vanilla ice cream, or slide the cardboard sleeves over the triangular Joystick water ices as they emerged from the frozen mould.

I was given a credit on the pre-war Joystick sleeve as Norman Abbetts – but only ever paid in ice cream!

A MAN OF SHEFFIELD

These visits, normally on Saturday mornings, were also made memorable by the dramatic film serials playing at the Manor cinema next door. I became addicted, and the 'To be continued' message at the end of every episode brought me back week after week.

After my father had served a short period as a special constable, the local police chief Superintendent Midgley appointed him head warden of ARP for the large Manor Ward. In the build-up to war, he was responsible for the development of Air Raid Precautions (ARP) in the area, and I have seen a notice in the local press in which 'EN Adsetts calls on all wardens to attend a general meeting at Prince Edward School on Prince of Wales Rd at 8.00 pm on Wednesday 3 May – Business important' – part of a very successful recruitment drive for more wardens.

Then came 3 September 1939 and the declaration of war. Within three hours the army had commandeered our new lorry, leaving our growing business of ice cream delivery to shops open to attack by the competition.

This was not the only worry, because on 6 October 1939 he appeared before Renishaw Police Court on a charge of selling two small barrels of beer for a party in the canteen at RAF Norton without a license. He pleaded guilty and was fined ten pounds. It was a minor offence – he was doing a favour, and had been told no license was needed – but I can remember just how distressed he was then. Perhaps it had some bearing on his decision to resign his position as head warden of the Manor to become a warden in Norton, where we lived.

Shortly afterwards there came another blow to the new business when my father's engineering background led to a tribunal decision, in the interest of the war effort, that he should report immediately to the Craven works in Darnall, where he was soon employed making jigs and tools for the production of aircraft parts.

My father was now working in munitions, and so my Uncle George, aged 56, came back from retirement to take over the running of the ice cream factory while his son Alf returned to Spear & Jackson, who were able to pay more than the struggling ice cream business could now afford. Pulled in all directions by his work in Cravens and a daily check with his brother on the ice cream business, my father was greatly relieved when, a year after he started working in Cravens, the government banned the manufacture of ice cream!

The enforced closure of the ice cream business triggered further official action, and once again my father was called before a tribunal, to learn that he had to do his war service in the forces; and before the end of 1941 he was in the Royal Air Force.

After training courses in Skegness, Cosford, and Grange-over-Sands he was commissioned as an equipment officer and finally posted to a maintenance unit near Market Drayton in Shropshire, where he was responsible for issuing parts for the repair of a wide range of aircraft. There were two RAF camps alongside each other – Ternhill and Stoke Heath – and my father was soon at home there, assuming responsibility for the camp cinema and incidentally making friends with a local farmer – hence the fairly regular deliveries of Pratt and Whitney cartons of carefully packaged eggs to the family home in Sheffield!

He was promoted to flight lieutenant, and assumed major responsibilities for all technical equipment, with several hangars full of stores essential for aircraft repairs and a very large staff. He enjoyed the pressures of service life in wartime, and gave little thought to his eventual return to civilian life.

From time to time we stayed in the town of Market Drayton nearby. I remember on one such occasion the thrill of going inside a Lancaster bomber being repaired after a mission. There was an equal thrill when my father took me to my first football match and I saw Stanley Matthews playing for Stoke City. I have never forgotten either experience. Nor have I forgotten the open-air party in the town square on VE Day with Mavis, my first girlfriend, while my parents were dancing the night away at a Celebration Ball in the Officers' Mess in Ternhill.

Late in 1943 Ernest had been hit by the bad news that the production of ice cream was being made 'legal' again; he saw immediately that this would give his competitors a head-start, and he was seriously tempted to remain in the RAF after the war. In the end, he decided to return to a riskier future in Sheffield, planning to create a new ice cream business named the Maytime Ice Cream Company for which he had big plans. For the manning of this new enterprise he turned to his family.

The first of these was his nephew, Billy Adsetts, with whom he had shared an adventurous life in Laneham and who had since joined the Royal Navy at the age of sixteen, enlisting as a boy entrant on 2 September 1925 at HMS *Impregnable* in Devonport. After 6 months' initial training as a 'Boy I' he had served a further 12 months at sea as a 'Boy II', first on the battleship *Emperor of India* and then the cruiser *Cambrian* in the Mediterranean, before signing on as an Ordinary Seaman for 12 years' naval service from 22 April 1927 – his eighteenth birthday. He left the Royal Navy in 1946 and joined my father in the ice cream business.

Billy Adsetts served most of his first 12 years in the Royal Navy with the Mediterranean fleet based in Malta, beginning with two years as an able seaman on HMS *Wanderer*, a 'W' class destroyer on which he was assessed as 'Very Good' for character and 'Satisfactory' for efficiency. In March 1930 he joined the commissioning crew of a new 'A' class destroyer, HMS *Anthony*, on which he served for another three years.

In the following six years of his twelve-year service, he was successively on HMS *Cardiff*, a 'C' class light cruiser, HMS *Scimitar*, an 'S' class destroyer, HMS *Frobisher*, a Hawkins class heavy cruiser, and finally, from August 1937, on HMS *Vindictive*, another Hawkins class heavy cruiser, built in 1920, but one which had been subsequently converted to an aircraft carrier – and back again! In April 1939 his 12-year service in the Royal Navy came to an end and he became a civilian – but not for long!

For a while he worked with my father in the ice cream factory, but within a few months war was declared and he was called back into the

Navy. On leave after training he got married, already an able seaman and a trained Shell Examiner, to 19-year old Joan Impey on 29 June 1940 in the Sheffield Register Office.

By April 1942 he was a temporary acting leading seaman and he joined the commissioning crew of HMS *Anson,* two months before this King George V-class battleship was handed over to the navy by the North-East shipyard of Swan Hunters, the handover having been delayed by the addition of fire-control radar and additional anti-aircraft weapons.

Billy served on HMS *Anson* between September 1942 and December 1943, providing the distant covering force for a succession of nine Russian convoys on the dreadful Murmansk run. She played the same role in February 1944 with cover for the HMS *Furious* air attacks on German targets in Norway, and then in April 1944 HMS *Anson* provided essential cover as the flagship for Operation Tungsten in its successful air strike against the German battleship *Tirpitz.*

HMS Anson on the Arctic Convoy – 'the worst journey in the world'.

A MAN OF SHEFFIELD

After such a concentrated period of action, HMS *Anson* was due for a refit, and after a few days leave in Sheffield, Billy was transferred in August 1944 to the sloop HMS *Whimbrel*, which was sent to the Pacific in early 1945 to continue the escort role that she had performed throughout the Battle of the Atlantic. Billy began this tour of duty as temporary acting leading seaman, then temporary leading seaman six months later. Finally, after HMS *Whimbrel* was present at the Japanese surrender, he reached in October 1945 the rank of temporary acting petty officer.

Four months later, back in the UK, he was 'released to shore', and met his baby daughter Linda for the first time. Shortly after his return, Billy took responsibility for the management and storage of the raw materials used in the ice cream factory. Jean Holmes, hired by my mother during the war at the age of 14, eventually took a supervisory role under Billy's direction.

Billy's wartime marriage to Joan didn't last, and their separation in 1952 came when their daughter Linda was seven. Divorce soon followed, and she remembers visiting the Maytime factory every month to collect her mother's maintenance money from Billy. Eventually, Billy and Jean married in April 1958 to become the stable core at the heart of the Maytime Ice Cream Company – and all that followed!

Linda married and went to live in Canada, but she did get the opportunity in the seventies, on a visit to the UK, to introduce Billy to his grandchildren. He was apparently very pleased to re-open a link with his daughter and her family, but there was no opportunity for further contact before his death. Linda has told me that 'my impression is that he was somewhat of a changed man after the war, much quieter and different from the country boy in Laneham'.

There was one other nephew of my father to whom he was very close: Billy Elliott, the son of his sister Alice, who was a toddler of four when my father first went to live with them in Manchester, had become a member of the Manchester branch of the Typographical Association. When war came, he joined the South Lancashire Regiment, and was posted to the 1st Battalion in 21st Army Group as Private CWE Elliott 3657354.

His niece Janet has traced the following commendation from General Bernard Montgomery: 'As C in C 21 Army Corps, I award you this certificate in token of the outstandingly good service you have rendered. I have given instructions that this should be noted in your record of service'.

Billy Elliott in Uniform.

Billy Elliott did not return home to his wife Peggy and son Michael after the war; he died on 6 June 1944 during the D-day landing on SWORD beach, and is buried in a quiet and peaceful graveyard in the village of Hermanville-sur-mer in Normandy.

The assault forces involving the 1st Battalion of the South Lancashire & 2nd East Yorkshire regiments had been led ashore 'in a heavy sea with bad visibility' by 25 direct drive tanks, with landing craft carrying armoured assault teams.

The troops landing on SWORD Beach had the most important task on D-Day – protecting the eastern flank of the entire landing area, where Lord Lovat had placed his 1st Special Service Brigade, including No 4 Commando. Their landing was concentrated on the beach in front of Hermanville-sur-Mer.

No 4 Commando was in the second phase of the assault, and landed just before the 1st Battalion of the South Lancashire Regiment, which included Billy Elliott, in the brigade that was assigned the task of clearing the beach.

They were led ashore by Lord Lovat, with his personal piper Private Bill Millin playing 'Highland Laddie', and the story goes that when the piper pointed out that there were specific orders forbidding this, Lord

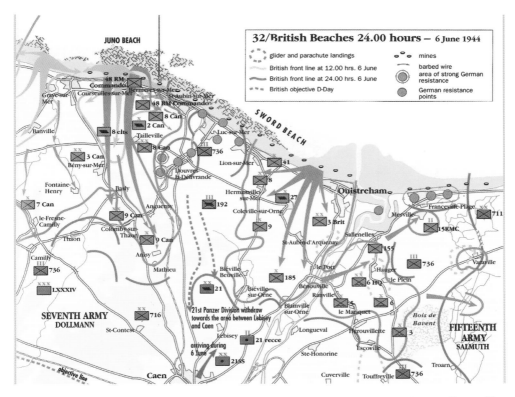

1st Battalion South Lancashire Regiment assault on SWORD beach and through Hermanville-sur-Mer to Caen Rd.

Lovat stated firmly that the orders came from the English War Office and did not apply to Scotsmen!

In the battle for the beach, the 1st Battalion of the South Lancashires broke out quickly, reducing German strongpoints behind the seawall and securing Hermanville by 9.30 am with the loss of 100 men, before heading for Caen, taking prisoners on the way. Billy presumably died in this hectic action – I do not know precisely where, but I do recall that my father, who was clearly very upset by this news of his young nephew, told me that he was shot in Hermanville.

Shortly after the end of the war in 1945, my father was demobbed and soon established the Maytime Ice Cream Company in the Ridgeway Rd factory. The post-war demand for ice cream was substantial, and despite the rationing which limited the ingredients that could be used, the booming cinema trade offered real opportunities. My father invested in a new continuous freezing process that increased production rates at lower cost; and he developed new products to meet changing demand.

He resurrected the Joystick, a triangular, sleeve-wrapped water ice, and was soon making 6,000 a day. It was closely followed by the more traditional Jolly-Lolly and by May-Joy, a chilled fruit drink in a carton. The ice cream range was increased with new flavours, and a new choc-ice machine, with a 'flow' coverage of chocolate, was much more efficient than the old 'dipping' process.

Uncle George stayed on as manager with responsibilities for accounts and administration, while his other son, Alf, came back from his wartime service with Spear & Jackson, and his friend Joe Goodhead also returned. A newcomer, Ernest Harris, who would stay with the family until the end, came back from the army, initially to take on maintenance duties for the growing fleet of van and cars. He eventually involved himself in the whole range of the firm's activities as the resident

FOR CHILDREN UP TO 90

THE "RAINBOW" RANGE

OF

JOLLY-LOLLY

THE MAYTIME ICE CREAM CO.,
Ridgeway Road,
SHEFFIELD, 12.

SIX
DOZEN

SIX
DOZEN

The Ridgeway Rd Factory with Uncle George in the centre and his son Billy Adsetts carrying trays of tubs to the cold store.

Jack-of-all-Trades. His pronunciation was often a bit 'hit and miss', and it was always a pleasure to learn of his adventures in the Sahara 'Dessert'. Later, when I worked with him in the insulation business, his reaction to any new idea was to suck in his lips, say 'Nooooo chance', and then go ahead and make it work!

This was a period in which I learned to know and love the Sheffield characters around me – my Uncle George, for example! I never wearied of sitting next to him in the tiny office of the ice cream factory when he handed out the wages on a Thursday. I would call out the name of each person before us, and Uncle George would slowly find the wage envelope before handing it over with a deep, shuddering sigh. The same process would be repeated with every one of the employees in a wonderful tragic performance.

My memories of Joe Goodhead had a strong impact. Quite apart from his vocabulary of swear-words, I recall his method of dealing with my father's reluctance to delegate, which was to gently rub the side of his nose and say, with appropriate expletives: 'Keep that out of it, Boss'. It always seemed to work. And if my father showed an inclination to let his temper explode, as it could occasionally, Joe would advise, 'Don't thee get t'bloody mask on'.

In 1946, however, the prospects for Maytime looked good: aged 15, I was able to contribute more to the business, and I was called on at weekends and during school holidays to sell ice cream, often working with some of my friends from school in the outside events like works galas and football and cricket matches.

Techniques varied, but real skill was needed when selling to the crowds around the pitch in the Sheffield Wednesday and Sheffield United grounds, when we had to deliver the choc-ices or tubs by throwing them to the buyers standing in the terraces, and being paid in coins thrown back; no wonder we preferred boys who could play cricket!

One of my school-friends, the late George MacBeth, who became a respected poet and author, described his ice cream selling experience in his memoir *A Child of the War* – he seemed to prefer the riskier technique of entering the crowd!

> "A slightly older boy, Norman Adsetts, had a father who was then the largest ice cream manufacturer in the North of England – after Wall's and Lyons – and he had the shrewd notion of inviting his son to employ boys from King Edward's to sell wafers at football and cricket matches in Bramall Lane, the home ground of Sheffield United. Every Saturday afternoon, a band of embryo salesmen would ride by van to the ground, assume the white coat and the shoulder-slung tray of the professional vendor and launch themselves raucous-voiced into the midst of the crowd on Spion Kop."

The Maytime team in Farm Grounds, with my mother, Aunty Madge, May, and my future wife Eve.

The Farm Grounds Gala, staged annually by *Sheffield Newspapers*, became a popular holiday event in the years after the war. From its small beginnings as a children's sports day organised by Uncle Timothy of the *Telegraph* and Aunt Edith of the *Star*'s Gloops Club, the event had grown to become a very large annual gala at which Sheffield families could enjoy a wide range of outdoor entertainments and all the fun of Joe Ling's fair over two weeks every summer.

My father had gradually increased his range of activities in Farm Grounds well beyond ice cream to include minerals, crisps, candy floss and a children's playground; and for this he needed a large team of temporary employees, including the boys from King Edward's and several family members (shades of William Tom!).

My early selling experience of manning a stall in the middle of Joseph Ling's fairground was memorable. The stall was set between a boxing booth and 'The Lady Entombed in Ice', lurid pictures of whom were mounted behind the barker, who had to build up a big enough crowd before enticing them to pay the entrance fee to walk around a large box made of blocks of ice delivered daily from Sheffield abattoir, staring in wonder, shock and horror at her fate.

The star of the show was a young woman of about my age, dressed in a bathing suit, who would lay motionless on a small piece of sacking in the box for about twenty minutes; and in between these tours of duty she would slip out of her tent to have an ice cream and a bag of crisps with me, hiding behind the candyfloss machine as we would chat about life.

Many years later, Professor Vanessa Toulmin, the director of the Fairground Archive at Sheffield University, introduced me to Ronny Taylor, the owner of the boxing booth on the other side of my stall. I told her of the night when, at a party after all the punters had gone home, Joe Ling, the owner of the fair, gave me the wonderful 1897 4-Abreast Galloper roundabout pictured below, only to take it back a few hours – and a few drinks – later because it wouldn't be fair to lumber me with 'that old thing'! I've been a frustrated fairground tycoon ever since.

There was an excitement about working for the Maytime Ice Cream Company in those years, and my father led a strong team, which he described in *The Ernest Adsetts Story* as 'a loyal, honest and hardworking staff of men and women who were unbounding in their enthusiasm';

The magnificent 4-Abreast Galloper, made in 1897, redecorated in 1948 and sold to Joe Ling: first shown at the Farm Grounds in 1950.

this simply reflects the quality of his leadership, and is a measure of the respect he earned from his people.

His mentor, CF Clark of Caribonum, had a simple formula for this, saying that 'Respect is earned by a combination of Trust and Fear', and my father lived by this maxim all his working life. Fear of the consequences of failure has a negative effect, but fear of letting the boss down is positive, and the best leaders are the ones who make sure that the right one predominates – as my father did most of the time. With this sort of team behind him my father was right to take an optimistic view of the future.

He was confident enough to try out an idea that had occurred to him in the Royal Air Force, when religious films in the camp cinema had attracted many more people than the churches. With the support of J Arthur Rank, the film giant of the day, and of a few cinema managers in Sheffield, he staged several Sunday cinema performances, with religious films, documentaries, cartoons and even a few hymns, aiming to attract children to his Sunday School.

It worked reasonably well, and there was even an article in the *New York Times* commenting favourably on the idea, albeit noting that a 2000-strong audience of Sheffield children reacted to the films 'roughly according to quality', but groaned when the hymns were announced. In the end, however, funding ran out, and the cinema owners and managers of the city were lukewarm about continuing.

In business, too, the odds were stacked against him. His decision to concentrate on the booming cinema and theatre market had been brilliantly effective, and he did manage to hold a major share of the regional market against competition from the large national makers of ice cream for nearly ten years.

I still have the Silver Medal awarded by the Ice Cream Alliance to The Maytime Ice Cream Company in January 1952 in a national competition open to all Ice Cream manufacturers. But it did not last. Gradually, the situation changed, as the post-war demand for cinema declined

following the explosive growth of television, which not only reduced the numbers going out to cinemas and theatres, but ultimately began to close them down.

This trend accelerated after the boost given to television ownership by the Coronation of 1953. As the demand fell, so the price competition between ice cream suppliers became fiercer, to the point at which only the giants could survive. My father sold the remaining ice cream business to Walls Ice Cream, and decided to concentrate on the new business of Maytime Catering that had carried out a number of catering contracts in the late summer season of 1955 – and made a profit!

The sale of two small shops helped provide the capital for the equipment needed to set up a full-service outside catering company, and a typically energetic personal sales drive by Ernest Norman Adsetts secured 36 outside catering contracts for the 1956 season.

The end-result can be summarised in my father's own words: 'The summer of 1955 had been the hottest and driest for years, but the summer of 1956 was the wettest! All my dreams of success sailed away on large black clouds which brought rain, rain, and even more rain'. The facts were almost unbelievable – out of 36 events, 32 were washed out. So my father approached the final event of the year, an Ideal Home Exhibition at the Edmund Rd Drill Hall in September, with the knowledge that he needed a miracle to salvage anything from a dreadful year.

The Edmund Rd Drill Hall was known as the Norfolk Drill Hall when it hosted the 1891 Industrial Exhibition, at which Ernest's father received a bronze medal for excellence. In 1955 it was going to help create a new business opportunity for my father. If anyone deserved an award for excellence in 1956 it was going to be William Tom's son Ernest, but it would take an incredible sequence of coincidental events to make it happen.

I had spent most of the time between 1950 and 1955 away from Sheffield. Two years of National Service with the Royal Air Force had been followed by three years at The Queen's College Oxford studying Philosophy, Politics and Economics, and so I had no direct knowledge of the dire situation in the family business.

I returned to Sheffield in July 1955 and helped with a few catering events before joining Fibreglass Ltd, a subsidiary of Pilkingtons, the largest glass manufacturer in the UK, as a graduate trainee.

I had just completed my training in St Helen's before moving to London as a Marine Insulation Specialist when I went to a sales conference in Southport sometime in June or July 1956, where we were told of the imminent introduction of Cosywrap, a new glass-fibre insulation packed in small rolls for the householder.

My father was preparing his stall in the Drill Hall a few days before the Ideal Home Exhibition when one of the organisers approached him, asking for help. A stand by the entrance needed a new occupant, and my father could have it if he could guarantee to fill it – which he did.

Later that day, I telephoned my parents from London to talk about some practical details to do with my wedding in Sheffield on 20 October. When my father told me of the offer of a stand at the exhibition and asked me what I thought, I suggested that Cosywrap was a sort of Ideal Home product – and agreed to talk to the product manager at Fibreglass to see if he could help.

And that was it!

THE BIRTH OF
SHEFFIELD INSULATIONS

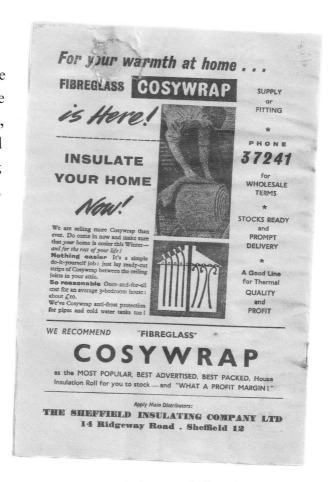

Needless to say, he didn't have a clue what to do with the stand, but he had never refused something for nothing and he had already begun, with my mother's help, to line the empty stand with decorative drapes and flowers whose colours fortuitously matched the Cosywrap packaging.

The approach to my colleagues in Fibreglass got a favourable response; and it was soon taken out of my hands as the local representative, Bill Vann, was cleared to help my father in every way possible. Since it was such a new product, the local Fibreglass stockist hadn't yet worked out a price, so my father borrowed twenty-nine out of his total stock of thirty rolls. Fibreglass helped with the literature and a salesman, and 1300 rolls were sold, many on a 'supply and fix' basis.

A new business was born and formally registered as the Sheffield Insulating Company. Some miracle! My father always put it down to the power of prayer – and he may have been right. Two new ventures were entered into within a few weeks of each other – the 1956 launch of a business selling insulation in September, and the marriage of Eve and Norman Adsetts in October – and both are still going strong sixty years later!

The events in The Edmund Rd Drill Hall in October 1956 offered a possible way out of the financial problems created by the awful weather that had wrecked the full-scale launch of my father's catering company. The salesman in Ernest sensed that he had found the right product at just the right time, but he knew that it would take all his experience, and some hard graft, to turn this opportunity into a profitable business.

These thoughts, and his outline plans for action, must have been swirling around in his mind in the few days before I was to marry Eve on 20 October. Working in London until the last minute, I had not fully realised just what an incredible change there had been in the prospects for the family business, and what a load had been lifted from my parents. Nothing was said during the very special day of the wedding, but I am certain that just as soon as Eve and I had left by the London train en route to our honeymoon in Holland, my father had begun working on the details of an intensive selling campaign for Cosywrap.

A MAN OF SHEFFIELD

The Maytime Catering stall in the Edmund Rd Drill Hall displaying Cosywrap at the Ideal Home Exhibition of 1955.

It took the form of a house-to-house sales drive based on the list of callers to the exhibition stand, a list to which the local Fibreglass representative, Bill Vann, who had helped on the stand, added his own contacts. Many additional orders were received, and Fibreglass Ltd quickly agreed to appoint the new Sheffield business as a Cosywrap stockist and distributor.

From this point, my father said, he never looked back. Cash-flow difficulties – the legacy of his earlier problems with the catering venture – slowed things down a bit, and at first he had a problem finding teams to fit insulation in lofts, but Ernest Harris, who had turned his hand to the running of catering contracts in 1955 and 1956, was now asked to run the growing business of putting Cosywrap in lofts for our new customers, and he made a good job of it; meanwhile Billy was put in charge of warehousing and controlling the stock of a growing range of insulation products.

In the fifties there were no set standards for the insulation of buildings, and the market largely consisted of 'supply and fix' contracts for the traditional use of insulation on the pipes, boilers and ducts in heating systems, or for its large-scale use in specialised processing plants or cold stores, and so my father hired a specialist contracts manager and successfully entered this branch of the market.

Once again, the results from diversification into a new market flattered to deceive: a building programme of new power stations massively increased the demand for the skilled men we employed, and pay rates tripled virtually overnight. There was no alternative but to withdraw from industrial contracting and concentrate on distribution, the unfashionable but ultimately more rewarding end of the insulation market.

At the same time, my own career was taking off as the demand for specialist insulation products was growing in all types of transport.

It was an exciting time, as shipbuilding for both the Merchant and Royal Navies kept UK shipyards working at full capacity: Warships needed hull insulation that was light and robust, a new generation of aircraft for passenger travel needed very light fuselage insulation with very high sound-absorption, the new diesel locomotives being introduced by British Rail were noisy and needed acoustic treatment, and new railway carriages needed insulation to replace the traditional sprayed asbestos treatment.

Some great ships insulated with *Superfine*

Aragon	Empress of Canada	Oriana
Arlanza	Empress of England	Southern Cross
Canberra	Ivernia	Transvaal Castle
Carinthia	Northern Star	Windsor Castle

In every area of the transport markets, new standards and new applications needed new products, and I worked closely with R&D

engineers to ensure that they met the needs of the customer. This was particularly true of the twin developments of moulded glass fibre for under-bonnet sound absorption and for one-piece decorative roof linings in new cars, on which I worked with a multi-disciplinary team in the product development department.

Meanwhile, my father's insulation distribution company was getting steadily stronger as his unique form of intense personal salesmanship got results in his dealings with both suppliers and customers. He now had stockist terms from Fibreglass on all their products sold to the construction industry. He was getting attractive prices for the sale of expanded polystyrene from the largest manufacturer in the UK, and there were other products like polystyrene ceiling tiles and flexible foamed plastic pipe insulation where a 'stocking' distributor was just what the manufacturer needed. His advertising encapsulated his vision.

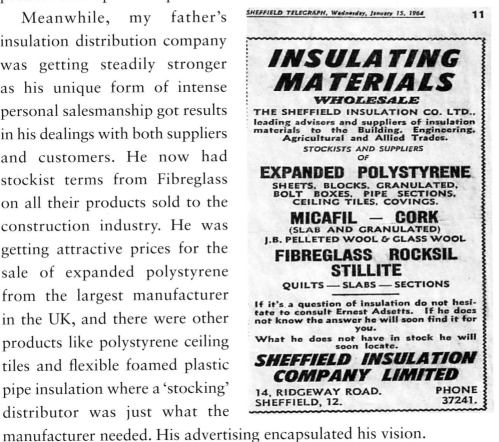

The demand for direct supply of insulation to builders was still small, and there were still some older specifications around; in my father's papers I even found a blotter advertising Cabot's Quilt, a quilt made from eelgrass, which as far as I was aware had last been used to insulate Captain Scott's hut in the Antarctic Expedition of 1910; this does raise the interesting possibility that in the 1950s my father had bought and sold this historic material.

The original insulation for timber buildings – quilted seaweed!

And why was there a case to be made for becoming a specialised distributor of insulation to the building industry? Insulation manufacturers were finding that, even though demand for these new products in the construction industry was rising as more architects were putting insulation into their specifications, the traditional distribution channels to the industry – builder's merchants – were not interested in holding stocks.

The explanation was simple. Insulation products are normally bulky, light and relatively fragile, so that the typical builder's merchant, with an open yard for storage and flatbed lorries for delivery, was not well placed to handle them. Add to that the intermittent demand for a new product and the fact that builders would often need guidance on its use, and most builders' merchants saw no easy return from handling insulation.

At this stage of the introduction of insulation to the building industry my father was slowly developing the classic model for a specialist insulation distributor. Operating from covered warehouses, he would use large vans instead of lorries, train his sales staff on the proper use of the products, and

SILK SHIELD

Tel. Day 37241   Tel. Night 73876

HAND LIST OF

Insulating Materials

THE

SHEFFIELD WHOLESALE INSULATING MATERIALS

14 Ridgeway Road . Sheffield 12

STOCKISTS & TRADE SUPPLIERS at WHOLESALE TERMS

INDUSTRIAL PIPE SECTIONS AND SLABS
BUILDERS' QUILTS AND MATTINGS
ROOFING MATERIALS
BOILER PLASTICS
ASBESTOLUX
VERMICULITE
LAGGINGS

Fibreglass - Asbestos - Rocksil - Magnesia - Mineral Wool

TELEPHONE

37241

PLEASE MAKE USE OF OUR FREE ADVISORY SERVICE

★ *What we do not know we'll soon find out for you*
        ★ *What we have not got we'll soon obtain*

THE SUPPLY BRANCH OF

The Sheffield Insulating Company Limited

on War Department and Air Ministry Approved List of Contractors hold stocks in anticipation of demand, acting all the time as a pro-active partner supporting the marketing plans of his suppliers as, one by one, they introduced new types of building product to a very conservative market.

This decision to be pro-active rather than reactive in his approach to the market was just what the insulation manufacturer wanted to hear. Ernest remembered Caribonum Ideal No 10: 'To use every incident as a positive occasion for improving the business'; and he was in a good position to do this!

Apart from the one lorry he bought before the war, he had only ever used vans for the ice cream and catering deliveries; and I recall from the early days of the insulation business that he had one vehicle – called the 'Sheffield' van – which had reversible panels on both sidewalls: one side advertising Maytime Catering and the other side the Sheffield Insulating Company.

The teams for fitting loft insulation and catering for bar mitzvahs and wedding receptions were similarly interchangeable in those early days. Covered warehousing space for stocks of insulation was available in the Hillsborough Barracks, where my father had established his new company after a brief spell in Ridgeway Rd.

Hillsborough Barracks had been built in 1848 and comprised quarters for both infantry and cavalry soldiers, with two parade grounds, stables, and a large block for officers' quarters on the Langsett Rd frontage. From 1932, by then renamed Hillsborough Works, it had housed the factory and offices of Burdalls Ltd, a manufacturing chemist whose best-known product was Burdall's Gravy Salts. Mr Herbert Burdall, a Sheffield character, had placed his factory in the stable buildings around the cavalry parade ground, and rented out the rest.

In the early post-war days of the ice cream company my father had rented a set of broken-down garages on the infantry parade ground of the Hillsborough Barracks at a peppercorn rent for the storage, repair and maintenance of the refrigerated cabinets that we loaned to cinema customers.

Subsequently, when this parade ground was sold for a new Sheffield depot for British Road Services, my father talked again to Herbert Burdall and got a bigger unit in the old infantry quarters at the same low rent. From then onwards, as the Sheffield Insulating Company grew, we were able to move into other parts of the massive barracks complex, and ultimately took over the whole Burdall's factory when it closed down in the '70s. Without this option the rapid growth of our Sheffield-based business would have led to difficult and costly decisions as we were forced to move premises to find more space for our warehousing and distribution operations.

My father's decision in the early '60s to shed the contracting arm and concentrate on the growing demand for specialist distribution of insulation was clearly the right one. The rate of growth, though limited by cash-flow difficulties, was significant, and continued to rise as my father built up a strong customer base in the Sheffield region.

At the same time, my own career was taking off as the transport markets for specialist insulation products grew. My specific area of responsibility was the introduction of the new Crown Superfine to transport applications. Superfine matched the performance of coarser-fibred materials at a fraction of their weight, and was particularly valuable when efficient insulation and/or sound absorption had to be combined with the need to keep weight as low as possible.

At roughly the same time, my father and I were recognising the changing needs of our particular markets and setting out to design and develop new products and services so as to more effectively meet those needs. We were following the same route as my grandfather, who had set up a shop to sell fishing prizes, or the path that had led my great-grandfather to re-model himself as a groom and a gardener to serve the successful entrepreneurs who were setting up home on the hillsides of the Don Valley.

In our own ways we were all entrepreneurs – and such risk-taking activity is, in my opinion, best achieved by treating it as a game: a serious game, but challenging and fulfilling! This was certainly true in my new role as sales development manager.

As I became more involved in the development of new products and new markets, it was increasingly difficult to keep tabs on what was happening in Sheffield. I was nevertheless made aware of the steady growth of the Sheffield customer base every Christmas when, like every family member, I was recruited to deliver my father's personal gift to every key customer.

A decision on the future was looming, both in relation to my own career path and the future development of the Sheffield Insulating Company. In 1965 my father would be sixty, and I was in my thirty-fifth year, and it was going to be a year of decision for both of us. How was the vision of a national insulation distributor to be turned into reality?

NORMAN'S EARLY YEARS

EDUCATION & INSULATION

London Office: 63, Piccadilly, W.1. Telephone, Hyde Park 2115.

W. N. Adsetts, B.A.
Marine Insulation Specialist.

Fibreglass Limited,
Head Office – St. Helens, Lancs.
Works – St. Helens & Glasgow.

Within ten years, the development of the new company led to my return to Sheffield and a new career in a small business run by my father. More of that later, but I need to say something about the years between the beginning of the war in 1939 and 1955, when first I entered the insulation business.

I did not want to become a businessman like my father, and to be fair nor did he want it for me, but when at the age of ten or eleven I decided that I really wanted to join the Royal Navy by applying for a place in Dartmouth College he wasn't very keen on that idea, either. The debate ended in 1942 when I got a scholarship to King Edward VII grammar school in Sheffield.

In 1942 my father was already in the Royal Air Force, and I saw little of him for the next four years. I watched over the progress of the war from my bedroom in Norton Lane, with maps and little flags covering the walls. I read a lot, beginning a lifelong obsession with book collecting, and at other times I played alone in the ruins of the disused Norton Aerodrome across the road, a great place for stimulating the imagination of a small boy.

Before he went into the RAF my father was a jig and toolmaker in Cravens, working on wings for warplanes – I remember the Westland Lysander (of which I had a model) and the strange-looking Barracuda, which then found a place in my war stories.

In November 1940, the Blitz came to Sheffield, and we crowded into the brick air-raid shelter in our garden. It had only just been built, and the benches and bunks had not yet been installed, so everyone, including the neighbours who were invited to join us, had to bring their own seats. The Ashworths from next door decided on deckchairs, which took up most of the floor space, and I was relegated to a small stool in the corner.

The resultant feelings of resentment and claustrophobia are still my main memories – not the bombs, nor the sounds of the anti-aircraft battery a few hundred yards away, which made the walls of the shelter vibrate, nor the red glow filling the night sky when my father took me outside the shelter to see Sheffield burn.

My father spent most of the night, on the two occasions when the bombs fell on Sheffield, on patrol with the local wardens of the ARP, and I recall two stories from his reminiscences. On one occasion, he was walking across the field next to my school when suddenly surrounded by a 'stick' of incendiary bombs that seemed to set the field on fire. In making his panic-stricken escape he jumped over a five-foot hedge to reach safety – an impossible feat!

The second occasion was more sombre. On Derbyshire Lane, near where he had opened his first shop, the wool shop received a direct hit from a German bomb. When my father and his team of wardens started looking for survivors they began to carefully remove rubble from the house site and stacked it in the backyard – only to discover later that the lady who ran the wool shop had died in the outside toilet during the raid, and they had covered her body with the rubble from the house. It was not an incident he ever forgot.

My memories of the war are more domestic. There was the first day of 'Home Service', when we didn't go to school and the lessons were taught in our back room, where the sounds and smells of soap, steam and wet clothing every Monday, washing day, created a unique atmosphere for learning.

From the top deck of the tram to town I remember seeing the piles of rubble and twisted girders along the Moor, where shops and a cinema had once stood, and the ruins of Walsh's, the department store, which had burned down for lack of water supply after the raid, taking with it (I thought) the football game which I had wanted for Christmas – but which miraculously turned up on Christmas morning! Simple proof that we were going to win the war!

Then came the new experience of going to King Edward VII School in September 1942: the school uniform, the long journey by tram and bus to and from school every weekday and Saturday morning, the Wednesday afternoon games which I was too small and untaught to enjoy, and the new books that we covered proudly in brown paper, and which I loved to handle.

The 'scholarship' boys who came to King Edward's in 1942 were all in form 2D – 25% of the full year intake; the remaining three forms, 2A, 2B and 2C, still consisted of fee-paying pupils. This situation changed two years later, when there were no fee-paying pupils – the only obvious change being that we sang the hymns in assembly from 'Songs of Praise' in place of the 'Public School Hymnal'.

For the first few years I was one of the smallest boys in the class, and, with no real experience of team sports, I was getting fed up of being knocked about by the other side whenever I played football. On the rare occasions when I managed to get my mother to write a note for me, I missed Wednesday afternoon sports and went to matinee performances in the Lyceum. My most enjoyable and memorable afternoon in the 'gods' was spent watching the American hit play 'Arsenic and Old Lace' on its post-London tour in November 1944.

Lyceum programme for the matinee on Wednesday 15th November 1944 when I should have been playing football.

The sudden surge in my growth to become taller than anyone else in the class, which eased my mother's concern that I would be smaller than my sister May, was repeated more than 50 years later when my grandson Simon went through the same spurt of growth in his teens – obviously a hereditary thing.

Immediately, and despite having no obvious ball skills, I became the left back of the unbeaten first XI of Clumber house, and got my own back on a few of the bullies who had knocked me about when I was small, ultimately managing to exploit this minimal ability to gain a half-blue in lacrosse playing for Oxford.

The 1945 General Election was an event of great excitement; I collected the political leaflets of every party and read the lot. Which party would I have voted for? My favourite, with a questioning approach which has remained my political stance, was Common Wealth, a left-leaning party founded by J B Priestley in 1942 to question the post-war plans of the main coalition parties. It had gathered a few seats during the war, when Labour or Liberal candidates were not allowed to stand against Conservatives in by-elections, but it disappeared without trace in the General Election.

And the best speech? There's no doubt about it – Harry Pollitt of the British Communist Party filling the Sheffield City Hall to bask in the reflected glory of our great ally Soviet Russia – my abiding memory is of dozens of white enamelled buckets full of money stacked on the platform from the collection after the speech.

I had joined the school Boy Scout troop 167B fairly early in my school career, and, despite my size and initial reluctance to enter into the more physical exploits of scouting, I progressed to become a patrol leader, then senior scout, king scout, and eventually a member of a South Yorkshire troop which went to the 'Jamboree de la Paix' in Moisson near Paris in 1947.

This was my first trip abroad, and the rail journey from the Channel port to the campsite near Paris was noteworthy for the rusting remains of tanks and other fighting vehicles in the fields of Northern France. My father was persuaded by my mother to go and make sure that I was OK, and so he too made his first trip abroad, stayed in a Paris hotel on the Boulevard Haussmann, and found his way to the opening of the Jamboree.

He was reassured by the organisation, and his main concern – that we were not going to get enough food – was dispelled when he saw what we were cooking on our own campfire that evening. For the rest of his life he complained to me that he was not invited to join us for the evening meal. He added to this his disgruntlement that he had to hitch his way back to Paris in the back of a pickup truck, the lack of food, and the uncomfortable ride. To cap it all, the damp sheets in the hotel were wrongly blamed for the back problems that actually began in the Royal Air Force. I just don't think he enjoyed his first experience of 'abroad'.

Being a bright pupil and a quick learner, with a conscientious application to homework, I was earmarked for the classic route to Oxbridge, and did quite well in Latin, Greek and Greek History in the School Certificate. Confusingly, I also did quite well in Mathematics, Additional Mathematics and General Sciences, and decided to take that route into the Sixth Form.

It worked to some extent, and I eventually got a Hastings Scholarship in Natural Sciences to The Queen's College Oxford, only to change my mind again and decide to take a degree in Philosophy, Politics and Economics instead of Biochemistry. Why? Because I had always liked the sound of it, and thought it would be interesting. Perhaps my experience of the political process during the General Election had something to do with it?

Aside from my academic interests, I also had some ability in ballroom dancing, being taught by the same teacher from whom I learned tap dancing before the war, when Joe had taught me to tell the time and a few other things. My partner was Norma, and we won some medals together and entered some competitions, though without any notable successes.

The pay back from this investment in social skills came when I was sixteen and met Eve Stefanuti, my future wife, at the Saturday night 'hop' in St Oswald's church hall. The first meeting was not encouraging – she slapped my face and strode off the dance-floor – but at least I earned the grudging respect of my friends, who wondered what I had done to deserve such a gesture – it was an innocent cuddle because she was cold!

Later on, Eve and I were friendly companions on the school bus every morning, and when her boyfriend left school to join the Army I moved in to take his place. Our subsequent relationship was for a while interrupted by my National Service, and then by our separation to colleges in Leeds and Oxford, but one night in Oxford when I heard she was engaged to someone else I got drunk and decided to do something about it. Since then we have been together for more than sixty years!

In 1948 and 1949 my father took us for family holidays in London, staying in the Strand Palace Hotel and going to theatres every night. My memories are a jumble of sightseeing, with random explorations of the Tube network, eating Knickerbocker Glories in the Cumberland Hotel, enjoying the great comedian Sid Field in 'Piccadilly Hayride' and the American play 'Harvey', and developing a fascination with theatre that has never left me!

I finished my final year as head prefect of the school, taking over when my best friend Geoff Garlick decided to leave early to join the army before Cambridge, giving me the dubious honour of needing to memorise the Latin speech of welcome to be delivered to our honoured guest at Speech Day – I can still declaim it now: 'Omnium eorum qui hoc tempore adesse solent hunc eo libentius excipimus…', and so on. I am sure you get the drift!

My academic record never lived up to its early promise, perhaps because I chopped and changed so much, but at least I received a general education at a time when it was hard to avoid being forced into early specialisation. The decision to change my degree course to PPE meant that I would have to do National Service first, instead of going straight to Oxford. So I joined the Royal Air Force and was sent straight to West Kirby on the Wirral near Liverpool for my 'square-bashing' course.

I learned a lot in the first few weeks. There were about twenty new recruits in my hut, and one day we were told off by the corporal in charge, who had been on leave, for having a scruffy hut. He sacked the recruit who had been made 'senior man' on the back of his experience in the Air Training Corps. I said that this was a little unfair – and was immediately appointed to be the new 'senior man'. (Lesson 1 – don't put your head above the parapet).

When I tried to raise our standards of housekeeping on the first 'Bull night', I found that I wasn't getting anywhere, until I remembered the vocabulary of swear words and obscenities that Joe had taught me on our runs to the dancing class. All at once we were talking the same language and my authority was accepted. 'Bull night' was completed quickly, and we went to the NAAFI for a few drinks. (Lesson 2 – learn the 'right' language).

The young man in the next bed, who signed our group photograph Al 'Jolson' Booth, was a professional rugby league player who also performed 'black-face' in the clubs around Wakefield, miming to records of the American singer. I had seen 'The Jolson Story' and 'Jolson Sings Again' several times and collected his records, so we had a common interest, and when the news came through that Jolson had died, I comforted this tough footballer and gave him my copy of the obituary from the *Guardian*. He became my minder and a useful friend! (Lesson 3 – mates are good to have around).

Then came the worst experience of all. I had been given one of the precious tickets for Reese's Staff Dance in Liverpool, and on the same day we had been on the obstacle course. My boots were soaked and muddy, so I placed them near the stove and asked my deputy to pull them away after an hour or so. Coming back in the middle of the night, my boots were baked and indistinguishable from the ashes surrounding them. (Lesson 4 – if you're thinking of asking anyone to look after your boots, DON'T).

I had been earmarked as POM or Potential Officer Material, and was Best All-Round Recruit at the end of our 8-week square-bashing. There was some pressure that I should join the RAF regiment, based on my record in the Boy Scouts, but I finally chose to become an equipment officer, following my father's example.

No course was immediately available, so I was allotted to Casualty Flight and given jobs to keep me busy. It was winter, very cold, and I was presumably literate, so I was set to work writing railway warrants at Station Headquarters. I was quickly sacked because I became so bored that I doodled over the back of a railway warrant book, and spent the rest of my time shovelling frozen coke in the early morning before keeping the fires alight in the offices of the commanding officer and his senior staff for the rest of the day – a much more interesting job!

A number of training courses followed: after West Kirby came Bircham Newton, Kirton-in-Lindsey, and then a brief stop in Finningley before my first posting as equipment officer to RAF Dalcross near Inverness.

Dalcross, now Inverness City Airport, provided almost fog-free conditions year-round, and was rapidly being returned to its wartime role as an RAF training school for aircrew, this time as No 8 Advanced Flying Training School (8 A.F.T.S.) for pilots who were being made ready to go to Korea. A large number of Airspeed Oxford training aircraft from World War 2 were made available to us, and they all needed to be brought back to operational readiness. My job was to find and order the spares.

This was combined initially with regular flights alongside the flying instructors who needed an observer with them during blind flying practice as part of their training. And so I got a few hours in, and was occasionally allowed to take the controls. I enjoyed my time in Inverness, and had a little BSA Bantam motorcycle to explore the countryside. I was then moved to Full Sutton near York, where I did a similar job before my final posting to RAF Driffield, where the last stages of pilot training on jet aircraft were being carried out.

At Driffield I was in charge of EPAS, the Equipment Provisioning and Accounting Section, responsible for all aspects of provisioning, stock control and accounting records. Then came the day when the Air Ministry auditors arrived, and what then happened is best told in the account printed in the *Independent on Sunday* forty years later. I had been interviewed for one of a weekly series of 500-word articles entitled 'My Biggest Mistake', which ran for over five years, in which 'eminent' people, mostly from the world of business and commerce, described what mistake they had made that merited this title.

The article began, 'My biggest mistake was losing an aeroplane', and I went on to describe the normal procedure to be followed when an aeroplane crashed. When this happened, the damaged plane was transferred from the squadron commander into the charge of the junior Equipment Officer (me), while at the same time the Air Ministry was advised by signal of the event.

It was standard procedure – so simple that nothing could go wrong, and so I had no inkling of trouble ahead when the auditor began to ask me questions about it. 'Flying Officer Adsetts', he said, 'what about this aeroplane?'. He showed me the ledger entry showing that I had responsibility for a two-seater Gloster Meteor Jet Trainer. The next question was: 'Where is it?'.

The article went on to describe my terror after committing the ultimate RAF crime of losing an aeroplane. It was ultimately found flying happily out of an airbase in West Germany, because of course it had been sent away for repair, but its departure had never been recorded.

I made a few remarks at the end of the article about paying attention to detail, saying: 'Don't be misled by your appointment as a manager – at

Gloster Meteor T Mk. 7 two-man trainer in flight.

whatever level – into thinking that it means you are supposed to sit at some isolated desk having deep thoughts about strategy'.

Six years later, in 1998 (46 years after my big mistake!) the results of a detailed analysis of over 200 of the *Independent on Sunday* articles were published in a book entitled *Ending the Blame Culture* by three researchers, two from Oxford and one from Dublin. In effect, the book makes the point that progress and learning come from making mistakes, and my interview is printed in full in the final chapter because I had made this point quite strongly.

A list of 'Thirty things to know about making mistakes' in the same chapter makes one point which I endorse whole-heartedly: 'Some lessons learned by making mistakes are not easily learned any other way'. This is one of the reasons that I learned later to take three-week holidays, because it gave my staff time to make 'real' mistakes with no real chance of avoiding them!

Apart from losing a Meteor, I got quite a few opportunities to fly them, being occasionally taken by instructors on test flights and the night-flying observer duties I had experienced in Dalcross. The experience was, however, very different from the slow-moving Oxford, and I will never forget the thrill of flying just above the clouds, and the fantastic feeling of speed as the wings scythed through the top surface of the cloud in a swooping turn.

Driffield was the final posting in my two years of National Service. It was close enough to Sheffield and to Leeds, where Eve was at college, for occasional trips in a rather beaten-up Ford Utilivan that had replaced my little BSA motorbike.

It was also conveniently close to Sheffield for my 21st birthday party in April 1952 at the Grand Hotel, which was the last occasion on which all five children of William Tom Adsetts – George, Annie Bellamy, Alice Elliott, Nellie Binge and Ernest – were brought together in a family reunion with many of their children. A group photograph survives, on

Family group photograph on my 21st birthday at the Grand Hotel Sheffield April 1952.

which I have been able to identify most of the relatives who play a part in the events recounted in the Adsetts Story.

In the front row, seated from left to right, there is my Aunty Annie Bellamy, my mother, myself, my sister May, and my father; then from left to right standing behind them are my cousins Bobby and Hazel Wheeler from Manchester, cousins Alf and Billy Adsetts, their father (my Uncle George) with his second wife Annie, my Aunt Alice Elliott, then Jarve Binge with his wife (my Aunt Nelly), then Billy's wife Joan, cousins Audrey Wheeler and Hilda from Manchester, plus cousin May (Alice's daughter) with her husband John Lappin, my mother's brother Bob and his wife Madge, my mother's sister Mabel, George and Jack Bellamy, and finally Nancy, Alf's wife.

I became a civilian again and returned home, to begin preparing for the opening of Michaelmas Term at The Queen's College Oxford. I was slow to recognise the opportunities available in both college and university to move beyond academic interests to enjoy other social and sporting activities, but I soon began to make ample use of this freedom.

I tried things because they were new, and in my first year I passed Prelims, learned to row and played football for the college. I also joined the Eglesfield Players to become a singing and dancing member of the cast in a Queen's College revue, '*Collaborations 53*', produced and directed by Norman Rae, a fellow student and future Trade Commissioner for Jamaica in Europe for 14 years.

During my two years in the RAF I had managed to save some money, which I spent on a low-cost skiing trip to Austria in December 1952 with the Oxford and Cambridge ski clubs. I had not skied before, and this holiday, my first for two years, was memorable for what went wrong.

When we began our journey it was the weekend of the great London Smog, the last classic peasouper in the capital, which virtually closed London down and was said to have killed 12,000 people in four days. Our cross-Channel voyage then lasted 18 hours, and the overall rail journey and sea journey from London to Zurs in the Arlberg took 43 hours.

I showed very little aptitude for the sport, but I enjoyed the social life, only for it to end in tragedy. As we neared the end of our holiday, weather and snow conditions worsened. On the morning of our return, the road from Zurs to the railway station in the valley was blocked, but a special effort was made to clear the road and a column of buses took our party to the station. On their return with incoming holidaymakers up the same route an avalanche swept the leading bus off the road, killing 23 people, including several British students. It could have happened at any time!

In my second year, I was treasurer and then president of the Taberdars Room (Queen's equivalent of a Junior Common Room), and I played for the Oxford University lacrosse team, whose practice sessions I began to attend with my friend from King Ted's, Peter Higgins, who was at Balliol. In

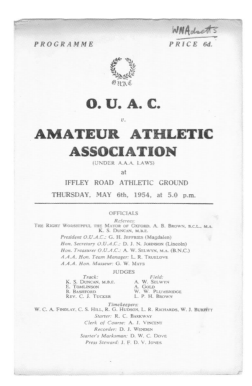

PROGRAMME   PRICE 6d.

WNAducts

O. U. A. C.

v.

AMATEUR ATHLETIC ASSOCIATION

(UNDER A.A.A. LAWS)

at

IFFLEY ROAD ATHLETIC GROUND

THURSDAY, MAY 6th, 1954, at 5.0 p.m.

OFFICIALS

Referees:

THE RIGHT WORSHIPFUL THE MAYOR OF OXFORD, A. B. BROWN, B.C.L., M.A.
K. S. DUNCAN, M.B.E.

President O.U.A.C.: G. H. JEFFRIES (Magdalen)
Hon. Secretary O.U.A.C.: D. J. N. JOHNSON (Lincoln)
Hon. Treasurer O.U.A.C.: A. W. SELWYN, M.A. (B.N.C.)
A.A.A. Hon. Team Manager: L. R. TRUELOVE
A.A.A. Hon. Masseur: G. W. MAYS

JUDGES

Track:	*Field:*
K. S. DUNCAN, M.B.E.	A. W. SELWYN
E. TOMLINSON	A. GOLD
B. BASHFORD	W. W. PLUMBRIDGE
REV. C. J. TUCKER	L. P. H. BROWN

Timekeepers:

W. C. A. FINDLAY, C. S. HILL, R. G. HUDSON, L. R. RICHARDS, W. J. BURBITT

Starter: R. C. BARKWAY

Clerk of Course: A. J. VINCENT

Recorder: D. J. WENDEN

Starter's Marksman: D. W. C. DOVE

Press Steward: J. F. D. V. JONES

lacrosse I found a ball game in which my size was an advantage as a body-checking defender. In the summer I played cricket, a game I enjoyed, but without any observable ability, for the Queen's Quondams, two or three times a week against village cricket teams around Oxford.

Thursday, 6 May 1954 was overcast and windy, with occasional showers, and although I had heard the rumours that Roger Bannister might attempt a four-minute mile in the annual match between Oxford and the Amateur Athletic Association that evening, it seemed unlikely. At four o'clock, an hour before the meeting was due to start, I was sitting with my anchovy toast and a cup of tea in the Taberdars' Room looking through the windows at the pouring rain.

As I got up to return to my books the rain stopped, the sky lightened, and on impulse I walked out of Queen's and made the short walk to the Iffley Rd Athletic Ground to join a small crowd of expectant spectators a few minutes after the meeting began with the pole vault at five o'clock.

It was still windy, and I learned later from Roger Bannister's book *Under Four Minutes* that it was not until the runners began to line up for the start of the mile race at six o'clock that the wind dropped and the flag over the pavilion began to flutter more gently. He writes: 'This was the moment when I made my decision. The attempt was on'.

I can recall every second of the next four minutes, and the lap times are written in my programme. Chris Brasher set the pace for the first two laps and Chris Chataway took over for the third lap, to be overtaken by

Roger Bannister with three hundred yards to go. He says that 'the world seemed to stand still' until he reached the tape and collapsed; and the feelings of those watching were somewhat similar as we all waited to hear the words of Norris McWhirter, the public announcer.

He prolonged the agony – pausing between each record in the list:

> *"Ladies and gentlemen, here is the result of event number nine, the One Mile. First, number 41 RG Bannister of the Amateur Athletic Association and formerly of Exeter and Merton Colleges, with a time which is a new meeting and track record, and which, subject to ratification, will be a new English, native, British, British All-Comers, European, Empire and world record [No one heard the rest but he completed the sentence] ... of 3 minutes 59.4 seconds!"*

He added later that Roger had also equalled the world record of 3 minutes 43 seconds for the 1500 metres.

It was simply a great occasion, and I am privileged to have been one of the couple of thousand people there on the day.

Philosophy, Politics and Economics was a degree of great interest and variety. I was more at home with Politics than Economics, and found Philosophy hard to deal with. Somehow I had lost a lot of the academic zeal for study that had been so strong at school, although I still found hours spent reading, surrounded by the books displayed in the beautiful library of Queen's, enormously satisfying and enjoyable.

My classical education had eventually proved helpful: my good friend and room-mate the late Anastasias Christodoulou or 'Chris', a fellow undergraduate reading Philosophy, Politics and Economics (and future founding secretary of the Open University) had the onerous duty, as Bible scholar, of reciting a Latin Grace before dinner in the Hall. His personal life interfered occasionally with this commitment, and my role was to take his place on those occasions when he failed to turn up in time.

It has often come in useful over the past fifty years to recite from memory: 'Benedic nobis Domine Deus, et his donis quae in liberalitate tuae sumpturi sumus, per Jesum Christum Dominum nostrum'.

In 1955, I led Oxford to a big defeat in the lacrosse match against Cambridge, and concluded that, although I had played reasonably well during the season, including for Oxford and Cambridge Combined against the University of Virginia, and for the South of England against the North in the first televised lacrosse match on BBC TV, my performance as captain of the university side had been poor and inexperienced – yet another mistake to learn from!

Garry Robertson of Brasenose College, from a lacrosse-playing school in Manchester, and one of the stars of the Oxford lacrosse team in this disappointing game, became my brother-in-law a few years later when he married my sister May, before they embarked on a globe-trotting career of research into the tropical diseases of the potato that took them and their family to Nigeria, Kenya, Pakistan and Peru before retiring to the UK.

During Eights week of 1954, I had rowed in the boat of the Eaglets, a small dining club in Queen's, and we had 'bumped' each day, a major achievement even though we were in a very low division as the college fifth eight. There was not the same involvement on the river in 1955, but the dinner in Michaelmas term was notable for the discovery of the beautiful Eaglet sorbet cups, used for the first time in twenty years. It was my decision to make room for a sorbet course, and the quality and cost of the accompanying menu led to a difficult interview with the Senior Fellow, our oldest member, and to the imposition of austerity measures.

I was awarded a second-class honours degree, thanked my tutors, and played my final game with the Quondams at Islip where, with the aid of a friendly umpire, I scored a record 34 runs playing without my glasses, which had been lost while punting on the Isis the night before. Eve also played well when the wives and girlfriends played a match after our ignominious defeat. It had been a wonderful day, and an enjoyable three years, but it was time to get on with some work.

It was the norm in those days to hunt for a job after university via the University Appointments Committee, and in our final year we received detailed reports on each company looking for graduates. I wanted a company with growth prospects offering an early opportunity to get working.

I found the answer in an interview with John Creek, the sales director of Fibreglass Ltd, who had been a graduate of Pembroke College Oxford in the thirties. He was looking for a graduate who had studied sciences at A level but read PPE for his degree, and who didn't want a long training scheme. We clearly spoke the same language, and after he put the starting salary up from £500 to £600 a year I accepted his offer, saying that I would start after working for the family firm in the summer.

I reported for work in St Helen's on Monday, 31 October, having delayed my arrival for several weeks, ostensibly to help my father in the difficult transition from ice cream to catering. But, if I am honest, Mr Escritt of the Oxford University Appointments committee came closer to the truth in the letter he sent to me just before I left for St Helen's.

> *"I am very pleased about your decision. In spite of what may have seemed to you latterly your tendency to procrastinate, you are in my judgement someone who ought to get stuck into something practical and constructive as soon as possible, would be most happy in doing that, and my bet is that you will be most successful having done it."*

John Creek obviously felt the same, because instead of going through the standard training course for an area sales representative I was immediately put through a more demanding training regime to become a specialist marine salesman, responsible for persuading ship-owners and ship-builders of the case for replacing traditional insulation materials like cork and asbestos with glass fibre insulation.

The market opportunity was very significant, because a massive shipbuilding programme was needed to replace the tonnage lost in the war. I would need to be able to talk convincingly to naval architects and superintendent engineers in the City offices of the world's ship owners about heat insulation, fire protection, refrigeration and acoustics.

I had to be able to explain condensation and how to avoid it, to make the economic case for lightweight insulation of the new air-conditioning systems fitted in ships' accommodation, to explain how to reduce the weight of insulation in the new aluminium superstructures of passenger liners, and to complete the conversion of the insulation fitted in refrigerated cargo ships from the traditional cork, which was in very short supply post-war, to glass fibre.

My predecessor and newly appointed manager, Bill Snowden, had been head physicist in the research and development department before he went to London as a well-qualified marine insulation specialist. Apart from A level Physics I had few similar qualifications, but I left university as a learning machine and I absorbed it all.

Later, I got to know more about the reason for my appointment. Senior management had argued that the London marine insulation specialist should be a retired naval officer with engineering experience who could speak with authority to the executives and engineers of the ship owners and ship builders. A man who met this job description was hired, but during his training and subsequent tour of the shipbuilding areas of the UK, he followed the naval tradition of having a 'girl in every port', and created an embarrassing situation for the company.

In the debate which followed his resultant dismissal it was said that John Creek, who had not been involved in the original appointment, argued that there was no need to go for specialist marine or engineering experience, because 'any reasonably intelligent arts graduate from Oxford could pick up all that was necessary in three months'. An apocryphal story perhaps, but the people I met around the company believed it, and my subsequent career was watched with some interest and trepidation!

My subsequent move to London, where I rented digs in Thames Ditton, was briefly interrupted by a trip back to Southport to be briefed on the introduction (of unknowable significance for my future career) of a new retail product that was eventually called Cosywrap. I then returned south to continue to introduce myself to the traditional ship owners and their technical advisors in the City of London.

I knew nothing then of the Caribonum Ideals, but I had learned about selling from my father, and so my first few months shared some similarities with the way he had sold carbon paper and ice cream. The first big test came when I met Douglas Timpson of Ferguson & Timpson, a company with exclusive rights for the sale of Fibreglass insulation to the shipping industry. Douglas was a likeable man with years of experience in the City, who lunched every weekday in the Great Eastern Hotel.

Douglas found me less abrasive than my predecessor, and he took me out from time to time to meet his contacts, but he was well aware that his position as our sole agent was vulnerable, because the whole nature of the market was changing and he didn't find it easy to change with it.

I was eventually able to bring the agreement to an amicable end, and I learned from this experience, to the long-term benefit of Sheffield Insulations, that in order to survive any middleman must market his services in two directions, and be as sensitive to the changing needs of the supplier as to those of the consumer.

A typical day in my life as marine insulation specialist began with a drive from Thames Ditton, parking in St James's Square for the day, and paying a shilling to the old man who watched over my car and occasionally washed it. It was a short walk to the Fibreglass offices above the NatWest Bank at 66 Piccadilly, then up to the room in the roof-space which housed four 'specialist' representatives: myself, along with Tom Hughes, who handled the air-filter market, Russ James, a Welshman who dealt in glass-fibre tissue for the anti-corrosion treatment of oil pipe lines, and Jack Mountifield, the daddy of us all, who was the expert on fibreglass-reinforced plastics.

After checking for letters and messages, I would take the Tube from Green Park to Aldgate, make a courtesy call on the Ferguson & Timpson office nearby, and then start my walking tour of the streets of the City of London. There would be follow up calls on ship owners about vessels on order or under construction, with the backing of reports on ship builders' progress from my colleagues in Scotland, Northern Ireland and the North East.

Perhaps a meeting with Royal Mail Lines, who were considering the use of polyurethane foam to insulate the hold in one of their three ships, Amazon Aragon & Arlanza being built at Harland & Wolff in Belfast – I think I won that one on price! And then a successful meeting with the superintendent engineer of British India Steam Navigation, whom I managed to persuade to reject an unsuitable polystyrene spec in favour of fibreglass slabs in their five ships being built in Govan.

The names themselves are a nostalgic reminder of the days when the British merchant fleet was the largest in the world: Port Line, Elder Dempster, Shaw Savill & Albion, Ellermans and the Blue Star Line. Plus the shipyards of Cammell Laird, Alexander Stephen, John Brown, Swan Hunters, and many more. A *Financial Times* article in 1956 stated that: 'The total order book of UK shipbuilders, comprising both ships already under construction and those not yet laid down is now equivalent to over four years work at the current rate of completions'. It was an exciting time to be involved in this industry.

I was engaged to Eve, due to be married on 20 October in Sheffield, and I was taking instruction in the Roman Catholic faith from Father Richard Mangan, a Jesuit priest in London, having decided to convert. I was eventually confirmed by another Jesuit, Tom Roberts, the former Archbishop of Bombay, who had left India after independence. Unprepared for the need to nominate a saint's name, which was customary, I could only think of one – Jude, after the saint who helps hopeless cases – not the normal choice, but a very appropriate ally in my future career!

As the wedding approached, I learned more of the weather problems experienced by my father in his first full season of outside catering. I could not have helped him, because I had been meeting the ship owner contacts in London and touring the whole of southern England to re-establish links with the smaller boat yards. I covered many miles, visiting the local ship owners in Cardiff, the shipyards and ship repairers of Southampton and the Isle of Wight, and a range of key contacts with the Admiralty in Bath and the naval dockyards of Chatham, Portsmouth and Devonport.

And then came the telephone conversation with my father in October that ultimately changed everything, as it indirectly gave him the opportunity to save the family business after the disastrous summer of 1956.

Eve and I married a week later, honeymooned in Holland, and returned to live together for a short time in Thames Ditton before moving quickly, and, with some relief, to a cosy apartment on the edge of Blackheath. This was a much better base for my work in the City, and Eve got a teaching job in Eltham. Our daughter Helen arrived in September, and after much hunting I found a larger flat on the other side of the Heath.

I happened to mention this happy result to my boss, Bill Snowden, on the way back from a visit to the Admiralty in Bath, and within days I was offered a promotion, replacing Bill as marketing manager of the transport division (MMTD), with responsibility for all transport uses of insulation, which meant a move to St Helen's. I accepted, and was given a small salary increase, but they took my company car away!

At first we rented a terrace house in Knowsley Rd, backing on to the ground of the St Helen's Rugby League team. It was a short walk from the Fibreglass factory, with the further advantage that if I stood on the toilet seat in the bathroom at the back of the house I could see most of every St Helen's home game without paying!

Helen and I at home in St Helen's working on the insulation needs of the UK shipbuilding programme for my monthly report!

Shortly thereafter we bought a new semi-detached house in Eccleston, a suburb of St Helen's, where Eve got a part-time teaching job, and we settled down to wait for the arrival of son Philip.

I was still responsible for three representatives covering the UK marine market from offices in London, Glasgow and Newcastle, but I also did a lot of travelling, because I was personally selling insulation to aircraft and motor car manufacturers while monitoring our sales for railway engines and rolling stock – the responsibility of a sole agent, W Gilmour Smith, an exclusive agent like Douglas Timpson, but with a very different style!

The initial business meeting with his team was in a cottage overlooking the River Clyde, and the plan was clearly to ply me with Scotch whisky and Havana cigars and bulldoze me into improving his agency deal. These old-style tactics didn't work, because I still had the head for alcohol that had been developed with pints of Queen's College ale. Once he realised this, we got on well together.

In the late 50s, Fibreglass planned a major move away from the original glass-fibre process invented by Owens Corning Fiberglas in the States that had been licensed to Pilkington's, the large British glassmaker, to meet the need for insulation in the post-war prefab building programme.

The French glass manufacturing giant St Gobain had developed a new rotary 'Tel' process that produced a cleaner and finer glass fibre, with advantages of cost, performance and handling which could not be ignored. Finer fibres improved on the thermal and acoustic properties of earlier products at lower densities, a combination of properties that was particularly important in transport, where noise and weight were often crucial.

I went a number of times to France to look at the transport applications for the new fibre. There were, of course, other benefits to be gained from a few days in Paris, and I recall one trip when Bill took me to the Crazy Horse Saloon, a high-class strip joint on the Champs Elysee; in return, I took him to a Gala performance of Tosca at the Paris Opera. Quite apart from the respective entertainment values, and even allowing for the evening dress we hired to go the opera, I think the 'free' champagne and food at the Paris Opera House provided better value for money.

There were other benefits, quite apart from the heavy concentration on technical issues and site visits. My link man with St Gobain, Marc Toledano, the head of relations with foreign subsidiaries and associates, who became a friend, gave me a signed copy of his book *Le Franciscain de Bourges*, describing the support that Marc and his brother Yves, with other members of the French Resistance imprisoned in Bourges, received from a Franciscan monk who was a prison guard in the German Army. Subsequently filmed, and published in English in 1970, it is a moving and inspirational true story.

Gerard Dubreuil, who was my guide and instructor on marine and other transport applications for St Gobain Tel products, also went with me to the theatre in Paris in 1960 to see the original production of the play

'*Becket ou L'Honneur de Dieu*' by Jean Anouilh, when I was astonished by the surprising effectiveness of my School Certificate French.

The insulation of refrigerated cargo holds could be a profitable opportunity for the Crown fibre (our brand name for the Tel fibre), but the key question was this: 'How would a low-density slab of Crown insulation compare with loose glass fibre unevenly packed in the large cavity between the lining of the cargo hold and the ship's side?'

Reports on research related to this question were to be presented to the Tenth International Congress of Refrigeration in Copenhagen in August 1959, and I went there with Alan Pimblett, who was the chief physicist of Fibreglass R&D. We listened to various learned papers, met numerous experts from glass-fibre makers around Europe, enjoyed the fairground rides in the Tivoli Gardens, and visited old Viking sites at the weekend.

The end result of this relaxed approach was that we recommended that a lightweight Crown 125 slab (weighing one and a quarter lbs/cubic foot) should replace Fibreglass White Wool (hand-packed at about five lbs/cubic foot) increasing our profit at lower cost and strengthening our hand against the emerging competition.

When the responsibility for marine sales was subsequently transferred to the Fibreglass area offices, I became sales development manager for all specialist fire protection and acoustic matters, while retaining responsibility for developing our business in the railway, aircraft and car markets. I had served my time as a salesman, and was now wholly involved in market and product development.

My search for a way into the car market led to the development of glass-fibre insulation moulded to fit under bonnets, onto bulkheads and to the underside of car roofs, replacing traditional materials and providing better acoustic properties and lower fixing costs. I became the leader of a multi-disciplinary team within the R&D department to take forward this project, which required the design and testing of a new production process.

Sometime later, when a new R&D director was recruited from the Atomic Energy Authority to bring a fresh approach to applied research and development at Fibreglass, both Bill Snowden and I joined his team with a brief to introduce change and deliver results.

I was given the job of introducing a project-based system of budgeting, while also researching the literature on fibre-forming processes, patents and licenses to identify the scope for developing our own production process. No longer a salesman, I was now more of a Jack-of-all-Trades; and I was revealing a range of abilities which finally brought me to the notice of our parent company, Pilkington's.

After ten years with Fibreglass Ltd, I was told in 1965 that I was being considered for a new position in a long-range planning unit within the Pilkington Group, which was to be headed by a top computer expert from outside the company. It sounded very interesting, with a lot of travel to assess the plans of subsidiaries around the world.

While I was considering this proposal, the Fibreglass managing director, John Creek, who had originally recruited me from Oxford, offered me the challenging position of managing director of Fibreglass India, and I asked for time to look closely at the current trading position and prospects of this company before making a decision.

And finally, at a dinner in Sheffield to mark my father's 60th birthday on 29 November 1965, my parents proposed that Eve and I should return to Sheffield to share with them the ownership of the Sheffield Insulating Company, with a view to becoming managing director in the near future. The company was growing rapidly, and the management of this growth was going to be more than my father could handle alone.

I tried to approach the choice between these options without making any prior judgement, and I was as objective as I could be. But the choice between the planning and FG India appointments was ultimately fairly straightforward, since I wanted to do my own thing rather than advise someone how to do his. Years later I read the following extract from

Robert Townsend's *Up the Organisation*, a book published in 1970, full of common sense about management, in which the author makes a similar point.

> *'Once I was asked to head up a new long-range planning effort. My wife listened to my glowing description of my new job. Next evening she blew the whole schmeer out of the water by asking: "What did you plan today dear?" Bless her'.*

The choice between India and Sheffield was clear. The salary and perks of the Indian job were much greater and the commercial risks were about the same if not favourable to India, but the family disruption in moving to Bombay was unacceptable. So, in the end, the decision was easily made. We sold the house in St Helen's, bought another in Sheffield, arranged for the children to go to Mylnhurst, Eve's old school, and I reported for work in Sheffield on 1 April 1966.

SHEFFIELD INSULATIONS

ERNEST & NORMAN
TOGETHER AGAIN

Joining together in partnership to entertain needy children are Ernest of the Magic Circle and Norman, a visiting clown.

When I joined my father in the insulation business he was 60 and I was 35, and it was a partnership which combined his enormous experience of selling and small-business management with my training in marketing, knowledge of the range of applications for insulation, and understanding of the technical aspects of heat transfer and acoustics.

Initially, they did not easily come together. I had studied the potential uses for insulation in the building market, but did not know much about the channels of distribution to small and large builders or to the numerous specialist sub-contractors active in the market. In the marine and rail markets for insulation I had radically reduced the traditional role of the sole distributors and agents who had not moved with the times, and I was determined that this would not happen to us. I found the answer by looking into the reasons why a middleman was there at all!

The middleman sits between the user and the maker in order to improve the effectiveness of their relationship, but it is only natural for both ends of the supply chain from time to time to resent the margin he makes on every transaction. The middleman's position is therefore inherently unstable, being at the mercy of every new manager wanting to change something; and so the middleman who wants to survive has to make it his business to provide exactly what both the manufacturer and the end-user needs, and to keep on doing so as those needs change over time.

It sounds straightforward and simple, but it isn't. It is much easier, and more natural perhaps, for the relationship between buyer and seller to be confrontational and not collaborative. My father's natural understanding that the best results are achieved when negotiators trust and like each other had helped to get his initial relationship with Fibreglass off on the right track, but we would need to make sure that it was an approach that was adopted by all members of our staff with every supplier. To this end, 'Relations with Suppliers' became the compulsory first item on the agenda of every business meeting, and I am told it still is.

This sort of thinking occupied my mind on one level, while on a daily basis I was learning how to operate effectively in a one-man business in which there were no real guidelines except the ones in my father's head.

I was based in the three small rooms of the old Warrant Officer's flat in the heart of the barracks between the cavalry and infantry parade grounds. There were no stock records, and the general rule seemed to be that we always assumed that things were in stock.

Similarly, with delivery times we would always promise to meet the customer's demands without regard to other commitments. As far as prices were concerned, this was for me a guessing game, because finding a clue to past trading with a particular customer was virtually impossible.

Strangely enough, this 'system' works very well so long as the level of business activity does not stretch the individual entrepreneur's memory beyond its limits; but we were on a rapid growth path, and the need for a more formal approach was becoming essential. My job description began to define itself!

The first challenge appeared in an area of our business of which I had no experience at all – the retail demand for polystyrene ceiling tiles, moulded coving, and wallpaper backing in the developing DIY market. Within a few months of my arrival, my father and I were invited by Michael Blaskey, whom my father knew from the RAF, to meet the three Blaskey brothers for talks about supplying polystyrene ceiling tiles to their large chain of wallpaper shops.

The interview actually developed into a remarkable confrontation in which the three brothers argued fiercely with each other while demanding impossible delivery price and quality levels for about 50 shops within a radius of 80 miles of Sheffield. Fortunately, my father understood what was going on, and we got the contract!

Meeting the logistic needs of our customers was clearly my job. I needed to become expert in the management of the warehouse and the planning of deliveries, because our sales were entirely dependent on maintaining a reputation for fast and reliable delivery from stock. The two young men who were carefully chosen to make the Blaskey deliveries both made a great contribution to the future success of Sheffield Insulations.

Gerry Timperley joined first in 1964 and worked on insulation contracts and in the warehouse before becoming a van driver. When he was old enough he took the tests to become a HGV driver, travelling around SIG branches with stock transfers. Eventually he became my driver as I travelled around the large branch network. He died young of lung cancer.

Cliff Robins, a friend of Gerry's joined two years later in 1966, a few weeks after I arrived; he was van driver for a short time, and then became warehouseman, eventually succeeding Billy Adsetts as warehouse manager in Hillsborough works, with an additional role as the trainer of most of the warehouse teams in new branches around the country. Retiring early, he still works part-time as a gardener for SIG. Now aged

73 he has been reminding me of the tough early days when he and his colleagues helped set the 'Sheffield' values of customer service.

Setting up the means to ensure that this standard of service could be maintained was new and challenging, and it turned out to be the best and most satisfying job I ever had in Sheffield Insulations! I found it a fascinating task each day to find an optimal solution to each customer's delivery needs, and to ensure that the right number and size of vehicles were available and went out fully loaded.

I kept a journal all through the early years recording the priorities, the problems and the daily difficulties of my work in Sheffield. The entry for 23 February 1967 provides some indication of the way in which the growth of the business was creating new problems.

> "Our dealing with collection customers is archaic and impolite. They wander all the way down to the office (looking for someone to serve them) then all the way back to the top warehouse. Problems: there is no recognisable place for the reception of customers, visitors, or delivery drivers, there is no one person made responsible for dealing with them, and there is no organisation for the efficient loading and unloading of vehicles."

By 10 March 1967 we had created a new space beside the entrance to the top warehouse with a sales office and a collection/reception counter, and had set aside an area for delivery planning. In my view, it had been a survival issue; and the beginning of a slow process of converting the former officers' quarters and mess on the Langsett Road frontage from the warehouse which it was when I arrived in 1966, to offices – ultimately to become the head office.

Then there was the problem of the warehouse:

> "The Burdall's premises in the old barracks gave us a large amount of storage space, which was exactly what we wanted as

the range and volume of insulation stocks grew to meet the needs of our suppliers and customers, but a lot of manhandling was needed to carry rolls, slabs and cartons of insulation in and out of doors, up and down stairs, and through windows at ground and first-floor levels."

My first spending decision followed – an essential investment in mechanical handling – when I bought a Cook Elevator intended for farm use as a grain elevator from a local agricultural merchant. It cost less than 500 pounds and produced a significant return in savings of time and labour. Another survival issue!

This investment was ideal in the first year or so of rapid growth in the sales of the Fibreglass range of products, mainly packaged in rolls larger than Cosywrap and in small packages of thicker insulation in slab form, most of which could be moved in and out of storage through the bedroom

Billy Adsetts and John Barlow with the mechanical handling investment.

windows of the officers' quarters. Relatively small stocks of the larger panels of expanded polystyrene were held in the dining area of the officers' mess, a larger space that later housed the central computer of the group.

We needed a sales force, and the first year brought in Geoff Dawson and Bill Smith, whose experience of selling to small builders and DIY shops was invaluable, and we also followed the example of William Tom Adsetts fifty years earlier by enlisting the family.

Eve and I were the new family recruits, but my father didn't stop there! Alf's son Philip Nigel Adsetts had no intention of applying for a job when he came in to see his uncle Billy Adsetts about some insulation for his house and made a courtesy call on my father. He went in as a contented and successful salesman working for Sutherlands Meat Products and came out with an offer he couldn't refuse! 'Join me in selling insulation', said my father, 'and I'll see you get a car!' In the event it was a battered blue van!

Philip joined the retail team with Bill Smith, while I learned my trade as a warehouse manager and planner of deliveries. There was one memorable occasion when a driver didn't turn up for work and I had to take a fully loaded lorry on a two-day tour of sites – Wolverhampton, Bedford, St Neots, Norwich, Boston, Lincoln and home – because we had to meet some definite delivery promises.

These were the days before you needed a Heavy Goods Vehicle Licence, but I'd never driven anything bigger than a Ford Corsair, and it was an adventurous ride! I have not before told anyone of my delivery to a building site in the centre of Walsall, after which I drove my lorry down a narrow lane from the site with parked cars on both sides. Hearing an unusual 'tinkling' sound, I got out and saw a line of cars with wing mirrors at strange angles. A fellow 'knight of the road', walking past and seeing my indecision, told me that I should drive away quickly – and I did.

Our delivery service was proving invaluable to the insulation manufacturers, whose salesmen were bringing us ever more enquiries and orders. It was clear that we could expect further rapid growth and that there was a need for better management of cash before the explosion of demand overwhelmed us. So I talked to my father about bringing in an accountant, and here we ran into our first major misunderstanding. 'We already have an accountant', he said, 'who comes in to audit the books every year, and that's all we need him for'.

He subsequently accepted that I was talking about something else altogether, and we went ahead with the appointment of Ian Hanson, a young and recently qualified chartered accountant from Barnsley who soon gained my father's trust. This helped to limit the number of calls I was getting from George Clarke the auditor, a good friend of my father who was getting increasingly jumpy about the absence of any financial controls, and wanted me to do something about it.

The real breakthrough in the marketplace, however, which helped to secure our position as the only specialist distributor of insulation in the country, came with two developments, both involving suppliers of polystyrene insulation who needed help with distribution of their products.

The first opportunity arose in 1967 with Vencel, a large supplier of expanded polystyrene with a factory in the London area. My father had negotiated an arrangement whereby we held stocks for them in Sheffield from which we delivered to all their customers in the North of England. Vencel now asked us to provide a full delivery service to the same customers from a second factory they were opening in the Manchester area.

This temporarily eased our stockholding problems, as we no longer held consignment stocks for Vencel, but I had to learn quickly how to run a large transport fleet serving the North and Midlands from two distribution centres, an essential requirement for our future expansion. For several months I drove daily, there and back, over the Snake Pass between the Clayton factory in Manchester and my home in Sheffield to make sure that the complex trans-shipping system that I had devised was working properly. In so doing I fell in love with a road that changed every day with the varying conditions of light and weather – an experience I would not have missed.

This experience with Vencel served us well a year later when a larger and even more challenging distribution opportunity arose from Dow Chemical, the American producer of 'Styrofoam' extruded polystyrene, a product not then produced in the UK. 'Extruded' polystyrene has a closed-cell structure, heavier and more expensive than expanded polystyrene, but more suitable when water-vapour penetration is a risk.

Dow was building a new factory in King's Lynn to produce Styrofoam, and looking for four distributors to cover the South East, South West, North and Scotland in support of a UK marketing plan for their extruded polystyrene products Roofmate and Styrofoam, initially concentrating on the demanding markets for the insulation of flat roofs, cold stores and farm buildings.

This was a massive opportunity for our small company, giving us the opening we needed to adapt our specialist distribution of insulation to the needs of a major supplier with a clearly defined marketing plan. Our stockholding policy, knowledge of the technical aspects of insulation, and distribution strengths, were more than enough to get 'Sheffield' the Dow contract for the North in 1968, and by 1969 to take over the South East as well.

I had always realised that in the end the terms we could negotiate with manufacturers would be dependent on our ability to give an efficient delivery service for the full range of their products, in the required volume, over the widest possible delivery area, and that this would eventually require us to develop a model distribution unit which could be replicated over the country. Only then would we be able to take on the role of credible National Insulation Distributor and maximise the return from this level of service to our suppliers.

Our distribution agreement with Dow for the North of England was based to a large extent on their American experience in supplying the whole country from one Styrofoam facility in Midland, Michigan. Dow were going to make direct sales of full loads to customers who could take them, but smaller quantities were to be bought from the full-service distributors (like Sheffield Insulations) with large stocks, who would be responsible for sales volume and service in a region.

This approach coincided exactly with my own preferred model of a marketing distributor. It meant that we had to accept new standards, and could rely on a long-term relationship if we met them. It was a unique model that was new to the UK. We were a small company, and it needed an act of faith by the Dow manager, Lee White from Atlanta, to award us the largest distribution area in the UK – he recognised an entrepreneurial style with which he was familiar, and we took the gamble together.

However there was one big snag. The Roofmate and Styrofoam products were all rigid panels, the largest of which were 10' x 2', and we needed to hold large stocks of the full Dow range of products to serve customers across the North and the Midlands. In 1968, as if by magic, the necessary open warehouse was made available in Hillsborough Works as we added the large barracks canteen, covered an open space adjacent to the cavalry parade ground, and created a maintenance workshop in which the new transport manager Roger Kay could service our expanded fleet of vans.

The cavalry parade ground and the surrounding stable blocks became the Sheffield branch.

The later extension to the Dow contract in 1969, when we were offered the South East area because of a disappointing performance by the first distributor appointed, gave us an opportunity to expand without risk, and we took the first step by opening a branch in Bedford.

There was yet another 'coincidence' that helped us through this period, in that the Dow roofing specialist, Mel Harding, had worked with me at Fibreglass as a young member of my Sales Development Team several years earlier. When we replaced the first South East distributor, a reputable builders' merchant based in London who could not get on with the Dow approach, Mel asked me if he could join Sheffield Insulations to run our new branch in Bedford.

Something similar had happened in Sheffield a few months earlier, when Ken Gore, the Fibreglass representative based in Sheffield who had encouraged my father to develop the distribution side of his business in the early '60s, and who, as a senior estimator at the Fibreglass head office in 1955, had trained me in the technical aspects of insulation, also asked to join Sheffield Insulations to provide a solid core of experience for our home base.

These 'involuntary' appointments, made without recourse to the job market, meant that in both Sheffield and Bedford we now had senior managers with sales experience and knowledge of the insulation market. This released me to build the national network that was to be the next step in cementing our relations with suppliers.

It was also very helpful that Ken Gore was a good friend of my father, and had worked with him for years as the company grew. He was also very calm and patient in dealing with my father's resistance to change, which I was finding difficult to handle. Ken was particularly helpful, as a former estimator, in addressing the need for quicker pricing of invoices, for example. In a personal note written at this time I had described the situation:

"There have been many changes in the organisation of SIC in two years. In April 1966, it was still in most respects a one-man business, but there has been a gradual separation of functions so that ENA now sees few of the actual orders and has little to do with the planning of deliveries. Initially I had believed that if I took over the operational control my father would be forced to concentrate on the administrative problems of growth: the control of credit, the pricing of orders and invoices, dealing with enquiries etc. This has not yet happened."

The problems mainly stemmed from my father's insistence that only he could handle pricing, creating a bottle neck which could have been avoided if only he had made some effort to pass it on in the form of a pricing policy or a set of guide-price lists.

I was impatient for progress, and I had under-estimated the difficulty of making a successful transition from the personal direction of one man who knows everything to the delegation that was essential as the scale of operations began to exceed his ability to remember every aspect of the expanding business. This move from the one-man business to a management structure of delegated authority calls for the reversal of the approach that had been so successful in the past and is never easy for the 'one-man' – in this case my father – to accept.

My notes went on:

"This is the crucial stage: we can either succeed in finding the people and the correct form of organisation to step out into greater profitability and continued growth or we can fail. At present it looks as though we may fail."

That we succeeded was due to love and mutual respect – and the simple fact that neither my father nor I was going to let down the other by allowing our natural differences of approach to stand in the way of success. Nevertheless, Eve could always work out what kind of day it had been by the slamming of the front door when I came home at the end of the day; but the door survived – and so did I!

The next big problem arose inevitably from the opening of branch operations around the country, all with large open warehouses in which our varied range of products could be stacked in orderly racking and handled with forklift trucks, often with vehicle bays for efficient and quick assembly of loads. The contrast with the labour-intensive and time-consuming operations in the original Sheffield base, on which every new branch depended to provide start-up staff, training, and back-up stocks, was unacceptable both to the employees who worked there and to me.

Once again, Hillsborough Works provided the answer, as Burdalls closed down in the early 70's and the whole of the cavalry parade ground and its surrounding stables was available for conversion to become the Sheffield branch, physically and administratively separate from the head office of our network of branches across the country – now located in the old officers' quarters and no longer a warehouse!

1963	£ 90,398.	
1964	£ 125,536	+ 35,000
1965	£ 151,886	+ 26,000
1966	£ 183,294.	+ 32,000
1967	£ 294,224	+ 111,000
1968	£ 392,663	+ 99,000
1969	£ 480,000	+ 88,000
1970	£ 617,500 (est)	+ 137,000

These were for a while the only sales statistics I had to work from; but it was all I needed!

I learned slowly from my father that neither the sales nor the profit levels were of direct interest.

The key measure of health was that there should be enough cash at the end of the week to pay the wages. The more profit you make the more tax you pay – so be careful what the accounts say!

In retrospect, 1970 was the breakthrough year: the newcomers to the management team – Ian Hanson, Ken Gore and Mel Harding

– had the experience and qualifications to move us into new systems for control, whether it be in the provision of sales statistics, the disciplines of pricing, the availability of basic stock records, or the elements of cash-flow management.

For the first time, I was able to set a budget for the following year's sales. I took advantage of a spell of flu, a new device called an electronic calculator that was about the size of a typewriter, and a bundle of purchase invoices that I converted into estimated sales – and I came up with a forecast for 1971 sales in excess of a million pounds, with £800,000 from Sheffield and £300,000 from Bedford. In the event, it was the most accurate sales forecast I had ever made!

Our annual sales had increased from £183,000 in 1966, to £294,000 in 1967, £398,000 in 1968, £486,000 in 1969, and then a further 63% to £793,000 in 1970. Actual sales in 1971 were exactly as budgeted at £1,100,000, an increase of well over 250% in the five full years from 1967.

The growth programme continued, and it was decided that the next branches should be in the West Midlands and the North East, both conurbations with growth potential too far away from Sheffield or Bedford to provide an economical delivery service. As I recall, this was the first occasion when my father used his 'negotiating raincoat' – while he was searching for warehousing premises in Worcester.

The search parameters were exacting. We were looking for a site outside the metropolitan area of Birmingham, but close enough to be able to provide a good delivery service, and preferably within reasonable distance of Bristol and Cardiff. Nothing sophisticated, but we wanted to be far enough away from the cities to be perceived as a minimal threat to existing merchants, and where the rental costs of our preferred warehouse, which needed to be the size of an aircraft hangar, would be low.

My father's technique was to look around the area, park his large, new Rover round the corner from the estate agent selected for the first call, and put on his raincoat with the frayed sleeves and a missing button at the front. 'We are a small company looking for a big building at a very low price – nothing fancy': that was the line, and it worked!

In the end, he found a massive vinegar factory in the centre of Worcester, with what was said to be the largest single span cast-iron framed roof in Europe! The appointed manager for this new site was Brian Cooper, a locally based adhesive specialist whom we had got to know as a salesman for Pittsburgh-Corning.

Meanwhile, to serve the North East we opened a new branch in Ferryhill, County Durham, near Darlington. The large colliery in the town had closed, and a disused building housing a water treatment plant on the site was available once the machinery had been moved out. It was a relatively small branch, and the offices were in a terraced house a few yards away, but it served us well until we opened in Newcastle a few years later.

The first manager was the late Geoff Dawson. He was a first-class salesman who shared my father's belief in using the methods that other people didn't try, and he had already made a good start of establishing our presence in the North East from a small office in Darlington.

In 1972 the overall sales of the four branches amounted to £1.5m, made up of £760k from Sheffield, £440k from Bedford, £240k from Ferryhill and £60k from Worcester; and plans were already being made for more branches to open in 1973.

There was a remarkable surge of confidence as we entered 1973 with a plan to establish a truly 'national' distribution network of eight branches, but the time had come to introduce a note of caution. In an open letter to all managers in March 1973, I did not dwell on our achievements 'remarkable though they have been' but on the new problems that will arise from continued growth.

"We must face up to the possibility that our strength, or the absence of direct competition in certain areas of activity, will blind

A Man of Sheffield

us to our own imperfections. There is some evidence that as we aim for even higher levels of turnover and profitability we are falling below the highest standards of service to our customers. The basic strength of our approach to the customer is that we put his interest first and try very hard to meet his requirements in full.

Looking back to the early days of the business that my father started, we should remember that his success stemmed from the introduction of a concept of customer service previously unknown in this market, an approach which is equally successful, relevant, and <u>necessary</u> today.

"I acknowledge that the administrative and communication difficulties we face are new and will take time to resolve, but they are secondary to the main issue, vital to all our futures, of achieving profitable sales."

Burscough near Ormskirk was opened to serve the North West, and Philip Adsetts, the son of my father's nephew Alf, became manager after a period when he was responsible for retail sales in Sheffield. Philip's original office was a garden hut in the middle of a large farm storage building.

One Saturday morning, Eve and I, with our two children, called en route to friends in Cheshire when an articulated lorry with a 40ft container full of Roofmate and Styrofoam from Dow drove in to make the first-ever delivery of insulation to the new branch – Philip enlisted the whole family to unload the delivery in the absence of any warehouse staff!

A new branch in the South East for sales and deliveries south of the River Thames was initially opened in Tunbridge Wells, and quickly moved to Tonbridge when the first choice proved too small and outside storage in containers proved to be a fire risk. The manager was another ex-Fibreglass salesman called Malcolm Ramsey who was a most enterprising and effective addition to our team.

Sheffield Insulations Group Offices on the Langsett Road Frontage.

A branch in Taunton to serve the South West was delayed, but the national coverage was just about completed by opening one in Wishaw, near Motherwell. Geoff Dawson, recognising the potential, had been pushing for us to open a branch in Scotland, and he was pleased to move from Ferryhill to Wishaw, while John Barlow, originally Billy's number two in the warehouse who had successfully made the transition into the Sheffield sales office, was promoted to take over the Ferryhill operation.

As a personal note to myself, in a period of expansion beyond my most optimistic predictions, I wrote the following words of advice, which I moved from one notebook to another as the progress from 1970 to 1973 took us from being a local company with growth prospects to a credible national distributor:

"It is essential to create a managerial style that becomes the pattern for others to follow; calm, deliberate, and just. I must not

allow myself to be forced into a different style of frenetic, crisis-ridden control, effective in its way, but ultimately self-defeating as others copy it."

Eventually the new owners of Hillsborough Works warned us that they were planning to sell the whole property and after serious discussion we decided to buy the whole of the buildings on the Langsett Road frontage, the old officers' quarters and the chapel, in which we had invested a great deal over the years as we converted it from an inefficient warehouse to a well-equipped and furnished head office.

The rest of our leased property in Hillsborough works was surrendered in 1989 when we moved the Sheffield branch to a new modern warehouse on the Parkway, and the cavalry parade ground, stables and associated buildings became a Morrison's supermarket.

In April 2018 the company will finally leave Hillsborough Works, 70 years after my father negotiated a rent of two pounds per week for some broken-down garages on the infantry parade ground in which to store and repair refrigerators for his ice cream business. The whole site was of immense benefit to the insulation business in its early years of explosive growth as additional flexible space was always available when needed.

THE 'SAVE IT' EFFECT

By the end of 1973 we had seven operational branches – six in England and one in Scotland – and I was expecting to reap the rewards from our stronger position with suppliers, who would welcome a credible national distributor. I had not expected that developments in the Middle East would change this picture overnight! Actions by the Middle East oil suppliers in the last three months of 1973 were to change completely the nature of the market for insulation in the UK and around the world. Supplies of oil were restricted and the price quadrupled, with major implications for the world economy.

In the immediate short-term, the impact was felt most directly in our distribution operations, with shortages of fuel and the declaration of a three-day week. This crisis tested our new managers and their ability to respond to new and challenging trading conditions. I sent a telex to all directors and general managers on 7 January 1974 in which the first few sentences described my approach to the new situation:

"In the short-term, 3-day working will have more effect on our suppliers than on our customers. As deliveries become extended there is an opportunity to capitalise on our high stock level. I see the present situation as a major sales opportunity in which we can gain benefits from the new attitudes towards insulation created by the fuel crisis.

There were other aspects to the situation. We had to find ways to get enough fuel for our vehicles and impose more stringent credit control with a closer monitoring of cash flow. These were essential elements of a co-ordinated response that tested our organisation and invited managers to demonstrate enterprise and innovation. Then came a miners' strike, and my next telex of February 1974 predicted more difficulties ahead and greater uncertainty about the future:

"Demand will fall, supplies will be uncertain, and cash will get tighter for everyone – so cut costs wherever possible, resist the temptation to hoard stocks, get drivers to report any sites with problems. We are entering a period of high risk!"

This experience helped to consolidate our increased number of outlets and create some sense of shared experience across a workforce with many new employees, so there were some benefits to set against a level of sales that was well below budget in Quarter 1 of 1974.

This did not last, and sales growth was well ahead of our expectations for the rest of the year, particularly in fibrous insulation products. Fibreglass Ltd had already withdrawn 1" roof insulation in favour of 2", and this move to higher standards was going to continue.

More about this later, because I must now turn to a crucial strategic decision made in June 1974 which helped to create the conditions in which Sheffield Insulations became market leader over the next few years. One afternoon in June 1974 I wrote a short situation report on the current market and the prospects for continued growth and sent it to my father, to all directors, and to the general managers in each branch.

> *"I propose that we should not 'consolidate' as we had originally planned but that we should accept the need to expand even faster and open more sales offices and distribution points before the local alternatives begin to develop and before the main supply difficulties have been solved."*

This strategic approach was unanimously approved at board and senior management level, and within twelve months we had opened another six branches and four sale offices. The risks were considerable – the problems of control, co-ordination and communication had not even been ironed out for seven branches before we committed to doubling their numbers. But my argument was simple.

> *"Whatever the risk, the prize was worth trying for: quite simply the aim was to achieve a position of pre-eminence in insulation supply before other firms could take advantage of the boom situation created by the energy crisis and associated government action."*

In 1974 we broke all sale records with a total turnover of £5m, which compared with £2.4m in 1973. Most of the real increase, in a period of high inflation, came from the sale of Fibreglass and Rocksil products, while other products showed a more-or-less uniform decline. 1974 had been a triumph of opportunism (see Caribonum Ideal No. 10), and it was pleasing to see that we had not lost the ability to recognise and exploit market opportunities as they arose.

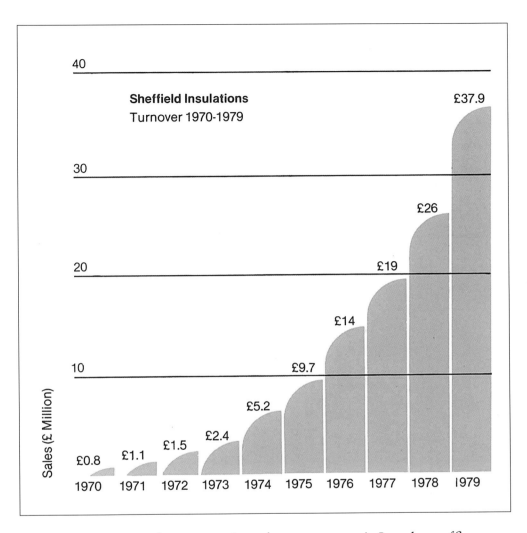

Sheffield Insulations
Turnover 1970-1979

Sales (£ Million)

£0.8 £1.1 £1.5 £2.4 £5.2 £9.7 £14 £19 £26 £37.9

1970 1971 1972 1973 1974 1975 1976 1977 1978 1979

1974 was a year of progress in other respects. A London office was opened in anticipation of the opening of a London branch early in 1975. Next came a Leicester office, and preparations were being made for the opening of a second branch in Scotland, in Blairgowrie.

Mike Pritchard, a property consultant who had sorted out the delays in opening Taunton, was now looking at sites in London, Loughborough, Manchester and Cardiff for the planned expansion of 1975; he was subsequently retained to handle all our property dealings – the days of the negotiating raincoat were well and truly over!

1975 was the year in which I began to address some of the other issues that had been by-passed in our drive for growth. We brought in an external advisor, Rob Hillman, to review our personnel management procedures in the light of new employment legislation, and Mike Wilson, a senior lecturer in Computer Sciences from Sheffield City Polytechnic, came to advise us on the introduction of computers to our central office administration, which was under great strain as a result of the recent growth. Both joined the Sheffield team in 1976.

We entered 1975 with plans for further growth, increasing the number of distribution branches and supporting them with targeted mailing and greater promotional spending so as to take full advantage of the new emphasis on energy saving.

Higher standards of insulation were now the norm, as its essential role in cutting costs to offset energy price rises was at last being realised. The government was committed to a major marketing effort to encourage householders and companies to 'Save It', and we had stocks in place to meet the demand generated by this campaign.

Our main aim was now to make sure that the central services that were needed to give efficient and timely support to the operating units were able to keep up with this growth, and this meant investment in training and in capital expenditure. The early introduction of a computerised system to link the centre with the branches was a priority.

We had also lumbered ourselves with a network of separate branches, each of which was an independent company – 'Sheffield Insulations (South) Ltd' and so on – the legal ramifications of which were complicated and costly to administer. At the time, this had helped each new general manager to feel as though he was running his own ship, and had encouraged enterprise. But we had reached a position where the tendency of our branch managers to think solely in terms of local interests was getting in the way of a coherent and consistent strategy for the company as a whole, and we needed to find a middle way.

A new regional structure was introduced, with four regional managers reporting to Mel Harding, who moved to Sheffield to become group commercial director. His task was to introduce central norms for pricing and to ensure local commitment to the terms of our national agreements with suppliers – maintaining our commitment to the trading autonomy of each branch, but setting it within new parameters.

Bill Smith, a schoolmate (and incidentally one of Eve's former boyfriends), had joined Sheffield in the early days to merge his own business selling polystyrene ceiling tiles with the retail business that my father had originally built up with specialist companies like Poron and PCL. He now moved to Bedford to replace Mel as the General Manager, and quickly showed his entrepreneurial imagination by unearthing an export market for the Dow products Roofmate and Styrofoam in the rapidly growing construction market of the Middle East. He later took on a roving development role, spending time in the Middle East and in the States.

My father, meanwhile, was exploring opportunities for new business by enlisting two old friends and employees in the contracting business: Joe Deakin was running a new subsidiary called Sheffield Ceilings and Linings, and Walter Lacey brought his insulation contracting business Durham Insulations into the Group.

So, a lot was going on, but the driving force behind it all was the energy crisis, which was still having a remarkable effect on our sales of fibrous insulation. My working week had for some time been spent visiting our distribution units around the UK, both to monitor progress and to give further training to managers and key staff in every small branch, and I soon had to take on one of my father's first appointments, a young man named Gerry Timperley, who had graduated from warehouse hand to van driver, HGV driver and depot manager, as my personal chauffeur and minder.

The priority for all of us, in this period of explosive demand, was to maintain the high quality of service to customers while we honoured our commitments to sales level and support of our key suppliers. Mel and his regional managers were now making real progress with this, and I moved on to the next big problem.

Which was cash. The sales turnover of £5,182,000 in 1974 had been a 115% increase on 1973, and in the first six months of 1975 the sales of £4,086,000 were already 80% of the full year total of 1974. In presenting our plans for 1976, I had warned that cash flow difficulties were bound to arise if any of our fine calculations of stock levels, profitability, or debtor payments were not realised.

Our bankers were uneasy, as the cost of opening new branches in the drive for growth of the first six months more-or-less wiped out our profits from trading, but I reassured them that actions were being taken to eliminate unprofitable areas and to control stock levels through the new regional structure.

At the same time, the massive increase of our purchases from Fibreglass and Rocksil led both companies to make firm proposals to reduce our credit terms from 90 to 60 days. By the end of 1975, the situation was eased by an increase of our overdraft, and by arrangements with the fibrous insulation suppliers to bring down the credit period by stages, but it became clear over the next few months that we could no longer rely on overdraft and extended supplier credit to finance the current level of over-trading.

We decided early in 1976 to enter into negotiations with a number of banks, aiming to secure a medium-term loan. By mid-1976 we were in serious negotiations with County Bank, Charterhouse, ICFC and Hill Samuel, and by the end of the year the final decision was made in favour of County Bank for a total of £650,000: 50% secured loan and 50% immediate equity.

The overall sales in 1976 were over £14m, with the combined sales of Fibreglass and Rocksil fibrous insulation at 60%, Dow and Vencel combined sales of Polystyrene at 15%, and a new high-performance polyurethane product from ICI at nearly 10%. We were now well set to continue the growth on a more secure financial base.

Sales turnover in 1977 grew yet again, to over £19m – an increase of 35% – while profits before tax jumped 60% from £390,000 to £635,000 as we neared the end of the major expenditure incurred in opening new branches. The record of sales and profit growth in the ten years since 1968 had been phenomenal.

There was still no real evidence that any other merchant was seizing the opportunity presented by the energy crisis and the government 'Save It' campaign to enter the insulation market with any conviction, but it was bound to happen sooner or later. We continued to strengthen our position by filling in obvious gaps in our coverage, and by some diversification into new products and services.

Sales continued to rise in the following years, 1978 and 1979, driven to some extent by higher insulation standards for new housing as Building Regulations were revised. From 1977, roof insulation requirements more than doubled, to 60mm from 25mm, and walls were included for the first time. Fibrous insulation remained at 60% of the value of all sales, albeit at lower margins as new distributors belatedly entered the market. One of these newcomers was Mel Harding, who left us to move to the south coast to set up Solent Insulations to compete with SIG.

Over the next few years this would become a familiar pattern, as a few young men trained in our hot-house of enterprise began to grow impatient with the disciplines of multi-product marketing – an unavoidable consequence of our growth. By definition they were one-man businessmen by nature, keen to exploit the opportunities of the 'Save It' campaign, and they brought energy into the marketplace and a healthy competitive challenge to our team.

The search was on for higher-margin products, and our sales teams inside the branches were encouraged to focus on the other products in our range – expanded polystyrene and polyurethane insulation, fire protection boards, adhesives etc – on which trading margins were either static or rising.

It was clearly very much in our interests to increase the return on existing products in the range, and we developed Styroliner, a single-sided laminate of plasterboard and Styrofoam, as a competitive product for insulated wall and ceiling linings in residential and commercial buildings. After a successful period of test marketing in 1979, a new factory for Sheffield Insulation Systems Ltd was planned.

The markets in the UK for which Dow products were suited, principally in flat roofing and cold stores, had been badly hit in the recession which followed the energy crisis, but our sales stayed up with the help of Styroliner and Bill Smith's enterprising sales of Roofmate to the Middle East from the Bedford branch.

I explored with Dow the potential for a Sheffield-type distributor in the Middle East to meet the rapidly growing demand for their products in the insulation of commercial buildings, and set up a sales office in Sharjah in the United Arab Emirates with Jim Davies, another young colleague from Fibreglass who had worked with me on the development of moulded insulation for cars before moving to Bombay to handle sales and marketing for Fibreglass India.

One surprising result was a profitable ceiling contract in the Ghurair Centre in Dubai, which helped Steve Wharton and his team in Sheffield Ceilings and Linings to weather a difficult time in the UK. We also built up significant Roofmate business with the Pakistani builders who were active in the Emirates.

In November 1979 I decided to call on building companies in Karachi before visiting the British embassy in Islamabad, combining this with a few days staying with my sister May and her husband Garry, who was working on an agricultural project in Pakistan.

On 21 November 1979, the day after I arrived in Islamabad, Pakistani students, enraged by a false radio report that the United States had bombed a holy site in Mecca, stormed the US embassy in Islamabad and burned it to the ground.

I was in a meeting with the commercial attaché of the British embassy when we saw a convoy of lorries heading for the neighbouring US embassy. They carried the 'Rentamob' from Rawalpindi, clearly with aggressive intent, and I was advised to leave immediately. As I walked to my car I heard the opening shots of the attack, which led to the death of four people, including two American soldiers.

The staff of the US embassy locked themselves in a secure area as the rest of the building burned, while the British ambassador unsuccessfully pressed the Pakistani president to send soldiers in a rescue mission. After a few hours, they escaped, and meanwhile my sister May and I were conscripted into a rescue bid to collect American children from their school outside the city. The mob had already been there, but the children had been safely gathered into a secure building, and we persuaded their protectors – several brave young American boys with baseball bats – to let us take them back into Islamabad.

This was not quite what I had come for; the situation remained tense, but my family members were safe and there was no chance to renew my business talks at the embassy, so I went home!

Back in the UK, we were beginning to feel some benefit from what was called the 'Benn Package', a massive Energy Conservation Scheme for public buildings announced in 1978 by Anthony Wedgwood-Benn, the secretary of state for energy in the Labour government. Extending over ten years, this £320m programme of government spending provided our whole industry with the confidence to invest in additional capacity.

A Labour Party policy paper presented to Tony Benn's National Energy conference of June 1976 had included the following statement: 'Although the government has taken a number of short-term measures to encourage energy conservation, more urgent and stringent action is needed if we are to make any worthwhile savings'. Tony Benn had certainly lived up to his promises, and it was now time for the industry to respond.

Up to this point, the main effort to save energy had been aimed at the housing market, and had been limited to increasing the standard of insulation in new homes. Now a publicly funded investment in a wide range of energy-saving measures in all types of government buildings seemed to be secure, and we all felt confident in planning further investment.

The suppliers began to build new factories, and we felt able to build a new warehouse and sales office in Birmingham. We began to move from smaller branches in Manchester, Bedford and the Isle of Dogs to much larger purpose-built units. A new factory in Sheffield, built to make Styroliner and other types of insulated panels, was opened in 1981, together with a separate warehouse for Micarta, an American decorative laminate that we had arranged to distribute in the UK for Westinghouse – a higher-margin item for the future that was already being sold in the US from our Atlanta depot.

These and other investments aimed at increasing margins were necessary and affordable, as a result of our new confidence in the growth of the core business. By 1979 our sales had risen to £40m, with profit before tax exceeding £1m (£1,335,000) for the first time; and in 1980 we were preparing to mark the 25th anniversary of our move into insulation in 1955.

We were not prepared for what then happened. Mrs Thatcher became Prime Minister after the election of 1979, and a few months later the 'Benn Package', the government commitment to energy conservation investment in public buildings, was no more. So, the period of growth was brought to an end. We had come down to earth with a bump, and the next few years were spent finding ways to survive. A few of our suppliers, competitors and customers didn't make it.

THE LONG ROAD BACK
THE CORE BUSINESS LEADS THE WAY

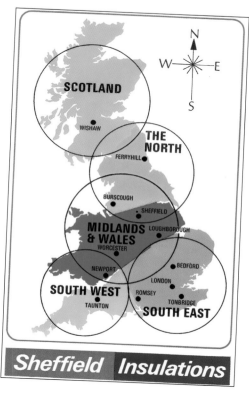

In 1981, the fall in the demand for the fibrous products which had grown to 60% of our sales coincided, unhappily, with our plans to celebrate the 25th anniversary of the first Cosywrap sales in the Edmund Rd Drill Hall. We had produced a special Annual Report that was full of bullish but now unrealistic forecasts of the prospects for further growth, with details of some of our newer products and services.

There were some positive developments. Sheffield Insulation Systems had now added Styrofloor and Styroclad to Styroliner for the growing retrofit market. The two small contracting companies formerly run by ex-employees of my father had been combined to form Sheffield Insulation Contracts Ltd. While Sheffield Supplies in Atlanta Georgia was making good progress in the regional insulation market, selling Owens Corning Fiberglas products in addition to the laminate sales of Westinghouse Micarta.

However sensible such diversification plans may have been, their impact was minimal in the short-term. Massive over-capacity for the production of insulation had been created in the UK by the expectation of increased demand, but after the complete reversal of the government policy that had created this demand there was a bloodbath of competitive price-cutting.

The Group Newspaper *SINews* reported on the developing situation in 1981, and in the December issue I summarised our position in a Christmas message.

> *"1981 has been, for the most part, a year of enforced consolidation: a year of struggle in which we have shared with the rest of industry the problems of static or falling demand for our products."*

These brief comments put a positive gloss on a root-and-branch rethink of the direction of our marketing efforts. We were still more reactive than proactive in our approach to selling, and it was time to make a change!

Bill Forrester, a man I knew well, had been the sales director of Rockwool UK before moving to the Middle East to run a new glass-fibre plant in Kuwait, and he was ready to return to the UK. He was exactly what we needed, a professional sales manager who recognised the need to strengthen our branch set-up in the new competitive market, and was ready to do something about it.

It was an uncomfortable period, because some of the staff who had been so effective in driving forward the company during the period of explosive growth were not performing so well in dealing with the developing crisis – and they found the enforced change to a drive for survival unpalatable.

We were not alone. The major suppliers in the energy-saving field had already realised this with the creation of the Association for the Conservation of Energy (ACE) in 1981 'to argue the business case for investment in energy conservation', bringing together a small number of those businesses whose interests had been most severely damaged by the withdrawal of the Energy Conservation Programme.

The main aim of ACE was to change the prevailing attitude to energy policy, which was still focussed on the development of new energy supplies as the only viable strategy to deal with a perceived fuel crisis.

In October 1981, the parliamentary under-secretary of state for energy, David Mellor MP, came to Sheffield to open the new factory of Sheffield Insulation Systems. Over lunch I argued strongly for a major national energy efficiency initiative by the public and private sectors acting together; apparently, Mr Mellor repeated this in a subsequent meeting with the governing council of ACE, as a result of which we received an invitation to join ACE, the first non-manufacturer to do so.

On total sales of £36m in 1981 the group made a loss of nearly half a million pounds, but it was clear that Bill Forrester was already making a real difference to the effectiveness of our selling effort in the UK distribution company, and in January 1982 he was made managing director of Sheffield Insulations Ltd, which continued with a steady improvement in results over the year.

Nevertheless, overall losses doubled in 1982. There was a disappointing result from the States, due to a nationwide collapse of housing starts. We had not expected this, and there was an immediate crisis as the local bank withdrew its supporting overdraft. NatWest stepped in to help, and I toured our major suppliers around the States to arrange for continued support, but the momentum was lost.

I also made the difficult and costly decision to take over Miller Insulation (the largest attic insulation contractor in the UK), to safeguard a very big debt. Peter Cohen, a management consultant who had already made significant improvements in Sheffield Insulation Contracts, took over the running of Miller, with a brief to restore it to profitability and begin repaying the internal debt, which he eventually managed to do.

Our bankers, NatWest, had remained supportive through this difficult period and had been kept informed of the actions being taken. Despite the signs of recovery in the core business of UK distribution, recovery elsewhere was very slow, and our financial position was still weak. NatWest therefore sought a second opinion, and after some discussion it was agreed that Arthur Andersen would carry out a review of our trading position.

On 7 January 1983, Andersen submitted the final report to NatWest on 'the financial status and prospects of the Sheffield Insulating Company Ltd and subsidiary companies'. An interim report had been submitted in November, and I had accepted the overall conclusions and recommendations, most of which were in line with our own thinking, but with a greater emphasis on getting quick results.

The Andersen report broadly accepted our forecast of a profit of £900,000 on UK distribution business in 1983, and noted our action plan for the other subsidiaries that was aimed at generating profits and a positive cash flow in the near future. This plan included the sale of the loss-making businesses of SI Contracts and SI Ireland, both already in hand, while the remaining subsidiaries (Millers, US operations and Systems) were expected to produce a profit of just under £200,000 in 1983.

It was also noted that the liquidity problem created by the losses of 1981 and 1982 was going to remain for a while, that this would require a continuation of short-term borrowing and extended supplier credit, and that we needed to introduce regular reporting of our progress with a fully documented strategy for recovery.

This led to the final and most significant recommendation, that there should be 'a detailed plan to improve the group's financial management and control procedures, and that we should implement immediate measures to improve the monthly monitoring of each activity'.

In my response to this report I stressed the central point about the return to profitability of the UK distribution company, Sheffield Insulations Ltd. The following extract from my letter to NatWest went to the heart of our strategy for recovery, and helped to put the problems of the smaller subsidiaries in perspective.

> *"In 1980, and to a much greater extent in 1981, over-capacity in the UK insulation market led to price anarchy. Priority was given to [dealing with] this problem. Actions were taken in 1981 and have continued in 1982 to restore profitability – organisational changes, new senior appointments, a new marketing structure and revised sales objectives, with better support and promotion from suppliers."*

We had enough confidence in our ability to get results in a sluggish market to move forward with the opening of new branches in Cardiff and Plymouth in 1984, and we strengthened our position in the growing fire-protection market by the acquisition of Dalton Ballard in Uxbridge, a move which also enabled us to open a new branch of Sheffield Insulations to serve West London.

Our over-dependence on the low-margin 'structural' sales of fibrous insulation was reduced with the formation of an Industrial Division of Sheffield Insulations, operating initially from three branches in 1983, which had risen to 13 out of our 20 branches by 1988. There was also a limited prospect of growth in the housing market as the further increase of roof and wall standards introduced in 1982 began to take effect.

However, the over-capacity in the insulation market claimed yet another victim late in 1984 when Cape Industries Ltd withdrew from insulation manufacture and sold their plants in Stirling and Queensferry to Pilkington's. A by-product of this decision was the resignation in 1985 of Bill Doughty, the founder-chairman of ACE, whose company was no longer a member, and I was elected by the members of the governing council to take his place.

The main event of 1985, however, came when I took over from my father as chairman of the Sheffield Insulating Company on his retirement at the age of 80, 30 years after founding the company. At the same time, Bill Forrester took over from me as chief executive, responsible for all Group companies.

We had begun the recovery from the low point of two successive losses in 1981 and 1982, which had now been followed by two successive year of profitability – £1m in 1983 and just over £2m in 1984, on sales of nearly £60m. The remaining subsidiary making a loss was in the US, and it was finally shed in a limited management buyout.

We continued to address the fundamental issue raised in the Andersen report regarding the weakness of financial management and controls. A new financial director of Sheffield Insulations with a management accountancy background had been appointed, and the plans for further investment in information technology included, from 1987, a main computer to provide on-line communication between central services and our branches.

In 1985 Frank Prust left County Bank to join the Sheffield Insulating Co Ltd as company secretary and become a member of the group executive board. Given his background, his banking experience, and his detailed knowledge of our company, I knew that Frank could make a major contribution to the improvement of our financial management and control systems.

A year or so later, I tried to introduce a new working relationship, which was in effect a job-swap, between Frank Prust as company secretary and Ian Hanson as group finance director. Ian could not accept the change of role, and we parted. Ian and his wife Jackie had been major contributors in the early years of the company and I was very sorry to see them go.

In 1985 and 1986 the recovery continued, but the lingering effects of the market pressures in the early '80s still had their effect on our trading margins, and while group sales grew from £69m in 1985 to £80m in 1986, profits in both years stuck at around £2m.

In 1985, the first evidence of a government commitment to energy saving came from Peter Walker, the secretary of state for energy, who declared 1986 to be Energy Efficiency Year – with the slogan 'Get More for your Monergy'. It was launched at the National Energy Managers' Conference in November 1985, and throughout 1986 there were seminars run by ACE around the country, at many of which, as ACE chairman, I made speeches in support of the Monergy message.

For the first time, I was working in a political arena, and with guidance from the ACE director Andrew Warren I was learning the trade and techniques of the lobbyist – not so very different from the lessons my father learned from Caribonum!

My experience of working closely with politicians and civil servants to help deliver one aim of government policy resulted in the award of an OBE! The contribution of ACE to the Monergy campaign, a series of positive meetings with Peter Walker and his team, and possibly some recognition of my partnership work in Sheffield, had taken me to Buckingham Palace with my family for the award from the Queen – an unbelievable result!

One of the recommendations of the Andersen review had been that we should seriously consider the negotiation of a second medium-term loan. This became a serious issue once we began to realise that we had weathered the storm, that we had got rid of the diversifications that hadn't worked out, and that the core business, having diversified its product range and improved its marketing skills, was going to be in a good position to continue its growth – but how would we fund it?

Having experienced the problems created when the rapid growth that had been funded by a combination of high borrowing and supplier credit was stopped dead in its tracks by the sudden withdrawal of government support, I was reluctant to enter into negotiations for yet another loan, and asked Frank to explore the possibility of a public issue of shares.

While these enquiries were going on, the trading results for 1987 and the prospects for 1988 were beginning to take shape and increase our bullish approach to the possibility of a float.

In 1987, sales rose to £85m and underlying profits to over £3m, reduced to £2.6m by the losses of two subsidiaries sold to local management in the States and the UK. In 1988, sales exceeded £100m and profits were £3.7m without any deductions for loss-making subsidiaries!

As a result of Frank's enquiries and the improved trading performance, the decision was made to 'go public', and shares in Sheffield Insulations group were successfully offered on the market in a placing of 6.1m 10p shares at 125p a share on 21 April 1989, when SIG plc was born, and I became the executive chairman of a public company, a position I held for five years.

I had a good team. We had just completed a detailed review of the operations of the company and had a positive plan for the future, so I had expected a fairly straightforward few months in which to get used to our new standing as a public company.

In normal circumstances this would have been the case; but these were not normal circumstances – they were over-shadowed by a catastrophic event at Hillsborough football ground in Sheffield on Saturday 15 April.

On the day before the Cup semi-final between Liverpool and Nottingham Forest at Hillsborough, Frank Prust and I had flown to meet my son Philip in New York. He was a shareholder of the company, and he needed to be briefed before giving his formal approval on some technical issue to do with the public offer of shares.

Philip's apartment in New York, where he worked for the Bank of Novia Scotia, was close to the United Nations building in mid-town New York, and we met on Saturday morning in our hotel room nearby. I rang Eve to give her a chance to speak to Philip, and she told me there was 'trouble' at Hillsborough, where the FA Cup semi-final between Liverpool and Nottingham Forest had just started.

We then saw live pictures on the hotel TV of an awful crush at the Leppings Lane end of the ground, where the Liverpool fans were standing. The sheer scale and horror of the disaster began to unfold in front of our eyes.

I realised that I would have to get back to Sheffield very quickly to play a part in the city's response to such an appalling tragedy. I had originally been invited to the match as president of the Sheffield Chamber of Commerce, and I should now represent the business community at the meeting of civic leaders called for the following morning.

Leaving Frank and Philip to deal with the formal paperwork for the float, I went straight to JFK, caught an overnight flight to Heathrow, rented a car, and drove to Sheffield in time for a meeting in the town hall, a visit to Hillsborough, and a decision by the mayors of the three cities to launch a Disaster Appeal.

I was then nominated by the local authority as the Sheffield member of a four-man board of trustees (one each from the three cities of Liverpool Sheffield and Nottingham, and one from Liverpool FC) to distribute the funds raised by the appeal to the benefit of the victims of the disaster and their dependents. Eventually, £12m was raised, and our task of distribution ended in 1997. The nature of our role, which was to determine and apply a basis for compensation appropriate to the high proportion of young victims of this disaster, was both detailed and demanding, requiring a lot of sensitive enquiries into the circumstances of each victim, and we were pleased that the end result was generally accepted as a fair distribution.

I had already moved away from full-time activities within SIG following the work on partnership (of which there is more in later pages) which led to my election as President of the Sheffield Chamber of Commerce. It became clear that I was being drawn into greater involvement with city regeneration and into a fundamental shift from running the largest public company based in Sheffield into a new career in which I would eventually acquire the media nickname of 'Mr Sheffield' for my range of activities within the city.

These changes marked a new phase of our life. My active participation in working with the city council and others, which began on the Board of the Sheffield Development Corporation, soon began to expand; and other aspects of my family life – my two autistic grandsons and Eve's health – played a larger part in my thinking.

Eventually, for a variety of family and heath reasons, I decided to retire. I first became non-executive chairman before finally deciding to step down from the chair and the board of SIG plc on 6 April 1996 my 65th birthday. I was subsequently elected to become Honorary Life President of the company. My successor as chairman was Barrie Cottingham, our first non-executive director and my former colleague in the Chamber's work on Sheffield regeneration. And so my thirty year career, beginning with my appointment as a director of The Sheffield Insulating Company on 1st April 1966, came to an end.

In the twenty years since I retired from SIG the company has continued to grow, both organically and by acquisition, and there has been a significant diversification into new products, services and assembly, with a major expansion of areas of operation.

That growth has recently faltered and a new chief executive from the Netherlands, Meinie Oldersma, has been brought in to explore the reasons for this and to reverse the trend. On reading my account of the period between our birth in 1956 and my retirement in 1996, Meinie's instinct, after in his own words 'capturing' the content of our history over forty years, has been to learn from our experience and go back to basics.

He argues that the business model which my father and I developed is still effectively in operation today and that the company is still acting in most of its current commercial activities as 'a middleman with a strong focus on customer service' He believes, as I do, that this model remains as relevant and as viable today as it was twenty years ago, but that the strong customer focus has been allowed to decline in some areas as the scale and complexity of the enterprise has grown.

Recognising that there is an inbuilt heritage of commitment to quality, not only in our company but in the traditional tools industry of the city (see pages 33 and 47), he believes that this is built on the strength and stability of 'a company still headquartered within the same Sheffield community'. Meinie has made the blunt assertion that SIG needs to retain, and where necessary return to, ' the same pragmatic customer focus that made the company successful'.

The company today has many more lines of business, and its communication, supply and advisory chains are more numerous than anything I ever had to deal with, but I can recognise and support Meinie's line of argument. He states that 'Sir Norman would continuously re-invent the organisation, turning risks into opportunities, to capture the growth of the market'. This was possible when the organisation was smaller and effective internal communication was easier, but it still remains the answer. Simplification of the structural and bureaucratic features which can inhibit change is the way forward, linked with good old-fashioned communication to get over the message that 50 years of 'Sheffield heritage' will work.

THE ADSETTS STORY

The Birth of a
New Career

Partnerships in Sheffield

NORMAN ADSETTS

REFLECTIONS ON
A CHANGING LIFESTYLE

When I took over from my father in 1985, the first questions I asked myself were: 'What does a chairman do?' and specifically, 'What should the chairman of SIG plc do?'

As chairman of the governing council of ACE I had already taken responsibility for a lobbying organisation aiming to raise the government's commitment to energy conservation and hence increase the demand for insulation. This was a role that kept me in touch with the leaders of the other companies in the energy conservation business, including most of our suppliers, as we worked together to promote the national interest in using our energy resources more efficiently.

I looked at other chairman-like interests. There was, for example, our membership of organisations like the Chamber of Commerce and the Confederation of British Industry. Both existed to speak in support of the interests of business and to lobby government on issues of particular note.

My question was: 'Were we getting our money's worth from our subscriptions?' Having questioned the heads of both bodies, I was invited to join both the Chamber council and the board of the regional CBI, from which positions I could observe and, where necessary, influence their actions.

After attending only one meeting, I had no difficulty in deciding on the first priority for the Chamber of Commerce. In order to fulfil its primary duty to support the interests of industry and commerce in Sheffield there must be a constructive working relationship with the city council to help in addressing the condition of Sheffield – and this required effective communication.

Instead, there was in my opinion a scandalous atmosphere of mutual blame, when what was needed was for both organisations to get together to work out what was to be done. The only remaining question for me was: 'Is it in the interests of SIG for me to try to do something about it?'

To me the answer was obvious, and with that in mind I accepted the invitation to join the Chamber Council in 1985; and in 1988 I began a year of office as president of the Sheffield Chamber of Commerce, having already chaired the Image Working Party of the Chamber for two years, arguing strongly that the main interests in the city needed to work together in partnership.

A year or so later I was invited to become the chairman of the regional CBI for Yorkshire and Humberside when the chairman-elect withdrew for company reasons, and I was then able to lobby more effectively on behalf of the wider business community.

Among other regional issues, my aims were to join the national Energy Policy Committee of the CBI, to support their proposals for an Inner City Programme of Regeneration, and to use the lobbying strengths of the

CBI and of John Banham, its director-general, to get some support for Sheffield's World Student Games in 1991. I made more headway with the first than the third!

The World Student Games event was planned as a major element in the regeneration of the city, supported by major investment in sporting infrastructure, including the new Don Valley stadium and the Sheffield Arena, with a refurbished Lyceum Theatre at the heart of its Cultural Festival. The successful recruitment of a very large team of volunteers was clear evidence of public support for the event, but lack of sponsorship caused financial difficulties. It was nevertheless an integral part of the plans for image and morale building that were becoming my major concern.

At this time, Eve was having a lot of difficulty with osteoarthritis in her right knee, and had the first of several knee replacement operations. There was real pressure from the family for us to move to a warmer climate in the winter. Eve and I were on holiday in Venice in June 1993 when I wrote a report to myself on the way in which our lives were changing, and what I needed to do about it.

In the early days of the company any holiday had always resulted in a small notebook full of my thoughts about the way ahead; this time, I typed the first sentence in my new laptop under the heading 'Reflections on a Change in Life-Style', the title I have chosen for this section of my memoir. It reads: 'Many things have been changing in the recent past and there has not really been time to adjust to any of them; this break is an essential period in which to think through the implications of change'.

Then came the moment for the first decision – Eve fell on an icy path in Sheffield in December 1993, just before we went away for a family holiday to Florida. She flew out with her leg in a pot, and, after a family conference, I bought a sea-front apartment in Boca Raton, and we began to spend more of each year in Florida.

Our son Philip spent a year in SIG after completing a Maths degree from University College London. For six months he drove a 40ft artic HGV around all our UK branches and in the other half of the year he worked in our new US branch in Atlanta as driver, salesman and warehouseman. After graduating with an MBA from Cornell he made his career choice to become a banker in the States, married an American girl, and began to live in New York, extending our family relationships over two continents!

Our daughter Helen, on the other hand, was living in Sheffield with five children, two of whom, by her second husband, were successively diagnosed with autism in 1995. A whole new shape to our lives began with the arrival of this new and puzzling condition.

My responsibilities were changing. From my position in the Chamber I was able to press for the leaders of the city to work together; this led to a place on the board of the Sheffield Development Corporation and subsequent regeneration projects. I also played a supporting role in the troubled World Student Games, in the refurbishment of the Lyceum and the management of Sheffield's theatre complex, and in leading the Sheffield Hallam University project to restore the fortunes of Kelham Island Museum and Abbeydale Industrial Hamlet.

In all these ways I was gaining the confidence of the local authority, and demonstrating that partnership could make a positive contribution to the governance of the city. The shape of this new career had been envisaged in the original 'Reflections on a Changing Life-Style' in 1993, and I wrote later versions in 1997, 1999 and 2003 as new events and possibilities emerged.

Together they give an account of my life and the career choices that were faced over the ten years since I ceased to be a full-time employee of SIG plc. The following sample of extracts from this series of personal 'reflections' will help to put my memories of this unstructured period of progress in proper context.

Written in July 1993

"If I look back over the last five years, beginning with my period as President of the Sheffield Chamber of Commerce, there has been a gradual process of education about the outside world after twenty years in which I had immersed myself in the business.

The longest association has been with the Sheffield Development Corporation, of which I have been a board member for over five years, and which directly reflects my interest in the regeneration of Sheffield [beginning with the Image Working Party]. With four years now to get some results, and with a clear allocation of marketing overview to myself as Deputy chairman, there is a clear challenge.

The chair of governors of Sheffield Hallam University, which I am due to take over in August, is a very new area of interest. It is an exciting prospect. There are a number of challenges – the management of change, the effective use of public funding, the marketing of research strengths – I intend to prepare myself properly for this job.

There have to be serious questions about my Arts interests – Sheffield Theatres, Yorkshire and Humberside Arts, and Opera North. Can I really keep them going? Perhaps only one, the theatre complex in Sheffield, can be retained.

I began to look into family history in 1986 and have never really returned to it since my involvement with the Chamber of Commerce and the CBI began from 1988 onwards. I am keen to return to this research and to link it to a history of the company while the basic information is still relatively easy to get at."

Written in September 1993

"The position of deputy chairman of SDC is going to carry on much as before with occasional action to support the chairman, particularly when there are sticky issues with the city council. Mainly I will be focussing on marketing activities'.

'Recent events in the administration of Sheffield Theatres will almost certainly call for more attention. There is a need for crisis management and for special efforts to convince our funders to continue to provide support." [I subsequently resigned].

Written in June 1997

"The real change in our lifestyle [after my 'retirement' to become non-executive chairman] came with an accident to Eve [in December 1993] that severely damaged her right leg. I bought an apartment in Boca Raton, Florida, and since September 1994 we have spent most of our time between September and April each year in Boca.

I finally retired fully from the chair and board of SIG in April 1996, and the SDC completed its task in the Lower Don Valley at the end of June 1997.

I am left with three major responsibilities, as chairman of governors of Sheffield Hallam University, of the related project Kelham Island museum, and of Sheffield Theatres Trust to which I returned as chairman in 1997. All three present short-term challenges: to find a new vice-chancellor for Hallam by October, to negotiate a wider remit for Kelham to take over Abbeydale, and to make a fresh start in Sheffield Theatres with board changes and a new chief executive.

The fundamental shift in my priorities over the past four years has been in another direction altogether. The recognition that two grandsons – first Stephen then Jonathan – were autistic has been a traumatic experience for the whole family. It has tended to overshadow all other considerations."

Written in October 1999

"Early in 1998 Kelham Island museum was renamed Sheffield Industrial Museums Ltd as it took over Abbeydale Industrial Hamlet. Later in the year I resigned to become chairman of the Kelham Riverside Development Agency'. [To avoid possible conflict of interest].

In 1999 I have taken on two other positions: first as chairman of Sheffield First for Investment; and then of Mount St Mary's in Spinkhill [which both Mark and Simon attend].

In July 1999 came my departure from Sheffield Hallam on the same date – July 20 – that I received a knighthood from the Queen for services to the community in Sheffield."

Written in June 2003

"On the day after the World Trade Centre disaster, while we were struggling with the fact that Philip had been in the neighbouring building and out of touch for several hours, Eve and I moved to Eckington to be near Helen [and her autistic boys].

I am no longer directly involved in economic regeneration in Sheffield after stepping down as chairman of Sheffield First for Investment in March 2002.

My commitment to work in the arts has grown. In July 2002 I became a member of the National Council of the Arts Council and chair of the new Regional Arts Council for Yorkshire. I have also been re-elected to a third three-year term as chairman of Sheffield Theatres, with the principal task of securing funds for a major redevelopment of the Crucible.

I am advising on the development of the new Autism Centre in Sheffield Hallam University."

Regeneration & Economic Development

The Image Working Party
Sheffield Development Corporation
Kelham Riverside Development Agency
Sheffield First for Investment

THE IMAGE WORKING PARTY

In the lead-up to my eventual election as president of the chamber I first became junior vice-president in 1986, and then senior vice-president in the following year, when Richard Field, the chairman of Dyson Refractories, was president. I asked him what I could do to help in his year and he said, 'Do something about the image of Sheffield'.

After a preliminary meeting with city council representatives in November 1986, I arranged for a paper to be delivered by the chief executive, John Hambidge, to propose that the Chamber should take the lead in developing a 'positive promotional policy', working with the council to do whatever was necessary to bring new investment into Sheffield.

As a result, the Image Working Party was formed, but not before meeting in secret with a few early 'believers' in partnership from the Chamber of Commerce and the city council, knowing there was no clear majority for this approach in either body.

I took the chair at the first meeting of the Image Working Party on 5 February 1987. It was not surprising that, given the lack of constructive communication between city and business leaders that I had noticed when I first attended a meeting of the Chamber Council, there was a tendency to start with the same old catalogue of complaints.

As chairman I ruled that the working party should initially ignore negative issues and focus entirely on the positive features of Sheffield. Surprisingly, this produced a list of nine points, together with a general commendation of the friendly attitudes of the people in the Sheffield 'village', a theme repeated over and over again in all meetings of the working party.

After two meetings, I made the first progress report to the Chamber Council in March. There were a few surprising conclusions and recommendations. The general view was that there was no need to be defeatist. Time was on our side if we were prepared to tackle the subjective image issues.

The key recommendation was a message to the Chamber Council pinpointing the need to direct a positive message on investment to our own members: firstly because they were already here and their decisions on investment or relocation were likely to include at least one Sheffield option, and secondly because 'we cannot hope to sell our attractions to others if we do not convince those already here, who could be our best salesmen'.

On re-reading the papers to do with the Image Working Party I note the name of one member who has played a strong role in my career ever since. Barrie Cottingham was then a senior partner of Coopers and Lybrand; some years later he was the first non-executive director of SIG plc after the flotation; and after I retired in 1996 he became my successor as chairman. [His quiet commitment to the community, specifically the Boys and Girls Clubs of South Yorkshire has just been rewarded with an MBE]

By July 1987, after six meetings, the Image Working Party had become a larger and more representative group, and our discussions now focussed on the experience of other cities, based on external research to which I had contributed after business trips to Atlanta and Boston in the United States, and following talks to business leaders in Glasgow.

These cities were very different from one another, but there were some recognisable common factors: there was a working consensus between local authority and the business community, and a willingness to place the economic development of the city in a different category to current political issues.

There was also, particularly in Atlanta and Glasgow, a long tradition of the business community entering into joint actions when called upon. And in each city, all parties had got together at an early stage of regeneration, planning to provide an economic review of regional strengths and weaknesses.

Oddly enough, when talking to the players who had been personally involved in these cities, there was a note of apology in every case for the 'messiness' of the programmes they described – no rigid master plan, and no neat and formal structure of organisation. In fact, it seemed that this readiness to let action flow from joint discussion and consensus was an important element in the dynamic growth of such efforts.

There was confirmation from Glasgow of the importance of flagship projects around which all communities could gather in support – the Cultural City bid for Glasgow and the World Student Games bid for Sheffield were examples – and the importance of local sponsors giving strategic guidance, such as the SDA and McKinsey in Glasgow and MIT and Harvard in Boston.

But I liked best the description of the Atlanta regeneration, which was built around nine task forces – Housing, Transport, Infrastructure, Parks, Communication, Retail, Conventions, PR, and Strategic Planning – involving at one time 400 members of the business community, including the bankers, working with specialists from public bodies, including the educators!

Kenneth Clarke QC MP, Chancellor of the Duchy of Lancaster and Minister of Trade and Industry, had been appointed 'supremo' for the inner cities in late 1987. In a bid to be included in his planned tour of UK cities in need of support, Irvine Patnick, MP for Hallam, and I joined forces to try to convince Kenneth Clarke that Sheffield should be on the circuit.

In January, shortly after his return from a US tour during which he visited Atlanta, I reported to the minister on the work of the Image Working Party, and stressed the case for a programme of regeneration based on partnership.

I told of my enquiries in Glasgow and Atlanta, and the lessons we had learned. 'There is a new spirit in Sheffield, but we will need some help from public funds' if we are to get results.

In his reply to me Kenneth Clarke welcomed 'Partnership in Action' as a 'good practical example of bridge building between industry, commerce and the local authority to provide a better focus for local commitment. I wish you every success'. And in his reply to Irvine, he said 'we have thought very carefully about the possible venues for the Action for Cities breakfast meetings, and I regret to say the list does not include Sheffield, but keep us informed of progress'.

No funds, no statement of intent even, but our actions were welcomed and 'collaboration' was clearly the right button to push. So we kept going, the talks aimed at collaboration between the different interests in our community continued across the city of Sheffield, and, in the 'messy' way mentioned above, various initiatives began to move forward.

The bid for the 1991 Universiade, or World Student Games, had already been successfully presented in Zagreb; the distribution of a regular newsheet, 'Success in Sheffield', was already helping to raise confidence and morale; the Cooper Report on the state of the Lower Don Valley, commissioned by the Sheffield Economic Regeneration Committee (SERC), was presented to the government.

The vision of the 'Partnership in Action' campaign then brought together coach-loads of Sheffield ambassadors from all sectors of the city, travelling to the Mansion House in London to 'sell' Sheffield to the City of London on 23 May 1988 – an initiative which received the following commendation from Prime Minister Margaret Thatcher:

"Congratulations to Sheffield on its enterprise and initiative. Local businessmen, councillors and others are not sitting back waiting for business to come to them, but going out to sell the skills and expertise of those who live in the city. This is what I call real enterprise and initiative, and I wish them every success as they visit London's Mansion House tomorrow to show investors and financial institutions what Sheffield has to offer."

The support across the city had been remarkable; there were over 200 ambassadors, many of whom had been given training in ½-day courses by Sheffield City Polytechnic on behalf of Sheffield Partnerships; and the *Star* had produced a 40-page supplement with direct sponsorship by all the leading companies in Sheffield.

These were all aspects, in one form or another, of the 'Partnership in Action' vision, which was beginning, without much central co-ordination or control, to bring together organisations – public, private and voluntary – to work together for the regeneration of Sheffield. It was decided therefore that from its 13th monthly meeting, held in March 1988, the Image Working Party should become a quarterly forum of all parties interested in the promotion of Sheffield, with its 'executive' role to be gradually taken over by other partnership groups and companies.

There was a postscript to the Mansion House initiative later in 1988, when Eve and I were invited to a meeting of the Per Cent Club in London by Hugh Sykes, who had been backing this movement in Sheffield by encouraging company contributions to charitable and community causes. The main speaker at the Royal Academy was Mrs Margaret Thatcher, the prime minister, who pleased me with a speech in which the economic and environmental benefits of conserving energy was a central theme.

Following her speech, we all moved into the galleries of the Royal Academy for a reception, during which Mrs Thatcher and her party moved around the various groups from different parts of the country.

When she came upon the group in which I was standing with Eve and a small number of people from Sheffield, her first question was blunt: 'Are you the man who believes in talking to the council in Sheffield?'

When I said I was doing just that, she moved closer, placed a firm hand on my forearm, and in an accusing voice said, 'You can't trust them'. As she forcefully developed her theme, I was for a moment transfixed (I think I was being 'hand-bagged'!) until I realised this was a technique aimed at testing my response.

I gave her a few examples of progress and she replied with a question, 'Who will get the credit?' I replied that I had not thought about that, but that the point of partnership was that we could all share it, quoting her message of support for the initiative and enterprise of 'business' in sending the Sheffield delegation to the Mansion House a few months earlier.

My brief meeting with Mrs Thatcher was memorable. As she focussed her attention on to me, the gaze was hypnotic, and Eve tells me that Mrs T held my forearm firmly all the time she was speaking – so that I couldn't run away! In our exchange of letters after the event, it was interesting that she returned to the central theme of our conversation:

"I was very encouraged to learn when talking to you at the Royal Academy earlier in the month how much better things are going in Sheffield, and the confident and active part that business is playing in the city's regeneration. But do not underestimate the problems of presentation. It is important to get across to local people what business is doing for the community as a whole and for them to feel part of the recovery, not merely passively dependent on local government to do things for them."

I can see why she stressed the point, but it was really quite unnecessary in the context of the Sheffield Partnership, because the involvement of business was at the heart of most of the new initiatives that were beginning in Sheffield.

One such initiative, which ran between 1989 and 1992, was Sheffield Partnerships Ltd, of which I was co-chair with councillor Helen Jackson, whose brother Chris Price, the Labour MP for Lewisham and a former Labour councillor in Sheffield, had been a friend of mine since we were students at The Queen's College Oxford in the 1950s.

Another was the Universiade company, a partnership set up to run the 1991 World Student Games, in which I took on a temporary role following the departure of the original chief executive. I tried to persuade government, both directly and through the CBI and the Chambers of Commerce at a high level, that the Games project was a true partnership venture with much community support, and that it would be right for the government to support the partnership – but with no success at all! Lots of nice words but no money!

Obviously the doubters remained; an industrialist at a private lunch in the Cutler's Hall sought to strengthen Mrs Thatcher's message of mistrust, pointing out to me that the leaders of the city council were 'Marxists' – clinching his argument by reminding me what they did to Kerensky! It's a good job I remembered enough of the 'politics' in my PPE degree to recognise this reference to the Russian Revolution 70 years earlier – but it seemed of dubious relevance to the current thinking of the Labour group in Sheffield city council!

In the gathering momentum of the Partnership in Action campaign the need for a more formal statement of our vision for the future of Sheffield was apparent, and an ambitious document, sponsored jointly by Clive Betts the leader and myself on behalf of the city council and the Chamber of Commerce respectively, helped to provide a framework for the partnership. A flavour of this is provided at the end of this section.

Perhaps it did the trick and provided the formal confirmation that there was a workable partnership in Sheffield, and that it wasn't just words. Eventually, the breakthrough came – we were offered substantial government support for a major partnership project – to do something about the state of the Lower Don Valley. We had agreed in the Image Working Party that this was the best candidate for a project we could all agree on, and this was the basis on which we had sought help from government.

A Natural Centre for Business and Industry

Regeneration of Sheffield's industrial heartland is the key to this; plus the Cultural Industries Quarter, Special Steels & Supertram

Britain's New Decision Centre

A City airport, new conference centre, business and financial services.

A World Leader in Research and Technology

The development of University, Polytechnic and Sheffield College as technology leaders.

An International Centre for Sport, Leisure and Tourism

Beginning with the World Student Games, new sports facilities, a theatre complex of international standard, more and better hotels.

A City of Life

A city in which all are valued and able to contribute, with an emphasis on conservation of heritage and environment.

A City with a Big Future

"A city with a big future which will reward the investor, Sheffield is an excellent place in which to live and work. Come to Sheffield and you will not regret it."

That, in a nutshell, is my message to our friends in Britain and abroad.

As one whose family has lived in the city since the 1850s, I might be accused of bias. It is not sentiment, however, but realism which prompts me to encourage you to consider expansion, investment, location or relocation of your enterprises in Sheffield.

Through the Sheffield Economic Regeneration Committee, which brings together decision-makers from both public and private sectors, this vision of Sheffield in the year 2000 has been produced and a simple, straightforward strategy established which will enable a series of key partnership ventures to be developed with maximum support and encouragement. The strategy has widespread support in the city of Sheffield and the goal is progress for the benefit of all sectors of the community.

I could, of course, say a good deal more: about our city's industrial and sporting traditions; about the excellent educational, health and other facilities; about the benefits of living and working in a city which is so pleasing on the eye, so good for the heart and so easy on the pocket.

I will settle for concluding that Sheffield is a good place in which to make a living, a good place to invest. And if you should choose to join us, or at least target your investments in our direction, I'm sure you will not regret it. Neither will your shareholders!

Norman Adsetts

Norman Adsetts
President: Sheffield Chamber
of Commerce

SHEFFIELD CITY COUNCIL

Partnership in Action

Suddenly people are talking about Sheffield again—and for all the right reasons!

In two short years the results of a decade of planning and hard work are starting to bear fruit as Sheffield—England's fourth largest city—emerges from a period of transition to turn decline and depression into optimism and opportunity.

In that time, public and private sector agencies have been working together and pooling resources to get Sheffield back on the road as one of Europe's main manufacturing centres, with future glories ahead of it, as well as past glories behind it.

And the good news about the city is not mere hype. It's based on solid achievement. Just look at what has happened. Six large-scale shopping centre redevelopments backed by six of Britain's major development companies. A new Science Park which already has a waiting list of potential tenant companies. A pioneering Audio-Visual Enterprise Centre with major recording studio, film and photography investment as a cornerstone for the growth of a thriving cultural industries 'quarter'. And crowning it all, the chance to be host city for the 1991 World Student Games, with all the privilege and prestige which that confers.

All these developments, which mean prosperity for Sheffield and jobs for our people, have been possible only through a genuine partnership involving the City Council and a wide range of local and national organisations.

It is to carry that partnership forward that we are extending an invitation to you to join our Sheffield Vision of a city emerging from readjustment and change, and on the threshold of a dynamic new phase of expansion.

This brochure outlines our achievements and aspirations to ensure we take Sheffield forward to the next century on an upward trajectory.

We hope you will join us!

Clive Betts
Leader: Sheffield City Council

A MAN OF SHEFFIELD

THE SHEFFIELD
DEVELOPMENT CORPORATION

The Sheffield Economic Regeneration Committee, of which I was an *ex officio* member when I became president of the Chamber of Commerce in 1988, had raised sufficient funds to engage the leading accounting and consulting firm Cooper and Lybrand to produce a report on the state of the Lower Don Valley and make recommendations on ways to restore it to become a productive centre for industry and commerce.

Given this evidence that the business community and the city council were prepared to work together, Sheffield was offered an Urban Development Corporation (UDC) and, despite strong political opposition to taking planning powers out of democratic control, the council eventually accepted the offer, on the understanding that the new corporation would work with the city on planning matters.

The Sheffield Development Corporation was designated in June 1988 with an expected life of seven years and a partnership board to be chaired by Hugh Sykes, a local financier and industrialist.

Richard Field and I, respectively the immediate past and present presidents of the Chamber of Commerce, were two of the business members of the SDC board. There were other business and university members, alongside councillors with planning and economic development responsibilities, and Fred Mulley, a respected Sheffielder and former defence secretary, was deputy chairman.

There was clearly a strong commitment to the concept of 'Partnership in Action', and to the marketing initiatives beginning to emerge from the Image Working Party; and part of Hugh's role was to make sure that the SDC worked closely with the council on a strategic approach to the future of the city.

However, before we could credibly promote the benefits of the Lower Don Valley for investment we had to deal with the limitations of our 'product'. Our small team of development specialists had quickly realised that with limited resources and a deadline set for completion of our task, there would need to be a disciplined approach to the specific problem of product development before we could expect to sell anything.

The SDC had no land with which to work, nor had it much information about the complex pattern of ownership in the Don Valley, and so the board initially agreed to issue a number of compulsory purchase orders aimed at opening up the property market. Richard and I both had companies within the valley, and were invited to a meeting of the 'threatened' owners, only to be asked to leave when our affiliation to the SDC was recognised. All very civilised, but an indication of some very strong feelings!

The number of CPOs actually issued was small, and a gradual process of site acquisition in face-to-face negotiation, alongside the provision of improvement grants on existing sites, became the norm, albeit a slow process.

Various large 'projects' – an opencast site leading to an airport at Tinsley, the redevelopment of the canal basin in the city centre, and the completion of a large retail park at Meadowhall – had all been identified, but the main, and ultimately the most costly and complicated, project was the completion of a new spine road running through the centre of the valley, opening up access to sites for development and significantly improving our offering to investors and developers.

The problems of complex land ownership in the valley were bad enough, but we were also working in the difficult trading conditions created by the nineties recession. Difficult decisions had to be made. The partnership was at times under strain, and the SDC model of governance, which sat somewhere between the private sector culture of entrepreneurial flexibility and the bureaucratic rigidity of the public sector, was not really suited to this type of management. The resultant strains affected the relationship between the chairman and the chief executive.

The pressures grew. The chief executive was asked to leave, and, after he complained to his employers at the Department of the Environment, a senior civil servant conducted an enquiry. The end result was that the chief executive was in fact replaced, with a recommendation to the minister that clearer guidelines in the future would prevent similar problems.

This decision, which is summarised in *Forging the Valley*, led to a 'much stronger emphasis on understanding the market, and putting more effort into focussing on the needs of different sorts of customer'. My sort of language! Clearly we were approaching the point, always a delicate one, when the product development phase has to be replaced by active marketing.

As a small example, we supported the Five Weirs Walk Trust, of which I was an early sponsor, building a walk along the full length of the Lower Don Valley from Lady's Bridge to Meadowhall.

The River Don had been hidden from view during the growth of industry in the nineteenth century, and was used for the disposal of liquid waste and cooling water. With most of the factories now gone, the river was visible again, and the emergence of vegetation and wildlife was changing the nature and appearance of what had been an open sewer. Our developments were now reversing the alignment of the buildings along the Don to provide a river view for the occupants, and so the interests of the SDC and Five Weirs Walk were similar.

I had been asked to become deputy chairman following the death of Lord Mulley, and welcomed the opportunity to work in a close and effective partnership with the chairman, Hugh Sykes. We had worked together both in Sheffield Partnerships and in the complex corporate structures needed for the funding and staging of the World Student Games, so we knew each other well. Our strengths were complementary.

Inevitably, the first few years of the SDC had been a steady and systematic building up of land, structure and access to possible sites. This was the vital early phase, an essential prerequisite for achieving results on the ground, and there had already been some impatience at the perceived lack of progress.

As we entered the second phase of our life, it was time to move to the marketing phase – or as I prefer to say – 'to become more sensitive to the needs of the consumer', and we set up a small group of board members with sales experience to monitor our promotional efforts and measure our final progress in terms of deals completed and the estimated employment levels likely to be reached.

We were now driven by a 'sales budget', not just an 'acquisition budget', and the culture and pace of the Corporation changed. Two new members of the board, Don Lyon, a news distributor and retailer, and Frank Eul, a London-based property man with both public and private experience, were very helpful at this stage, and the technical and negotiating team of SDC employees soon picked up the pace.

The SDC completion date was extended by two years from 1995 to 1997, and by a combination of determined effort and imagination the devastated acres of the Don Valley had begun to be transformed. It was an exciting and fulfilling enterprise, led by Hugh Sykes, which completed its task on time and on budget – a great achievement by a pioneering partnership.

THE KELHAM RIVERSIDE
DEVELOPMENT AGENCY

Unlike the Sheffield Development Corporation, within whose area there had been very few residents, the Kelham Riverside area housed a relatively large community living alongside a mix of small – and medium-sized businesses in a historic area that had seen the birth of Sheffield's industrial might in the nineteenth century.

My work with KRDA in the regeneration of the Upper Don Valley drew on my experience with the Sheffield Development Corporation in the Lower Don Valley, but the starting point for recovery was very different in the two areas.

The common factor, however, which I discussed at some length with John Mothersole and with the new chief executive of the city council, Bob Kerslake, shortly after his arrival, was the need to encourage investment enquiries and convert as many as possible to firm investment decisions.

The vocabulary of regeneration, with its emphasis on the need to develop the right conditions for investment and growth, creates an impression that it was all about business and profit; but this does not help the building of a common purpose in partnership bodies and working parties.

The appointment to the board of Laura Moynahan, the director of the Netherthorpe and Upperthorpe Community Alliance in the heart of the Riverside area, who had also known my daughter at school, was a great help in building a constructive link with the community.

The simple fact that the emphasis on new investment is a means to an end, and that the aim is to achieve an increase in employment, took a while to get through, but when it did we had one of the most effective 'partnership' boards that I ever worked with.

Similarly, the deputy chairman Nick Hutton led a most effective Business Forum, and produced a valuable assessment of the specific needs of this varied complex of small – and middle-sized businesses plagued with access and parking problems in the narrow roads of the early industrial heart of Sheffield.

It is difficult now to realise just what a major step was being taken by this unique combination of interests in one area of Sheffield – city council, communities of the Riverside, and local businesses all working together to deliver the following mission statement, printed in the KRDA Annual Report for 1999-2000 – one of the early products of debate in the new board:

> "*To bring business and community together to realise the full potential of Kelham Riverside's unique heritage and waterfront as an excellent place to work, invest, visit and enjoy.*"

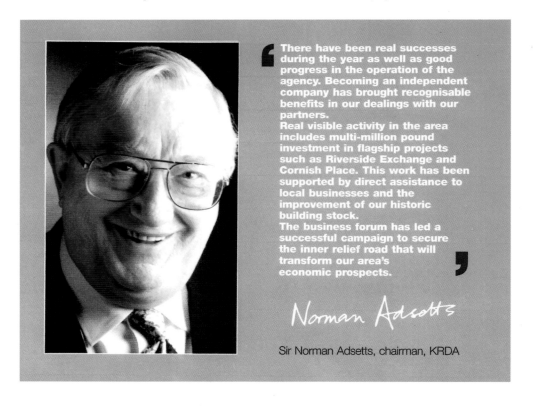

There have been real successes during the year as well as good progress in the operation of the agency. Becoming an independent company has brought recognisable benefits in our dealings with our partners.

Real visible activity in the area includes multi-million pound investment in flagship projects such as Riverside Exchange and Cornish Place. This work has been supported by direct assistance to local businesses and the improvement of our historic building stock.

The business forum has led a successful campaign to secure the inner relief road that will transform our area's economic prospects.

Sir Norman Adsetts, chairman, KRDA

SHEFFIELD FIRST FOR INVESTMENT

The final paragraph in the introduction to the SDC Regeneration Statement of February 1997 had stated:

"It is now essential for others to build on the successful regeneration in the Valley both to continue the momentum established and to secure regeneration more widely in Sheffield."

The Kelham Riverside Development Agency had made a promising start, and was to become the prototype of future agencies for local development within the city; and the decision to bring in the specialist firm of Civic Regeneration to help achieve the aims of the agency was another successful precedent.

Larger trusts maintained the momentum in the city centre, and in the development of the Arts, the Galleries and Museums of the city.

Although I was not by then a member of the partnership team working on an overall strategy for Sheffield, I had been sufficiently impressed by the marketing progress made in the SDC's final years to believe that a model for repeating this process for the whole city could be effectively introduced.

This did not happen in the immediate aftermath of the successful completion of the SDC project, but shortly after the arrival of the new chief executive Bob Kerslake, as part of his general briefing about the city we talked about my experience with the Image Working Party, the Partnership in Action campaign, and specifically the SDC model for site development and marketing.

As a result, I was asked in 1999 to set up a new city-wide agency to increase the level of new investment in Sheffield by promoting the benefits of such investment, developing new sites and providing professional services to interested parties to help bring negotiations over new prospects to a satisfactory conclusion.

In a draft note of May 1999 I set down my thoughts on the nature of this new body. It needed to have credibility with its partners and clients. It must have the ability to close deals and to provide a helpful service to any enquirers, increase the level of enquiries, and, beyond that, increase the conversion rate in bringing them to a final investment decision.

Council approval had been given for the formation of Sheffield First for Investment under my chairmanship, and I was given a free hand to name the private sector members of a board on which the chief executive of the city and other senior officers would also sit. My views were recorded as follows:

> *"Norman has strong views that if the board was to be effective then members should not be on it simply as representatives of any organisation but as a team of individuals who would bring strong skills and experience to the board, and who would work well together."*

In naming this new board, I was determined to find senior executives from business, land and property professionals and senior academics with direct personal experience of handling major new investments. I wanted board members who would know what it takes to make such decisions and what support would be needed when doing so.

Not for the first time my guide was my school friend Ralph Windle, alias Bernie Ramsbottom, whose poem 'The Decision Makers' from *The Bottom Line*, his book of business ballads, reminded me that:

> *Decisions, my friends,*
> *Are a means not an end,*
> *And its 'how' more than 'what' that may matter,*
> *And the wise are, as ever,*
> *More use than the clever –*
> *Since there's more to decisions than data*

In taking this approach, I chose not to nominate an executive of the Chamber as a representative of the business community, knowing that my selections, including three past presidents of the Chamber with members of the current Chamber council and the Cutlers' Company, had the wisdom of experience. My list included a relative newcomer to the partnership in David Grey, one of a new generation of Sheffield industrialists, who would go on to play a leading role in the future development of this project.

The new organisation was formed and its aims and objectives agreed, the first being 'to market Sheffield as the place for business', followed by 'the promotion of investment opportunities' and 'the provision of a high-quality, one-stop service for potential investors', with associated after-care to do with sites, training, grants and appropriate support from the council and private agencies.

An experienced professional was engaged as chief executive and city centre offices were occupied, and we began to show early results. As agreed in 1999 on my accepting the position of chairman, I stepped down in 2002 and handed over to Don Lyon, an experienced chief executive of a large local company with whom I had worked on the board of the SDC and on the Universiade, and who had been president of the Chamber of Commerce!

It was the right time for me to leave. Sheffield First for Investment had extended its remit to cover the KRDA, now renamed Sheffield Riverside Development Agency, and its boundaries were enlarged to take over more of the Upper Don Valley.

Education & the Arts

Sheffield Hallam University
Dealing with Autism
Ernest Gordon, Glass Designer
Kelham Island Museum
Sheffield Theatres Trust
Mount St Mary's College

SHEFFIELD HALLAM UNIVERSITY

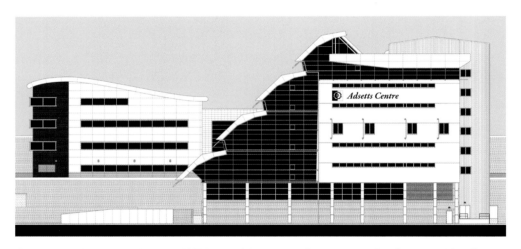

Illustration by local artist Jonathan Wilkinson of the Adsetts Centre on the City Campus of Sheffield Hallam University.

Shortly before the SDC reached the end of its life, I was invited to take over as the chairman of governors of a second university in Sheffield, to replace the Sheffield City Polytechnic in 1993. One of my colleagues on the board of the SDC, Peter Newman, was handling the formal transition, but he was being moved south by his company Davy McKee, and suggested, with support from the principal, John Stoddart, that I should join the interim board of the new university in preparation for taking over as chairman when he left.

A few years earlier I had received an Honorary Fellowship from Sheffield City Polytechnic in recognition of my work as 'a leading figure in the move towards the regeneration of Sheffield'. I had worked before with John Stoddart and members of his senior team, and I welcomed the opportunity to be involved with them in the further development of higher education in Sheffield; I had not worked in an academic environment since Oxford, and this was going to be very different – I looked forward to the challenge.

I was just on the verge of becoming the chairman of the governors of the newly created Sheffield Hallam University when the Queen came to open the new buildings around the striking Atrium which was at the heart of our new city centre campus. As chairman-elect I was asked to speak to the assembled great and good of Sheffield in the large new lecture theatre, and 'keep them happy' while the Queen toured the new buildings with my predecessor. No one knew how long it would take. I was essentially a warm-up act, a role – as I explained to my audience – which would in the old music hall be entrusted to a patter comedian or an eccentric dancer.

I was neither, so I told them stories about my three grandchildren. On the school run that morning, I said, I had asked them for advice on how I should deal with this situation before the Queen arrived. I told the audience of the serious advice offered by the two elder children, but that the youngest had entered into the spirit of the occasion by pointing out that we should have plenty of balloons, and that I should dress up and wear a funny hat.

Since I was festooned in a gilded gown and hood, wearing a mortar board with more scrambled egg on it than the Marshal of the Royal Air Force, the auditorium exploded into uncontrollable laughter – and just then the Queen came in!

By this time, we had already been through a complex and long-running process to decide upon the name of the new university. Sally Neocosmos, the clerk to the governors, was our main representative in the process of change from a local authority backed polytechnic to the formal structure of a university, and had already completed this onerous passage through complex legal negotiations, when the final decision on a name became the biggest issue of all.

The established universities were quite naturally keen on maintaining their identity free of the possibility of confusion with the newcomers. The Privy Council became involved, and various rules were laid down. Our own initial favourite, Sheffield City University, which retained two key elements of the original name, was not allowed.

Recognising that this was a branding exercise, we engaged a company that provided advice to business on such matters and there was an interesting debate before we finally chose the name of Hallam. As I recall, its plus points were that this historic region around Sheffield was nearly the same as our catchment area, that the name would be meaningless (i.e. with no negative connotation) to anyone who lived outside Sheffield, and that it had only two syllables and so was fairly easy to remember, a factor which hadn't done Harvard any harm!

One of our first tasks on the new board was to consider ways of reducing the number of university sites around the city from 12 to two or three, clearly a long-term project. We had an inadequate central library to meet the needs of the new university, with books scattered around all the different sites. The Higher Education Funding council was not impressed and called for immediate action to remedy the situation.

As a result, Sheffield Hallam built a new Learning Centre on a sloping site in the City Centre. It cost about £12m, mainly met by reserves and a matching grant from HEFC, but we also raised money from an appeal, to which I contributed. It is a striking building, packed with state of the art electronic wizardry, and led the way in international design, providing a modern approach to the demands of a university library; and the board decided to name it the Adsetts Centre.

In this new and unfamiliar environment it was clear from the start that the changes in governance, culture, objectives and identity were going to present some real challenges to the board, management, and members of the university. Most of this programme was naturally the preserve of the educationalists, but I had learned the hard way about the management of change when faced with the explosive growth of Sheffield Insulations, and there were similarities.

The executive team led by John Stoddart had already begun to address these issues, and it was clear that they had a professional grasp of the changes required; but there was one theme in particular I wanted to explore: who were the users of our services, what were their needs, and how well were we meeting them? And will they change as we become a university? We had to identify the changing needs of this new culture, address the expectations for the new image and, as necessary, meet competition from other universities.

In making this point so strongly I made the mistake of using the vocabulary of my own experience in entering new markets, and my talk of product development, competition and the management of change was not necessarily appropriate. In some quarters, it was even suggested that I was threatening 'academic freedom'.

I learned a lesson of real value – which came in handy when faced with similar reluctance elsewhere – that, rather than use the word 'marketing', with its connotation of encyclopaedia selling, I should stress the need for 'sensitivity to the needs of the consumer', an acceptable formula which did not carry with it a commercial stigma, and which had the benefit that it actually made sense!

In this period, my strategic thinking was focussed on two simple thoughts: we should take a professional approach to the growth possibilities in new areas of applied educational need, and we should take every opportunity to 'change the product mix' by increasing our research output; nothing very radical in that, but it was worth saying!

Over the next year the quality of the academic team that was reviewing the opportunities offered by university status was very apparent, and the new board, of which I was chairman, was beginning 'to learn the trade' and work with the executive.

I soon got an opportunity to make a small contribution. In July 1996 a holiday in San Remo Italy had been arranged for the whole family, including both our children – Helen with her second husband Peter, Philip with his American wife Dina and a total of seven grandchildren. The dates had clashed with a Board of Governors meeting and I had planned a quick trip back to Sheffield for this, just as Helen learned that Jonathan had been diagnosed with autism in addition to his elder brother Stephen.

Having already started the difficult process of adjusting to this condition with one child this news was difficult to handle. I cancelled my flight back for the Board and arranged an early meeting with John Stoddart the Vice-Chancellor on my return to Sheffield. I asked him what he or any other member of the university knew about autism, because I needed advice.

As I recall there were four or five people, all in different parts of the university, who knew something about autism and we arranged to meet to begin my learning process. Twenty years later much has changed and the Autism Centre in Sheffield Hallam is now a research and education centre with a national and international reputation.

The full story is told in a later section, but the point to be made is that this fortuitous introduction to an educational and research need has helped to create a valuable asset in the university.

Since the naming of the new universities had been a delicate issue from the start, John Stoddart and I had decided that, once it was resolved, we should meet our counterparts in the University of Sheffield, Gareth Roberts and Jim Eardley, in the interests of partnership.

I sat for this painting by Robert Priseman in 1994 to be displayed in the boardroom with various past chairs of Sheffield City Polytechnic. The portrait was hanging in the middle of the wall facing me when I was chairing meetings of the board, and I soon began to realise that I was gradually and unconsciously adopting the same pose as the painting!

Gareth and I were colleagues on the board of Sheffield Development Corporation, and I had for a while worked with him on the council of Sheffield University. Jim Eardley and I were respectively the sons of Sheffield's leading manufacturers of mineral waters and of ice cream, who had worked alongside each other on the big gala events of the 1940s; we were also prominent spokesmen for the Cutlers' Company and the Chamber of Commerce respectively in arguing for partnership across the city.

So, the scene was set for a rapprochement. A joint eight of the two universities was rowing at Henley, and John Stoddart, a member of Leander, arranged for us to spend a day together supporting our crew. Unfortunately, Jim couldn't make it, and the Combined Universities eight from Sheffield had been beaten in the first heat before we arrived, which meant that the remaining trio of Gareth, John and myself enjoyed the social amenities along the river bank and a long lunch in the town – to great effect. Quite a lesson on the way to establish a partnership – beginning with a decision on joint promotion of some masters' degrees! [At least I think that was what we achieved!]

My lasting memories of Sheffield Hallam are of the annual fortnights of graduation ceremonies in the City Hall, when I had the pleasure of presiding over the conferment of degrees and diplomas to thousands of graduates every year. I enjoyed every moment, and used often to dispense with the car which was there to take me back to the university for lunch and walk through to the front of City Hall, mingling with the assortment of families gathered there, each one celebrating this major event in the life of someone they loved.

I once spoke at a graduation dinner about my first appearance on the City Hall stage as a tap-dancing rabbit in the 1938 production of 'Starlets of Steelopolis'. I relished the opportunity, I said, to tread the boards again, dressed not as a rabbit this time, but still in fancy dress, with the funny hat that my youngest grandson recommended for such occasions.

This was the biggest job and the most valued role in my post-SIG involvement in the Sheffield scene, and Sheffield Hallam has remained an important part of my life since I ceased to have any formal connection with its affairs. In a university that aspires to provide an applied education of international quality, the continuing development of the Autism Centre in both research and education is of real significance and impact in the wider community. The continued growth of Kelham Island Museum, Shepherd Wheel and Abbeydale Industrial Hamlet, and the innovative developments within Sheffield Industrial Museums owe much to the University's ethos of partnership which continues to be its strength today. Added to which there is my family link to the Sheffield Institute of Art and my personal involvement with the reading project based in the Adsetts Centre. Now one of the largest and most accessible universities in this country I am proud to be writing this on the 25th anniversary of Hallam's founding.

LIVING WITH AUTISM

Even after stepping down from my role as chairman of governors in 1999, I have retained strong links with Sheffield Hallam, and a joint involvement with autism is one of them.

In 1996, early in my chairmanship, when first one and then a second of my young grandsons was diagnosed with autism I sought help and advice from within Sheffield Hallam.

One of the early pieces of advice was that I should make contact with the National Autistic Society. I arranged a meeting with Geraldine Peacock, the chief executive of the charity, who explained that NAS was established by parents of autistic children, who still have a strong role in its governance.

Stephen, Gaga and Jonathan.

She gave me a copy of a booklet published in 1996 by the National Autistic Society entitled *Autism – The Invisible Children? An Agenda for Action*. One of the authors of this document, she made a strong case for action in a number of key areas. She stressed the uneven level of awareness and understanding of autism among the professionals with whom parents had to deal, especially in local health agencies, and the great need to provide support for parents when the bombshell of an autism diagnosis is finally delivered.

My family had already experienced the traumatic impact of such a decision, not once but twice in the space of a few months. Fortunately, my daughter was subsequently supported by the local authority of North East Derbyshire, who paid for both Stephen and Jonathan to travel daily to Sutherland House, a special school for autistic children in Nottingham.

After my briefing by the NAS, it seemed to me that the central problem was one of education. There was clearly a growing need for the 'professionals' – the doctors, the nurses, the teachers and others in regular contact with the affected families – to be taught more about the nature of autism.

I then suggested to John Stoddart, the vice chancellor of Sheffield Hallam, which had inherited strong teacher training and other vocational teaching of professionals from the constituent parts of the polytechnic, that the university was in a good position to meet this emerging need, and perhaps to gain a competitive edge by doing so.

From these simple beginnings arose a small education and research unit in the university that became known as the Autism Centre, and with it a general awareness of the need for support services in schools and universities so that adequate mainstream provision can be made available to students with autism. I also began to notice a slow growth in the number of graduation awards making specific reference to autism.

My own involvement with autism support services continued after leaving my formal role in Sheffield Hallam. In a speech I made in 2011 at the Sheffield City Region Business Dinner I said:

> *"Over the past 20 years the regeneration of our city has moved forward from the first tentative steps of collaboration to develop an impressive array of strategic, arts, and educational partnerships. The readiness to work together which served us so well in the past can still be our greatest strength, not only in the economic regeneration of our region, but in improving the quality of life for*

the most vulnerable in our society, and in harnessing their abilities to the benefit of the local economy."

In this context I can refer to an initiative that my wife and I decided to back shortly after I became a trustee of the charity Research Autism in 2006.

The NAS booklet in 1996 had described the effect on parents of the diagnosis of autism in the following words: 'their world fell apart and they were sent home to cope alone'; and, based on our own experience, this was an accurate description of the despair and confusion of our family when the puzzling nature of autism was described to us.

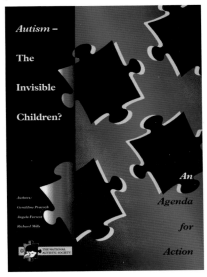

In the absence of anywhere to go for reliable advice on what we should do to help our child we were all exposed to a 'bewildering array of services, treatments, therapies, and approaches' from the internet and elsewhere that offered to improve or even 'cure' autism, and yet how were we to distinguish the false, misleading, biased or downright harmful 'interventions' from the helpful ones?

The Research Autism charity in 2005 proposed to set up a website which would provide 'reliable and impartial information about treatments and therapies for autism'. Recognising just how much pain and distress the lack of such a trustworthy source had initially created for our family, Eve and I made a substantial contribution to help it get off the ground. It is now part of the National Autistic Society, and is claimed to be one of the biggest, most up-to-date and reliable sites for information about autism interventions in the world.

Much has been done in the past 20 years to improve the services for children with autism; more remains to be done, and this will continue to be the case. But as the years go by, the number of adults with autism is steadily increasing, and the challenge of making it possible for these people to live a fulfilling and productive life is the next big priority.

This was a central aim of Autism Plus over the period in which I was its chairman, beginning in 2007 when Philip Bartey the chief executive took over the small Yorkshire arm of Prospects the London-based NAS employment scheme. He negotiated new funding, and established Jobsteps, a subsidiary that was to focus on finding employment for adults with autism.

Initially we were successful in achieving 1800 jobs for autistic people over three years, but the new Work Programme introduced by the coalition after 2010 was unsuitable for the disabled. Regrettably we had to withdraw from the government scheme due to lack of the specific funding that had been expected, and Jobsteps was closed down.

We made more progress with The Adsetts Partnership, launched in 2008 to bring together different charitable interests with the aim of establishing a number of social enterprises offering work to people with autism. At present they include a working chocolate factory and horticultural project in partnership with the Ampleforth Charitable Trust, a community centre in Hull providing meals on wheels by electric bicycles, a musical instrument maker in Sheffield and another horticultural project in Rotherham.

The Adsetts Partnership, with Autism Plus, is now based in the historic Exchange Brewery in the riverside heart of Sheffield, in which a new leasing enterprise provides much needed space for local small businesses and charities. Following the merger of Autism Plus in 2016 with Turning Point, a national charity offering complementary strengths, there is now an opportunity to plan ahead for growth of autism services in other areas. Before this I had stepped down from the chair to become Honorary President and now look forward to the enterprising future of the Adsetts Partnership within the new Autism Plus.

My two autistic grandsons are now in their mid-twenties, and I know from experience the difficulty in finding an appropriate framework for their employment, whether it is paid or unpaid, hobby or pastime. Apart from their involvement in family life and in social activities like the theatre, they now enjoy part-time work in a charity shop, and are training for work in film animation.

Stephen and Jonathan live with a degree of independence in the family home, sensible young men blessed with powerful memories, pursuing their own interests and hobbies – albeit facing to varying degrees the personal difficulties with social communication and high levels of anxiety that often accompany autism.

It has been of great benefit to their development that they have grown up in a family of five robust children, which now forms a group of mutually loving and supportive siblings. Their sister is now a senior fund-raising manager in the National Autistic Society, and with her two other brothers she has a unique understanding of the autistic condition that is of real benefit not just to Stephen and Jonathan but to the rest of the family, both now and in the future.

While we have been, as a family, getting on with our own lives, accepting and adjusting to each other with love without bothering about approved interventions or labels, further research and practical experience of autism has continued to guide the work of the Autism Centre in Sheffield Hallam.

The former teacher of autistic children, Nick Hodge, who was an early member of the Autism Centre team 20 years ago, now leads it as Professor of Inclusive Practice, and he is recommending a 'rights' approach to autism in children, which involves making a pledge to treat them always with respect, and with a proper awareness of their legal, moral and human rights – contrasting this with any approach which tries to force them into a state of 'normality'.

All I can say in support of this is that our family approach, guided quite naturally by love, has been precisely that which Nick recommends – and will continue to be so. It has to be recognised that the autism of every child can take different forms, each difficult to understand – Stephen for example has difficulty with communication, while Jonathan has to cope with occasional high levels of anxiety – but I have noticed that, autistic or not, we are all capable of handling such issues in the normal give-and-take of family life.

I now have an advisory group of five grandchildren in the UK and three in the USA; the two with autism bringing with them a special brand of humour and wisdom! Their dependence on memory of past experience as a guide to present behaviour earns my respect, and their reliance on literal truth is a reminder of the value and occasional hazards of straight talking, as when Jonathan described me as a nice man who is 'good at paying for things'.

Paraphrasing Will Rogers, we should all guide our future actions in the field of autism with the motto: *'I never met a child I didn't love!'*

The Adsetts Partnership sign over the door to the former Lady's Bridge hotel in the Exchange Brewery building – back to my grandfather's favourite pub!

A Man of Sheffield

ERNEST GORDON, GLASS DESIGNER

One of Ernest Gordon's Swedish Vases.

A family connection with Sheffield Hallam had emerged when my cousin Ernest Adsetts was identified as a 1940s graduate of the Sheffield College of Art, one of the constituent parts of Sheffield City Polytechnic and hence Sheffield Hallam. I was asked to provide background information for his entry in the Special Collections of distinguished alumni.

During the war years, while I was taking the first steps in secondary education in King Edward's, my cousin Ernest Gordon, Uncle George's son from his second marriage, who was five years older than me, was recognised as a promising young artist, and in 1941 he was admitted to the Sheffield College of Art, where he specialised as a sculptor.

In 1944 he received a scholarship to study at the Royal College of Art; his three-year course was extended by a year with another scholarship, and after graduation he entered into partnership with George Fullard, another sculptor from the Sheffield College of Art, and they shared a studio on the Kings Rd, Chelsea, where they produced joint exhibits for the Festival of Britain in 1952 and for the Ideal Home Exhibition of 1953.

When my father took the family to see the Festival on its opening day (he had no tickets and talked us in with the VIP guests) we stared in pride and admiration at Ernest's creations – he and George Fullard had been commissioned to make models of 'Queen Shu-bad's harp' and a Celtic chariot!

A year later, for the Ideal Home Exhibition in Olympia, they modelled an ambitious piece called 'All the Queen's horses and all the Queen's men' for the Coronation Cavalcade, an exact reproduction of the State Coach, two-thirds life size, drawn by eight Windsor Greys, with an escort of eighteen men ranging from postillions to mounted officers of the Household Cavalry', which stretched 30 yards down the centre of the Grand Hall.

All the figures and the horses were modelled and cast in a Kensington studio by Ernest Adsetts and George Fullard, and the *Daily Mail* of 15 December 1952 described their exhibit as 'a work of art in its own right', commenting: 'There is no question of mass production in this work; each of the heads they have modelled is different, and with a striking gift for portraiture they have made of each one a recognisable military type'.

A MAN OF SHEFFIELD

A few months later, in the *Yorkshire Evening Post* of 2 March 1953, it was reported that these two young sculptors from Sheffield had used 300 feet of steel tubing, 3 tons of modelling clay and 2 tons of fine plaster to make the horses and men in their Kensington studio for this exhibit!

In 1952 Ernest married a Swedish girl, Stina Jonasson, in London, and in 1954 they moved to live and work in Sweden, where Ernest got a job as design consultant with the famous 150-man Aafors glassworks.

Ernest drawing shapes on the floor of the workshop for the guidance of the glassblowers (ca 1955).

In 1955 the *Sheffield Telegraph*, under the headline 'Leading Designer – in three years', reported on an interview with Ernest Adsetts, who said that early in 1954 he had arrived in Stockholm with 'no experience of glass, no connections and no capital, just a book of sketches, a lot of ideas, and a Swedish wife whom I met in England'.

The article went on to say that 'he has now established himself as one of the leading designers in Sweden's world-famous glass industry', and quoted him saying that he would like to come back to establish a similarly design-based business in Britain, but that it would take a radical change in the British glass industry to make this possible.

The article quoted his final words: 'I see no sign of this being possible – about as much chance as there would have been 12 months ago in the

DOLISHING UP this 17 h.p. Lancia for its next run is Mr. E. A. Adsetts, 107, Mansfield Road, Aston, brother of the owner, Mr. Ernest Adsetts, now in Mexico.

THE "JALOPY" IS ASTON'S PRIDE
21 Years Old, Lapped Gamston at 75 m.p.h.

family ice cream business'! He was clearly well aware of my father's problems in coping with the arrival of TV, and, according to my sister May, he had some experience of selling ice cream on his occasional visits to Sheffield in the early 1950s.

She has told me about a trip they both made to Gamston in his old jalopy, with the joint aim of racing the classic car and selling the ice cream they took to the racecourse from a refrigerated box perched in the dickie-seat!

Over the 12 years he worked in Sweden, Ernest was a designer for Kosta and Aafors under the name of Ernest Gordon, promoting Swedish glassware and staging exhibitions of his own work around the world.

The owner of Aafors glass factory, Eric Aafors, asked Ernest to make something to decorate the new community hall in Aafors in 1956/57, Ernest made a sculpture (2.5m x 1.4m) showing the glassworkers who worked at Aafors at that time - Ernest could name every one of them.

Ernest, on a visit in 2007, repairing some damage to the artwork of his sculpture in the Aafors community hall.

A MAN OF SHEFFIELD

In the early 1960s he moved back to the UK and worked in partnership with Bill Smith (an old school-friend who later worked with me in Sheffield Insulations) for a company called Scandesco, which was later merged with the Swedish firm Konstsmide, of which he was a director and designer for over 20 years. His second wife, Lisbeth Orum, whom he married in Sheffield in 1965, was from Denmark

He married his third wife, Marjorie Falconer, in Chesterfield in 1975, but later returned to Lisbeth his second wife and married her again, The two of them worked together to create a retail outlet in Derbyshire selling Swedish lighting and Christmas decorations. Philip Nigel Adsetts, the son of his stepbrother, Alf, joined him as a director after leaving SIG plc in the late 1990s.

Ernest died in 2008, aged 81, after living in Derbyshire for more than 30 years. His designs were wide and varied, and a private collection of 60 of his early pieces was featured in the Cambridge Glass Fair of February 2010. He was a gifted painter and sculptor and a teacher of fine art, with a love of nature and a particular interest in beekeeping.

In 2017, to mark the opening of the new Sheffield Hallam Institute of Arts in the former Post Office building in Fitzalan Square, with the support of Gareth Taylor a London-based collector, there was a display of the work of the late Ernest Gordon Adsetts, a distinguished alumnus of the university.

KELHAM ISLAND MUSEUM
SHEFFIELD INDUSTRIAL MUSEUMS TRUST

In the early days of my tenure as chairman of Sheffield Hallam University I had been approached by Professor John Brooks of the Engineering department about the possibility of doing something about Kelham Island Museum, which was being starved of council funds and was in danger of being closed or severely cut back.

The museum had been opened in 1982 in a disused power station that had once supplied electricity for the city's trams, to provide both a physical record and a demonstration site displaying the industrial heritage of the city. In its day it had been a pioneering example of best practice in this new field, but was now in a state of decline.

With support from Councillor Peter Horton, who had also been a prime mover in the fight to save the Lyceum, the idea of forming a new trust to take over Kelham Island Museum was thrashed out and a proposal for a three-cornered partnership of Sheffield Hallam, the Cutlers' Company, and the council in such a pioneering trust was finally approved. I became its first chairman in 1994.

A MAN OF SHEFFIELD

An early decision was made to recruit a director of the museum with curatorial experience that focussed on industrial heritage, and John Hamshere arrived later in 1994. He reported a small increase in visitor numbers over the next year, and we began to plan for a large exhibition to mark the arrival of the new Kelham. Then came one of the 'coincidences' that have peppered my career.

The transport manager of SIG, Malcolm Dungworth, came to my office and asked me whether I had ever heard of Sheffield Simplex. He then told me that it was the name of a firm founded by Earl Fitzwilliam in the early years of the twentieth century to make cars in Sheffield. The purpose-built Sheffield factory stopped making cars shortly after the end of the First World War, but one of the last cars it ever made – the Sheffield Simplex 1921 model – was now back in Britain after years spent in overseas collections.

'Can you find a way to make sure it comes back to Sheffield?' he asked. After trying, and failing, to think of a way to assemble sufficient funds from old car enthusiasts to buy the Simplex, I went to see it in a car showroom in Batley, was taken out in it, drove it, and bought it! On the way back to Sheffield I tried to think of ways to tell my wife that I had just bought a 72-year-old car, but there was no apparent need – she said it was quite a good idea (now she tells me she thought I was mad!). I went ahead anyway.

SIG also employed Steve Myers, an expert on the Simplex car who had written a book on the subject (yet another coincidence!) and he set about servicing the car. The body was in mint condition, and there was no need to do much more than tackle engine and chassis maintenance and make the minor running adjustments needed in an old car that in Steve's opinion had not done enough miles to be properly run in!

From the beginning it had been looked after. Firstly, as Earl Fitzwilliam's chauffeur-driven car, then in the hands of a succession of collectors in Ireland and America before it came back to the Ferranti collection in the

UK. I learned more about its history when I went with Eve to Dublin for an operation on her knee, and met the sister of the Simplex chauffeur in Coolatin, the Earl's Irish country seat, to which the car was shipped for every summer season.

The problem of our opening exhibition was solved: called *Sheffield on Wheels*, it was to run from June to December 1995, and John Hamshere still talks of the day when I gave him six months to clear the large first floor hall in the museum of all the 'junk' that filled it – he chided me gently and I never again made the mistake of referring to our collections in that way.

The Simplex was displayed with other items from the Kelham collection. There was a stagecoach, several bicycles and motorcycles, a milk float, and other makes of small car made by Sheffield-based companies. The Charron Laycock was brought back on indefinite loan from GKN headquarters in the Midlands, and we also borrowed a single-decker Sheffield tram from the Crich Railway Museum. The exhibition was a great success and our new venture was on its way.

The Melting Shop play area at Kelham Island Museum.

A Man of Sheffield

Following this initial boost John Hamshere recognised the need for a more permanent attraction to maintain the momentum. Next door to the River Don engine he created a children's play area called the Melting Shop, 'a children's activity that shows how steel is melted, poured, rolled and hammered through play'; an innovative move that is now recognised as a crucial step forward in establishing the new Kelham. Originally I donated a vintage clock from my father's old firm to enable children to 'clock in' with their own card – but it can't handle the present level of use, so it's been 'retired' to the collection store!

Kelham's rebirth from a near-terminal decline stems, in this decision as in others, from the long-held belief that John and I share in a simple formula for decision-making – 'If in doubt do something, because the new situation you create may be easier to understand than the one you face today'.

Kelham Island Museum made steady progress, as John Hamshere proved to be a master of bid management, chasing the sources of funding for an independent trust that were simply not available to the council. A new crisis soon emerged. By June 1997 the council had decided that it could no longer afford to save Abbeydale Industrial Hamlet from closure. Faced with this 'opportunity' the new partnership board of Kelham took action.

By November, after a takeover by Kelham had been agreed, we changed the name of the Trust to Sheffield Industrial Museums Trust, gained formal support from English Heritage and other official bodies, and started talking to the city council about a new funding agreement.

Generous sponsorship from Meadowhall for a new education programme was crucial to a successful relaunch of the Abbeydale site. In addition, I gave the Simplex car to the new Trust, both to secure the car's future and to strengthen the balance sheet of the Trust in our negotiations with potential funders.

At a gala dinner on 25 March 1998 to mark the formation of SIMT and initiate local fundraising from Sheffield industrialists, I announced

Back from the brink: Abbeydale Hamlet now has a brighter future

Thanks for backing heritage rescue bid

I WANT to thank your newspaper for the very positive support you have given to the campaign to re-open Abbeydale Industrial Hamlet. The recent success in forming the new Sheffield Industrial Museums Trust, bringing together Abbeydale, Shepherd's Wheel and Kelham Island has, as you have been able to report, resulted in support from the private sector as well as an additional £30,000 from the city council. Naturally I am delighted by these developments, which confirm the view expressed by myself and others in the City Council that working towards Trust status for the Hamlet would bring advantages which were not possible whilst it remained as part of the City Council's direct provision.

Norman Adsetts

I have always emphasised that it is because the Council valued that part of the city's industrial heritage celebrated by the Hamlet and Shepherd's Wheel that we took the decisions to protect and enhance their future in this way.

As well as thanking those organisations who have now offered sponsorship, I should like to pay my tribute to the many people who have worked so hard to achieve this success – especially those members of Abbeydale, Shepherd's Wheel Action Trust. In particular I would give my thanks for all the hard work put in by Norman Adsetts who is now the Chair of the new Sheffield Industrial Museums Trust.

Councillor Viv Nicholson, Chair, Leisure and Tourism Services.

that the trust set up for Kelham three years earlier, and now extended to Abbeydale, had already achieved remarkable success both in retaining and strengthening a cultural asset of the city, and in providing a visitor attraction which would be a base for future regeneration of the area.

In a report to the board just before the dinner, John Hamshere had announced that 'the trust has raised visitor numbers by 40% and increased the earned income by 76% over the first three years of its funding agreement with the city council'. He went on to say that 'some three hundred thousand pounds in various grants has been received over this period, plus more than one hundred and fifty thousand pounds in cash and in kind from the private sector'.

A sound basis for the future development of Sheffield Industrial Museums had been achieved, and the Kelham Riverside, the historical centre of early Sheffield industry alongside the Don, became the next priority for regeneration. I was asked to become the chairman of a new trust, the Kelham Riverside Development Agency, and on accepting this role I stepped down from the SIMT board to avoid any appearance of possible conflict of interest.

The late Raymond Douglas, the former Master Cutler who followed me as chairman of SIMT, was very effective in gaining the support of local industry. His successor was Alex Pettifer (formerly of Sheffield Hallam), who had been responsible for our early negotiations with the local authority. Under his strong leadership there has been significant development of both the Kelham and Abbeydale sites – including the miraculous survival of the Simplex in 2007 when the Museum was flooded!

MOUNT ST MARY'S COLLEGE

Two of my grandsons enrolled at the Mount, a Jesuit independent school in Spinkhill, shortly after my daughter Helen and her family had moved away from Sheffield to a house in Eckington that could accommodate her five children.

The two boys, Mark and Simon, went to the Mount junior school in Barlborough Hall, where they had their first introduction to rugby football, and I became one of the group of proud fathers and grandfathers who weathered the elements to watch them on Saturday mornings; I was also chairman of governors of Sheffield Hallam University, a local link to higher education which got me invited to present the prizes at Speech Day.

In my speech I referred to an earlier experience of Barlborough Hall in 1943 when I camped in the grounds with a Boy Scout troop from King Edward's and took a ride in the punt on the ornamental lake... when the boat sank! A Mount governor who had been a pupil at the time exclaimed loudly, 'So that's what happened to it', and only the fact that I was being targeted as future 'governor' material saved me from getting a bill.

A MAN OF SHEFFIELD

Some years later, when I was reaching the end of my term at Sheffield Hallam in 2001, I was told of a plan to change Mount St Mary's College from a Jesuit foundation to an independent school trust, and I agreed to become the first lay chairman of governors in order to prepare the ground for the necessary changes in governance, structure, and presence in the local community, while still retaining the unique atmosphere and ethos in the two schools, neither of which had a majority of Roman Catholics in their student numbers.

It took about ten years to complete the transition. In many respects, it was a familiar situation, in that board members and management had been slow to recognise changes in the nature and needs of their normally stable market.

Maintenance of the traditional balance between boarders and day-school pupils was difficult in changing market conditions. Weekly boarding was one option, but the development of a new demand for full boarding places to replace the declining traditional links with the armed forces abroad and the colonial civil service was going to need a long-term marketing plan aimed at rebuilding international credibility.

It was therefore very important to build up the numbers of pupils in the school by establishing a new role for the Mount as a local independent day school. This had implications for the membership of the board of governors, shifting the emphasis to local knowledge, experience in the management of change and appropriate introduction of financial and quality controls.

There was a need for more investment in long-delayed maintenance, for new teaching resources to meet the needs of a changing syllabus, and for effective promotion to address the changing needs of our marketplace.

The greater provision of residential, catering, and sporting facilities appropriate for a student population living on the premises had to be made available to a wider audience, as part of a general move away from the isolation which I remembered from my schooldays.

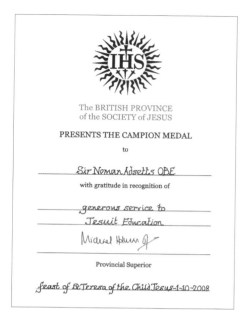

The BRITISH PROVINCE
of the SOCIETY of JESUS

PRESENTS THE CAMPION MEDAL

to

Sir Noman Adsetts OBE

with gratitude in recognition of

generous service to
Jesuit Education

Michael Holman sj

Provincial Superior

feast of St Teresa of the Child Jesus 1-10-2008

The sons of the local Catholic families in Sheffield and neighbourhood often went to the Mount, played rugby football in a national network of schools instead of the local soccer scene, and were to an extent separated from the social life of the city. This was occasionally demonstrated to the amusement of our children when I identified in team photographs lining the great corridor, a number of the boyfriends well known to Eve who were all members of the close group of Catholic families in the Sheffield of the 1940s.

The completion of the move to independent trust status was finally achieved. Many of the developments which have been introduced in the schools, including a major upgrade of the sports facilities for which the college had a proud reputation, were made possible as part of the takeover negotiations with the Society of Jesus. In 2011 the Provincial, Father Michael Holman, awarded me the Campion Medal for 'generous service to Jesuit Education'.

Father Richard Mangan the Jesuit who was my guide and mentor in Farm St in 1956 before I married Eve, would have been pleased!

My successor Jim Kelly, formerly the headmaster of All Saints the Catholic secondary school in Sheffield, and past national president of The Catenian Association, had the credentials to tackle the next phase, which was to upgrade the administrative and educational standards of the Mount; and the new headmaster Nick Cullihy is now successfully working on the balance of day and boarding numbers - the key to the future.

SHEFFIELD THEATRES TRUST

Restoration of Lyceum Theatre Sheffield 1990.

In the 1940s and early 1950s the Lyceum theatre was an important part of my life. 'Arsenic and Old Lace' was the best of the plays I saw on Wednesday afternoons whenever I could avoid school football. As a family we always went to the annual Lyceum pantomime, where I first saw Frankie Howerd, Morecambe & Wise, Jewell and Warriss and others, who set my taste in comedy for life. And once I got my driving licence, I delivered ice cream to a refrigerator in the Lyceum roof-space!

Three years after our return to Sheffield in 1966 the Lyceum theatre closed, and this magnificent building had short spells as a Bingo Hall and a venue for rock concerts before a bold private campaign to list the building saved it from destruction. It survived into the 1980s as an unused Grade II listed building in a state of disrepair.

In the run-up to the World Student Games planned for 1991, Councillor Peter Horton proposed that the cost of refurbishing the empty theatre should be included in the total funding package for sporting and other facilities by making it the centrepiece of the Cultural Festival included in the Games programme.

I had learned from my talks in Glasgow and Boston that investment in the arts could be a kick-start to city-centre regeneration, and so I agreed to support the council-led bid for European money for the Lyceum, and became a business member of the Lyceum board. The bid was successful, and the Lyceum opened with a Gala performance to mark the start of the Games.

Once restored to its nineteenth-century splendour, and fully operational as a modern theatre, the Lyceum took off with a vengeance and began to outstrip, in every sense, the Crucible next door. Sheffield Theatres, with its three different stages – the Lyceum, the Crucible and the Studio – was the largest theatre complex outside London, and the Business Plan spoke of the need for 'balanced programming' – easier to say than to achieve!

In the immediate aftermath of the Games I joined a new board created to run the complex of theatres under the name of Sheffield Theatres Ltd, with members nominated from the two trusts of the Crucible and the Lyceum. It was in effect a management committee watching over the operations and performance of the theatre complex.

By mid-1993 it was clear that there were problems with this structure, and our main funder, the Arts Council, was advocating change. I was a supporter of the Arts Council position and wrote the following notes as a basis for arguments to put to the chair and board of Sheffield Theatres.

29 September 1993
Fundamental weaknesses are beginning to emerge in a system of governance that was introduced at speed to secure Lyceum

funding. The legal framework of authority is upside down, with the STL board subordinate to the two trusts, mandated by them, and charged with carrying out policy decisions made by them.

As originally intended the Sheffield Theatres board does determine strategy, make operating decisions, and behave like a corporate entity, but it can only do this because of mutual goodwill and understanding between individuals. There is no guarantee that this cosy but unstable relationship will continue, so a change [in this management structure] is essential.

24 March 1994

A lot has been made of unfair 'threats' from funders. This is simply a dramatic way of expressing their power of patronage. They are like bank managers who 'suggest' certain courses of action and have the power to manage our overdraft terms accordingly. It always pays to take such 'suggestions' seriously.

In theory the problem of structure has a simple solution. Instead of being a management committee for the theatre complex with powers delegated from the two trusts, Sheffield Theatres needs to be an independent body to which a chief executive will report directly on the running of the theatres.

This would replace the present cumbersome structure with its costly, confusing and time-consuming reports and debates on identical issues at three separate meetings every month. It works, but only just!

I was therefore convinced that changes in structure were essential, both in the interest of effective operation of our theatre complex, and in the proper use of public money. In 1994 I decided to leave the Lyceum board after expressing my opinion that it would not be sensible to ignore a

The Lyceum, a jewel of Victorian theatre architecture.

formal appraisal from the Arts Council, a major funder, which was similarly critical of the management structure.

The necessary structural changes were made, and in 1996 I was invited by the city council, the other major funder, to become the new chairman of Sheffield Theatres to deal with a cash flow problem threatening its survival.

The Stage of 17 October 1996 announced this change of leadership under a headline of 'Adsetts to end Sheffield Turmoil'.

> *"Norman Adsetts has been named as the new chairman of the Sheffield Theatres Trust. Staff at the trust's three venues – Lyceum, Crucible and Studio – are hoping that his appointment will end the turmoil that has hit Sheffield this year."*

The audiences for productions put on at the Crucible were falling rapidly, and it seemed there was no realistic plan for recovery. There were financial problems caused by a serious theft several years earlier that needed to be brought to a close. I decided to inject a sense of urgency into the organisation.

So I started asking questions. My first stop was with the middle management, and I asked them what could be done to increase audiences in the Crucible. They said that we should bring in well-known actors, and when I asked why they didn't do so, they said it was too expensive.

Proceeding along a well-trodden path in such situations, I asked how much it would cost, and then pointed out that it would only require the sale of a few more seats to pay for the increase. Clearly, the management had become fixated on cost cutting as the only possible strategy for recovery, to the point at which it was weakening our dramatic product and making it unattractive to the customer! We decided to bring in some names.

Then I reported to the board and told them the situation was dire, and there were going to be changes at all levels. There were a few dissenting voices: I recall one in particular: 'we're already sorting out the chief executive job – the relationship with the artistic director is so critical that we're having an Away Day to decide on an appropriate job description'. I begged to differ, pointing out that the brief for any chief executive was very simple and straightforward and there was no need for an Away Day.

New members joined the board, Grahame Morris became chief executive, Angela Galvin was recruited as marketing manager, casts were changed, we sought a bigger grant from the Arts Council, and eventually the situation was brought under control.

I am not sure that we ever really solved the problem of balanced programming, but with the kick-start provided by the Crucible production of 'Brassed Off' written by the deputy chairman Paul Allen, and improved deals with touring shows in the Lyceum, the new chief executive Grahame Morris was bringing the theatres back into profit.

The annual return of the World Snooker Championship to the Crucible had become an important factor in the fortunes of Sheffield Theatres. I had become a snooker fan as I watched John Spencer win the 1977 final in the unique arena that had been designed by Tanya Moiseivitch for classic drama.

The Crucible Production of 'Brassed Off'. The single most popular piece of drama ever staged at the Crucible, it successfully undertook a unique transfer to the National Theatre.

In the beginning the rental for the use of the Crucible building and necessary support staff each year was negotiated between Sheffield Theatres and the governing body of the sport, but as the scale and attraction of the event grew Graham saw that time had come for them to do their deal directly with the City Council.

Our role, in the new circumstances, was to create the stable background of a strong and profitable theatre complex within which this unique event and vital part of the image and visitor appeal of the city could flourish.

Given the power of such features in the regeneration strategies of a city, as we had discovered in the work of the Image Working Party, I was totally committed to making a success of this theatre complex, and welcomed the steady restoration of a 'quality' culture to the management and production standards of our theatres.

A MAN OF SHEFFIELD

Paul Allen, Grahame Morris, Sir Norman Adsetts and Angela Galvin with theatre staff after winning the "Best Regional Theatre Award" for 2001.

This was not the end of the story, however. There was a perception in the Arts Council, observing our slow emergence from crisis, that we no longer needed their support, and I had to remind them that there was a significant difference between the success of a survival strategy based on tackling short-term issues at the expense of everything else, and the achievement of recovery in the longer-term, for which we still needed their help with stabilisation funding. This argument was accepted.

We also confirmed to the Arts Council, whose view had been that the Lyceum would not receive their support as a presenting or touring theatre, that we could and would produce and present theatre work in all and any parts of our theatre complex. As a result they agreed to fund Sheffield Theatres for the totality of its work.

With the subsequent arrival of Michael Grandage as associate director, and the confidence that Grahame's calm and professional management style brought to the theatres, the period of recovery was relatively short, and the Crucible returned to a position of pre-eminence among provincial producing theatres.

After ten years as chairman of the board, I became honorary president, handing over to my successors the responsibility for the next phase of development – a complete refurbishment to bring the Crucible up to modern standards – to meet the technical requirements of productions, to provide safety and disabled access, to improve facilities for hospitality and dining, and to work in partnership with the local authority to keep the Snooker World Championship in the Sheffield Crucible.

I wrote the above sentence on the day after the 40th World Snooker Championship in 2017, when it had just been announced that the event will be staged in the Sheffield Crucible up to 2028; and shortly before the Arts Council funding for Sheffield Theatres, as a National Portfolio Organisation, was confirmed until 2022.

PARTNERSHIPS IN ACTION

A REVIEW

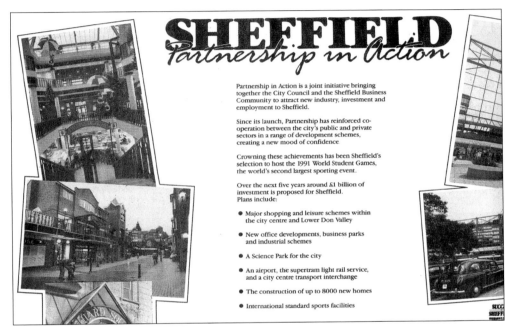

Partnership in Action is a joint initiative bringing together the City Council and the Sheffield Business Community to attract new industry, investment and employment to Sheffield.

Since its launch, Partnership has reinforced co-operation between the city's public and private sectors in a range of development schemes, creating a new mood of confidence.

Crowning these achievements has been Sheffield's selection to host the 1991 World Student Games, the world's second largest sporting event.

Over the next five years around £1 billion of investment is proposed for Sheffield. Plans include:

- Major shopping and leisure schemes within the city centre and Lower Don Valley
- New office developments, business parks and industrial schemes
- A Science Park for the city
- An airport, the supertram light rail service, and a city centre transport interchange
- The construction of up to 8000 new homes
- International standard sports facilities

Extract from the Star Mansion House Supplement of 23 May 1988.

In tackling the challenges of business, I had always looked for the common factors that would enable collaboration to replace conflict. This approach had been directly relevant to our vital relations with suppliers, and it had helped us to realise the corporate aim of getting government to promote energy conservation.

Such an approach was even more applicable to the regeneration of our city, because it was the way to get the council and the business community to talk to each other, and to build new areas of partnership to the benefit of the city of Sheffield. The apparent inability of our city leaders to move beyond public bickering was damaging confidence all round, and it looked as though it was going to be quite difficult to change things, so I had just what I needed – a challenging task.

In 1993, Patrick Seyd, a senior lecturer in Politics at the University of Sheffield, wrote a chapter on 'The Political Management of Decline 1973-1993' in a 3-volume *History of the City of Sheffield*. His perceptive account of the early moves towards a public-private partnership in the city, and of the examples of collaboration in the Image Working Party, the Sheffield Economic Regeneration Committee, the World Student Games and the Sheffield Development Corporation, is accurate, but it only covers the first tentative moves that were made towards mutual understanding and effective partnership.

In 1993, when his article was written, there were still plenty of issues on which confrontation and blame remained the easy option, while development of the trust and understanding essential for constructive debate and longer-term consensus was a relatively slow process.

Patrick pointed out that despite claims that Sheffield had developed a distinct form of collaborative politics, it was often difficult to sustain it and see the benefits. That was certainly true in the early stages, when we were trying to do something quite new and difficult; but we were trying hard to get better: and we did!

In a speech to the Chartered Institute of Bankers in March 1989 I had addressed this point.

"We should not expect too much of partnership – if we do, the inevitable occasions when we differ are going to seem like disasters. It never did mean that we would always agree, but what it will increasingly mean is that we can talk openly – and know each other well enough to be honest about our differences and seek to find solutions."

Patrick identified one weakness of our partnership strategy as the failure to concentrate more attention on the city's human resources. In his article, he remarked that one of Sheffield's major strengths in the past had been its skilled labour force, a scarce commodity that could attract capital to the city. He also argued that there should have been more intervention to enable the benefits of investment to be spread more widely.

I recognise the strength of these arguments. The Training Enterprise Council (TEC), led by Richard Field in Sheffield, was an effective addition to the partnership agenda, but it seemed to me at the time that before we could add the full range of regeneration options to our partnership approach, we would first have to learn how to live – and work – together.

Nevertheless the general argument that if we talk together and begin to understand each other's problems and points of view we will be able to make things happen, had already had an impact. The presence of more than 200 ambassadors speaking for Sheffield in the Mansion House had demonstrated the power of the message, but that was the easy part – we had to try harder; we had to prove that we could make it work; we had to get results!

Plenty of people were trying to achieve this in specific projects between 1988 and 2000, and I got involved in a few of them, beginning with the SDC and the Five Weir's Walk, both in their own way taking a partnership approach to the state of the Don Valley.

My successive involvement with Sheffield Hallam and Kelham Island Museum, the World Student Games, Sheffield Theatres, Kelham Riverside, and Sheffield First for Investment, earned a level of media coverage which got me the nick-name of 'Mr Sheffield', but the underlying purpose was to set an example that would encourage more people from different communities around the city to experience both the practical difficulties of, and the benefits to be derived from, working together on their chosen projects.

On reflection, I believe that the strategy we adopted was, in the circumstances of the time, the only option. Our apparent inability to work together to face our problems had to be addressed first, because it was necessary to restore the trust, confidence and common purpose without which no other strategies could have succeeded. This was necessarily a random process, in which the problem areas and participating partners selected themselves, and the confidence bred of success began to spread in the 'messy' way described in other cities.

Reviewing the progress made since 1993, Patrick has recognised that the shift in attitudes, particularly among local politicians and business leaders, which was generated by the Image Working Party and the Partnership in Action campaign, 'was seismic and paved the way for institutional structures and attitudes which prevail today, much to the benefit of Sheffield'.

A few years ago I spoke to a group of SIG managers on a development course in Sheffield Hallam. After a review of my business career, I was answering questions when one of the Business School academics asked to what I attributed my success. I had not been faced with this before, and after a brief pause I said, 'Trust'. To my surprise he followed by asking where I had learned about trust-based leadership, the subject of his research, and my answer was, 'on the job'.

Trust, empathy and acceptance of mistakes are often mis-interpreted as evidence of weak or gentle management; there will be times when a firmer style is appropriate, but my experience suggests that the percentages are all in favour of trust. My father's mentor in Caribonum insisted that respect, which has to be earned, comes from a combination of trust and fear – but I question the use of the word 'fear'. Fear of what? Certainly not of mistakes!

The motto chosen for my coat of arms is an argument for taking risks and not fearing mistakes, and I stick by it. However, it is also important how you do it, and if I could have chosen a second motto I would have taken it from Will Rogers, the 1920s Hollywood film star, who said that he would like his epitaph to read: 'I never met a man I didn't like'; and when I first heard this in a Broadway musical about his life I recognised it as the approach to others that I had first learned from my parents.

These are the kind of lessons you learn when beginning to build any partnership, and its what this book, at least in part, has been about. It's an approach worth trying – and it works!

A Postscript from John Mothersole
August 2017

I arrived in Sheffield in January 1998, and whilst there was a lot of momentum there was also a bit of a hiatus. The Sheffield Development Corporation had been and gone and everyone knew that the job was not finished. The choices were do nothing, more of the same or a new approach for the new era. We chose the latter, and Sir Norman was one of the few at the time who had the trust and confidence to work with us on an ambitious new agenda. The preceding chapters describe those ventures. Looking back, Sir Norman acted as the bridge between the first flush of the city's revival and the next phase of seeking to thrive.

The real test of impact though is its longevity even when the "actor" is not on the stage. The truth is that our inward investment activity now is still based on the framework established by Sheffield First for Investment, Kelham is now a sea of cranes and regarded as one of the nation's top urban neighbourhoods and the Lower Don Valley is becoming home of Europe's largest advanced manufacturing district.

The irony is that Sir Norman says that you should not expect too much of partnerships. The problem is that because his efforts have created such a high bar that now we do. A great problem to have!

John Mothersole
Chief Executive of Sheffield City Council

APPENDIX 1

THE STAR LAD

A poem written and composed by
William T Adsetts in 1883.

Hav've gotten mi pen i mi hand once moor
An 've a drop of ink left yet
Soa aw'll scribble away as as've done before
Abaat sumaat that aw can'tt forget

It wor' t'other neet while walking abaat
Aw met a poor lad i the street
He said to me we 'bea'ating heart
Will you buy a Star sur tneet

His feet they wor bare his face war wan
And his hands wor black and blue
The sufferings of that child no man
Wod dare to brave them throo.

Soa 'aw tuk a star and gave t'h pay
A haarpenny for ow't aw knew
Then walking on to read the news
As aw'd now't else to do

Wo'll sauntering on aw' throw't two sad
What that poor child must feel
But looking raa'mil 'the'poor young lad
Wor 'tramping at mi' heel.

Then luk'in up he said please sur
Aw 'think you've made a mista'ak
You gave to me a shilling sur
And sur aw've brought it back

Aw cud'dut find I 'me' heart or soul
To tak' that shilling agean
Son 'aw taw'd him to keep it all
A his eyes how they did glea'am

He thanked me 0er and oer agea'an
And trying his greaf to smother
Aw'll you and buy some bread he said
And tak to to mi' mother

Aw' axed him what his name might be
He said it was poor Joe
Aw' had a sister once he said
But she' dee'd long ago

And mi' brother he is dee'ad as well
Mi' mother shoo is blind
Mi' fa'ather deed two years ago
And left us two beho'ind

Aw da'at mi mothers'll not last long
Shee's gett'in worse and old
Soa ' awll get some coil and leet a foire
For aw think shoo must be cow'd

And as aw' luk'ed into his honest face
Aw' cud'ent help a sigh
Soa aw' said goa'hoo'am at once mi' lad
But pray thee don'not cry

Aw know there's troubles I this world
Enough for thee an' me too
Soa trust in God an then tha'll see
He's sure to pull us throo

He touched his hat and off he ran
And aw'd noa' where to roa'am
Sa' we lecter heart aw' turned mi'ra'and
There slowly sauntered hoo'am

Aw' throw't if these flash toffs but knew
What their bothers I poverty feel
They'd spare a trifle more of'the'coin
And help 'him' to a meal

Nah friends if hwen yo'gor'aat
Yo' hear a poor lads cry
If you've a copper then to spare
Doo'nt pass them heddler ?

For all the lessons aw've been taught
On all ? tha aw've had
The beset of all aw'think aw knor
I'wor by that poor Star lad

APPENDIX 2

THE FRIEND OF THE MUSIC MAN

A poem written by Ernest Adsetts
on 24 November 1938

I shall never forget how I met him
It's so seldom you meet his kind
One needs courage no end, to be a friend
To a fellow like me who's blind.

Not once did he ever mislead me
He was faithful and true to the core
I did, and I shall, always call him "Old Pal"
And I'll love him for evermore.

We started together at Clapton,
At a fair – near a yellow van.
I'll remember that scene for ever,
They called me the "Music Man".

Yes, remember that scen for ever
Though I told you that I was blind.
"Old Pal" you see, had eyes for me
He could paint scenes in my mind.

We have stood at times near "Crasher"
The boxer of days gone by.
By the light of the stars, you'd have seen his scars
As he yelled by the Cocoanut shye.

Round I would turn the handle
Of the music box at my side,
As Old Pal danced to a crazy tune
Kids laughed until they cried.

He'd wink as he took the cap round
At little girls he saw,
A somersault then for boys and men,
A frozen face he'd thaw.

"Fat Emma" would shout "Say Tiny"
Make money while you can
Give them a chance with your ragtime dance
Play up "Music Man".

Round went the Herdy Girdies
Over went the swings,
When the kids went high, Old Pal would sigh,
I'm sure he thought they'd wings.

Off went "Tom Pooleys" Dragons
To music loud but bright
Mixed with the yells of boys and gells
Joys of a fairground night.

From fair to fair – Yes anywhere
The whole of our native land
Was covered in time by he and I,
Some called us the "Village Band".

We sometimes struck a hard patch
Plodding along – though broke.
He'd dance – I'd sing – we did anything,
Each playing "The cheery Bloke".

But fate played its hand in our friendship
And took "Old Pal" from me.
One night last March at a gala
Near "Southend-by-the-sea."

My musical Box I was playing
Near the swings of "Smoky Dan"
When suddenly "Crack" and someone yelled
"Look Out" Music Man.

A jerk at my wrist was a signal
That danger was at hand,
A jerk by the pull of a leather lead
It made me understand.

I leaped and was conscious of something
Falling closely by my side.
"Crash" it went to the ground and then
"Poor Monkey" someone cried.

That meant more to me than a death knell
Forget it I never shall.
It meant that my life's joy had left me,
The monkey was "Old Pal".

Forgive me if I may have bored you,
But surely with eyes you'll see
That whilst to the crowd he was just a pet
He meant all the world to me.

I took his small frame to a cottage
Where now – to my end I'll stay,
And I buried him near to the window
Where I always sit and play.

I've covered his grave with sea shells
From Southend-by-the-sea.
Where he played his last act in the drama
Which left me in misery.

At his head is a stone that I carved alone,
Of course its just rough and free
From neat decoration – that sight could design
But he'll know that its good for me.

The kids love to come on a Sunday
And sing by his little grave.
Then I tell them of days at Clapton Fair
And the wonderful help he gave.

At dusk I sit at his graveside
And I picture the Yellow Van.
Then I play whilst I know he is near me
The friend of the Music Man.

BIBLIOGRAPHY

Addison, Paul (1994). *The Road to 1945 – British Politics and the Second World War*. Pimlico.

Algeo, Matthew (2015). 'Pedestrianism – When Watching People Walk Was America's Favorite Spectator Sport'. *Chicago Review Press*.

Austin, Michael (2004). *'Under the Heavy Clouds' – The Church of England in Derbyshire and Nottinghamshire 1911-1915*. Merton Priory Press.

Bannister, Roger (1955). *First Four Minutes*. Putnam (with original programme for the meeting).

Barr, James (2011). *A Line in the Sand – Britain, France and the Struggle that Shaped the Middle East*. Simon & Schuster.

Barton, Peter, Peter Doyle & Johan Vanderwall (2004). *Beneath Flanders Fields – The Tunnellers' War 1914-1918*. Spellmont Ltd.

Bean, JP (2008). *The Sheffield Chronicles*. D & D Publications.

Carruthers, Tom (2012). *Running for Money; A Decade of Corruption and Violence in Athletics*. Matador Imprint of Troubadour Publishing Leics.

Carter, Joseph H (1991). *Never Met a Man I Didn't Like – The Life and Writings of Will Rogers*. HarperCollins New York.

Cassar, George H (1998). *The Forgotten Front – The British Campaign in Italy 1917-1918*. The Hambledon Press.

Catherwood, Christopher (2004). *Winston's Folly – Imperialism and the Creation of Modern Iraq*. Constable and Robinson.

Chamberlain, Joseph (2015 [1903]). *Imperial Union and Tariff Reform*. Forgotten Books.

Clark, Charles Frederick (1918). *Caribonum Ideals*. Caribonum Company Ltd.

Clark, Charles A (written by those who worked with him 1945). *Clark, Charles Frederick – A Brief Biography of a Great Character*. Caribonum Company Ltd.

Day, Dave (Ed.) (2014). *Pedestrianism*. MMU Sport and Leisure History.

Dyos, HJ & Michael Wolff (Eds.) (1973). *The Victorian City – Images and Realities, Vol 1*. Routledge & Kegan Paul.

Eaton, Reg (1989). *The Ultimate Brace: A Unique Product of Victorian Sheffield*.

Farnsworth, Keith (1986). *The Ernest Adsetts Story – 'For Children up to 90'*. Privately published.

Farnsworth, Keith (1987). *Sheffield's East Enders – Life as it Was in the Lower Don Valley*. Sheffield City Libraries.

Faulks, Sebastian (1993). *Birdsong*. Folio Society.

Fisk, Robert (2005). *The Great War for Civilisation – The Conquest of the Middle East*. 4th Estate.

Furness, JM (1893). *Fifty Years' Municipal Record in Sheffield 1843 to 1893*. William Townsend.

Griffiths, Paul (1999). *The Five Weirs Walk*. The Hallamshire Press.

Haigh, Bernard (Compiled) (1994). *Around Bolsover – Old Photographs*. Alan Sutton Ltd.

Hart, Peter (2013). *The Great War*. Profile Books.

Harvey, Peter (2001). *Street Names of Sheffield*. Sheaf Publishing Ltd.

Hatfield, WH (1943). *Sheffield Burns*. JW Northend Ltd.

Hey, David (2005). *A History of Sheffield* (Rev. Edn.) Carnegie Publishing Ltd.

Hey, David (1986). *A Regional History of England – Yorkshire from AD 1000*. Longman Group.

Hey, David, Olive Martin & Martin Liddament (1997). *Forging the Valley*. Sheffield Academic Press.

Hilliard, Christopher (2014). 'The Twopenny Library – Book Trade, Working-Class Readers & 'Middlebrow' Novels in Britain, 1930-1942'. *Twentieth Century British History*, 2014, Vol 25, No 2, pps 199-208

Holliday, Joyce (1987). *It's a Bit Lively Outside – The Story of the Sheffield Blitz*. Yorkshire Art Circus.

Holmes, Richard (2004). *Tommy – The British Soldier on the Western Front 1914-1918*. Harper Perennial Paperback.

Humphery-Smith, Cecil R (Edited) 2002. *The Phillimore Atlas and Index of Parish Registers* (3rd Edn.). Phillimore.

Jolly, Emma (2013). *Tracing your Ancestors using the Census*. Pen and Sword Family History.

Lamin, Bill (2009). *Letters from the Trenches – A soldier from the Great War*. Michael O'Mara Books Ltd.

Lejeune, Anthony (Ed.) (1998). *The Concise Dictionary of Foreign Quotations*. Stacey.

Lewis-Stempel, John (2007). *Six Weeks – The Short and Gallant Life of the British Officer in the First World War*. Onion Books.

Light, Alison (2015). *Common People – The History of an English Family*. Fig Tree, an Imprint of Penguin Books.

Lloyd, Nick (2006). *Loos 1915*. Tempus Publishing Co Ltd.

Lomax, Scott (2014). *The Home Front – Sheffield in the First World War*. Pen & Sword Military.

Lombo, Gustavo and John Christy: 'The 100 Best Small Companies in the World – Sheffield Insulations'; *Forbes Magazine* (7 November 1994). Vol 154, Issue 11, pp 302-304.

Lovesey, Peter (1970). *Wobble to Death*. MacMillan & Co.

MacBeth, George (1987). *A Child of the War*. Jonathan Cape Ltd.

MacDonald, John & Zeljko Cimpric (2011). *Caporetto and the Isonzo Campaign – The Italian Front 1915-1918*. Pen & Sword Military.

McKenzie, Robert & Allan Silver (1968). *Angels in Marble – Working Class Conservatives in Urban England*. Heinemann.

Mackay, Francis (2001). *Asiago – Battle in the Woods and Clouds 15/16 June 1918*. Leo Cooper.

Man, John (1994). *The Penguin Atlas of D-Day and the Normandy Campaign*. Penguin.

Marshall, GW (Ed.) (1894). *The Parish Registers of Worksop 1558-1571*. Private printing 1/50.

Marshall, PS (2008). *King of the Peds*. AuthorHouse Ltd.

Mathers, Helen. 'The City of Sheffield 1893 – 1926'. *History of the City of Sheffield Vol 3: 'Politics'*, pp. 53-84. Sheffield Academic Press 1993

Middleton, Michael (1991). *Cities in Transition – The Regeneration of Britain's Inner Cities*. Michael Joseph.

Minnitt, Bernard A (1978). *A Soldier's Memoirs*. Private printing 49/100.

Muir, Frank (1997). *A Kentish Lad*. Bantam Press.

Mullaly, Colonel BR (1957). *Bugle and Kukri – The Story of the 10" Princess Mary's Own Gurkha Rifles*. Wm Blackwood & Sons Ltd.

Norton History Group (Compiled) (2000). *Norton – Images of England*. Tempus Publishing Ltd.

Parry, David (1984). *Victorian Sheffield in Advertisements*. Moss Valley 'Heritage' Publications.

Parry, David (1985). *200 Years of Sheffield Cutlery and Edge Tool Making*. Moss Valley 'Heritage' Publications.

Pawson & Brailsford, Sheffield (1985 [1862]). *Illustrated Guide to Sheffield*. Amethyst Press.

Pawson & Brailsford, Sheffield (2012 [1879]). *Guide to Sheffield* (abridged). ACM Retro.

Peacock, Geraldine with Angela Forrest and Richard Mills. (1996): *Autism – The Invisible Children? An Agenda for Action*. The National Autistic Society.

Pearn, Michael, with Chris Mulrooney and Tim Payne (1998). *Ending the Blame Culture*. Gower Publishing Ltd.

Pike, WT (Ed.) (1984 [1901]). *Edwardian Biography – Sheffield*, from Pike's New Century Series No 4, reprinted by Bell.

Piper, Glenn (2014). *Peds of the Past 1837-1920*. Glenn Piper.

Pollard, Sidney (1959). *A History of Labour in Sheffield*. Liverpool University Press.

Public Record Office (1990). *Tracing your Ancestors in the Public Record Office*, 4th Edition.

Ramsbottom, Bertie & Windle, Ralph (1985). *The Bottom Line Book of Business Ballads*. Century Hutchinson Ltd.

Riden, Philip & Dudley Fewkes, Dudley (2008). *Bolsover Town, Castle and Colliery*. Phillimore & Co.

Roberts, Monty (2001). *Horse Sense for People*. Harper Collins Publishers.

Star Supplement Monday May 23 (1988). *Sheffield Comes to London*. The Star

Syed, Matthew (2015). *Black Box Thinking – The Surprising Truth about Success & Why Some People Never Learn from Their Mistakes*. John Murray.

Syed, Patrick (1993). The Political Management of Decline 1973-1993; *History of the City of Sheffield Vol 3: 'Politics'*, pp. 151-185. Sheffield Academic Press.

Thompson, Mark (2008). *The White War – Life and Death on the Italian Front 1915-1919*. Faber & Faber Ltd.

Toledano, Marc (1967). *Le Franciscain de Bourges*. Flammarion Paris.

Townsend, Robert (1970). *Up the Organisation*. Michael Joseph Ltd.

Townshend, Charles (2011). *'When God Made Hell' – The British Invasion of Mesopotamia and the Creation of Iraq 1914-1921*. Faber & Faber Ltd.

Tripp, Charles (2000). *A History of Iraq*. Cambridge University Press.

Trounce, Harry Davis (1918). *Fighting the Boche Underground*. Charles Scribners & Sons.

Tweedale, Geoffrey (1995). *Steel City – Entrepreneurship Strategy and Technology in Sheffield 1743-1993*. Clarendon Press.

Walton, Mary (1948). *Sheffield – Its Story and its Achievements. The Sheffield Telegraph & Star.*

Walton, Mary & JP Lamb (1980). *Raiders over Sheffield*. Sheffield City Libraries.

Ward, Richard (1988). *In Memory of Sheffield's Cinemas*. Sheffield City Libraries.

Wylly CB & HC Colonel (1930). *The York & Lancaster Regiment* Vol 1-1919.

OTHER AVAILABLE SOURCES

The Ernest Adsetts Story, written by my good friend Keith Farnsworth after a long series of interviews with my father, has been a prime source of information about his career; my father wrote a lot of notes in preparation for his meetings with Keith and not all of them were used in the final version of the book. In conjunction with other research about Laneham and my own memories of the early days of the ice cream business I was able to make a fuller record of the period between the death of his father in 1913, and 1943 when he joined the RAF.

I also have a collection of 28 file-boxes containing relevant records and papers: eight contain personal records, certificates, maps, correspondence and photographs relating to the Adsetts family history. Two contain papers to do with my time in Fibreglass Ltd; 12 contain journals, diaries, promotional literature, correspondence, reports and assorted paperwork covering the 30 years from my move back to Sheffield in 1966 to my final retirement from the Sheffield Insulations Group in 1996.

The remaining boxes contain an assortment of documentation, mostly to do with my involvement in the regeneration of Sheffield and my specific responsibilities as chairman of Sheffield Theatres, Sheffield Hallam University, and Sheffield Industrial Museums.

The amount of information now available from the Internet has been a revelation, and it has gradually become more extensive and useful as my enquiries have extended beyond the records of Birth, Marriage, Death and Census returns to the databases of newspaper coverage.

These have been invaluable in exploring the lives of some of my forebears: my grandfather's political activities as a working-class Conservative in Sheffield between 1890 and 1910, for example, and, even more remarkably, the 'pedestrian' road-walking career of William Henry Adsetts between 1860 and 1880 in both England and America. The international media coverage of his son's murderous activities in Hong Kong was also wide-ranging.

Keil Green of Washington DC has been particularly helpful with additional information from family sources and from the US media, with regard to William Henry Adsetts the pedestrianist and his son William Henry, who was hanged in Hong Kong.

Friends and family members have shared their memories or have recommended new avenues of enquiry; in particular, Lisbeth Adsetts, the widow of my cousin Ernest Gordon Adsetts, provided valuable information on his eminent record in Swedish glass design.

David, John, and Ian Adsetts, with their sister Wendy Baka, added new interest to the story of the Bolsover Connection; and my cousin Philip Nigel Adsetts gave a new slant to the early days of Sheffield Insulations. Jacqueline Benner, nee Adsetts, and her brother David added to my knowledge of their grandfather, Tom Adsetts; Joyce Adsetts is the remaining descendant of the two boys killed in Treeton Colliery in the 1880s; and Clifford Adsetts, the grandson of William Tom's elder brother George, who helped him with the shops, gave me a hint of the family stresses involved.

I must also thank the staff of the National Archive, and of the Local Records and Archive Centres in Sheffield, Rotherham, Doncaster, Matlock, Retford, Reading and Nottingham, who have gone out of their way to help and advise me. The editing support of Jeremy Lowe was invaluable.

The local history group of Elmton-with-Creswell made a major contribution to my research into the Adsetts presence in this lovely village over five generations, and the information I obtained from the tiny room in which the records of Handsworth local history are kept was really valuable. Karl Noble of the York & Lancaster Regimental Museum in Rotherham was helpful in identifying the two Adsetts boys who enlisted in the regiment in 1914.

Nancy Fielder the Editor of The Star, and Jane Salt the Librarian were very helpful in locating and providing the photographs we needed.

My good friends John Stoddart and Sally Neocosmos, respectively Vice Chancellor and Clerk to the Governors during my time in Sheffield Hallam University provided excellent advice after reading drafts; as did Patrick Syed, Emeritus Professor in Politics at Sheffield University, in his comments on my review of the Partnership in Action campaign.

I could not have done without the help and support of the late Rowland Walker who was Master Cutler in the early stages of our work together on Image and Partnership, leading up to the Mansion House lobby and the Development Corporation.

There were a number of politicians, local and national, who helped to support the notion of partnership as a response to current difficulties, and I am grateful for their co-operation, friendship and advice: David Blunkett, Irvine Patnick, Richard Caborn, Clive Betts, Helen Jackson, David Heslop, Jan Wilson, Nick Clegg, Mike Pye, Mike Bower, Julie Dore, Peter Price and Angela Smith are members of an incomplete list, in no particular order, of those who worked with me as true partners.

Professor Nick Hodge of Sheffield Hallam University was a valuable source of information about the history and the aims of the Autism Centre.

The most unexpected contributor of background information on the life of George Albert Adsetts on the Italian Front in 1918 has been my publisher Martin Edwards, whose grandfather served in the same unit,

9 Battalion Yorks & Lancaster, winning the Military Medal in the Battle of Vittorio Veneto; and who introduced me to *Letters from the Trenches* by the grandson of another veteran of the 9 Battalion in Italy.

I am sure I have forgotten to mention the help and advice I have received from many others, and for this I apologise. I am grateful for the occasional words of encouragement or correction from my wife, children, and grandchildren, whose recollections of the early days of my business career in St Helen's and Sheffield are often more accurate than my own; and of course all the errors are mine.